Adopting .NET 5

Understand modern architectures, migration best practices, and the new features in .NET 5

Hammad Arif

Habib Qureshi

BIRMINGHAM—MUMBAI

Adopting .NET 5

Copyright © 2020 Packt Publishing

Group Product Manager: Aaron Lazar
Publishing Product Manager: Richa Tripathi
Senior Editor: Nitee Shetty
Content Development Editor: Ruvika Rao
Technical Editor: Pradeep Sahu
Copy Editor: Safis Editing
Project Coordinator: Deeksha Thakkar
Proofreader: Safis Editing
Indexer: Pratik Shirodkar
Production Designer: Jyoti Chauhan

First published: December 2020

Production reference: 1291220

Published by Packt Publishing Ltd.
Livery Place
35 Livery Street
Birmingham
B3 2PB, UK.

ISBN 978-1-80056-056-7

www.packt.com

To my wife, Sidrah, who assumed a disproportionate share of our responsibilities so that I could focus on this book. And to my children, Shanzay and Aaliyah, both of whom are now excited to resume playtime with me.
– Hammad Arif

I would like to dedicate these efforts to my beautiful wife for her support throughout my life, to my mother for my upbringing, and to my two children, who look up to their father and who one day will build on the things they aspire to and give back a lot to this wonderful world in which we live.
– Habib Qureshi

Packt.com

Subscribe to our online digital library for full access to over 7,000 books and videos, as well as industry leading tools to help you plan your personal development and advance your career. For more information, please visit our website.

Why subscribe?

- Spend less time learning and more time coding with practical eBooks and videos from over 4,000 industry professionals

- Improve your learning with Skill Plans built especially for you

- Get a free eBook or video every month

- Fully searchable for easy access to vital information

- Copy and paste, print, and bookmark content

Did you know that Packt offers eBook versions of every book published, with PDF and ePub files available? You can upgrade to the eBook version at packt.com and, as a print book customer, you are entitled to a discount on the eBook copy. Get in touch with us at customercare@packtpub.com for more details.

At www.packt.com, you can also read a collection of free technical articles, sign up for a range of free newsletters, and receive exclusive discounts and offers on Packt books and eBooks.

Contributors

About the authors

Hammad Arif is a passionate IT leader and speaker with over 16 years' experience in architecture, design, and implementing cutting-edge solutions to address business opportunities for enterprise applications. He earned his bachelor's degree in computer science and has previously worked as a solutions architect on Microsoft platforms. Based in Sydney, Hammad is currently leading a software development team that builds solutions on Azure and AWS platforms that serves all the top-tier financial institutions in Australia.

> *Comparing my initial drafts with the final copy, I can see a noticeable improvement that would not have been possible without the expert guidance from the Packt editorial team. In particular, I'd like to thank Ruvika Rao for the painstaking effort of thoroughly ensuring content quality and proposing improvements, often multiple times. I also wish to thank my experienced co-author, Habib Qureshi. His advice was invaluable during every step of my first book authoring journey.*

Habib Qureshi is an integration architect and lead developer with almost two decades of professional experience in the software industry. He has worked with start-ups and enterprises, successfully delivering high-quality solutions in an agile manner. He has experience in multiple countries and cultures with on-site, off-site, and remote teams. He is a go-getter and teams always look up to him for technical reviews and solutions.

> *First of all, I would like to thank Neha Sharma for reaching out to me at a time when I was ready to author another book. Next, I would like to thank all of the Packt team, who were very helpful and communicative from start to finish, especially Ruvika as the content editor, who was very interactive and helped us to reach our set targets on time.*

About the reviewers

Omprakash Pandey, a Microsoft 365 consultant, has been working with industry experts to understand project requirements and work on the implementation of projects for the last 20 years. He has trained more than 50,000 aspiring developers and has assisted in the development of more than 50 enterprise applications. He has offered innovative solutions on .NET development, Microsoft Azure, and other technologies. He has worked for multiple clients across various locations, including Hexaware, Accenture, Infosys, and many more. He has been a Microsoft Certified Trainer for more than 5 years.

Senthil Kumar is a Microsoft MVP in Visual Studio technologies. He is a co-author of the book *Windows 10 Development Recipes Using JavaScript and CSS*, published by Apress. Senthil has been working in the IT industry for over 9 years now and has had exposure to a variety of languages, including C#, JavaScript, PHP, and others.

Packt is searching for authors like you

If you're interested in becoming an author for Packt, please visit `authors.packtpub.com` and apply today. We have worked with thousands of developers and tech professionals, just like you, to help them share their insight with the global tech community. You can make a general application, apply for a specific hot topic that we are recruiting an author for, or submit your own idea.

Table of Contents

2

What's New in C# 9?

Section 2: Design and Architecture

3

Design and Architectural Patterns

4
Containerized Microservices Architecture

Section 3: Migration

5
Upgrading Existing .NET Apps to .NET 5

6

Upgrading On-Premises Applications to the Cloud with .NET 5

Section 4: Bonus

7

Integrating Machine Learning in .NET 5

Preface

.NET is a hugely successful framework with 20 years of legacy behind it. There are millions of developers using it to build all kinds of applications and solutions. .NET 5 is not just a mere iteration on previous versions; it also signifies the future of .NET technology, which is meant to be run on all platforms and devices with consistent capabilities and language features. .NET 5 unifies the battle-tested reliability and adaptability of .NET Framework with the open source, cross-platform, face-paced, and cloud-first philosophy of .NET Core, answering the ever-evolving needs of the modern application development landscape.

This book provides detailed coverage of all the new .NET 5 features using practical exercises for the reader to understand the tools and technologies that form the .NET 5 tech stack. It provides guidance on when and where to use the .NET 5 features and covers the best practices for architecting, developing, and deploying the applications to the cloud.

A section of the book has been dedicated to transforming the legacy applications to the latest .NET 5 platform. It discusses the scenarios in which the migration does and doesn't make sense for applications that have been built on previous .NET runtimes. The migration guide is written from both a code transformation and an architectural transformation perspective, so you'll learn about upgrading your legacy monolith applications to the cloud and microservices with minimal disruption.

While we couldn't possibly cover machine learning development in full detail in an introductory book, a bonus chapter has been included to enable .NET developers to incorporate intelligent machine learning services in their applications using the ML.NET library. By the end of this book, you will have a foundational understanding of building new and transforming existing applications using .NET 5's features and capabilities.

Who this book is for

The book is intended for intermediate and advanced developers with some experience of .NET and C# application development. It is also aimed at solution architects who wish to grasp the differentiating features and the future roadmap of the .NET technology. Knowledge of **.NET Core** or cloud development is not assumed. No prior machine learning knowledge is required to complete the bonus chapter on **ML.NET**.

This book discusses various transformation use cases for legacy applications written using **Windows Presentation Foundation (WPF)**, **ASP.NET**, **Entity Framework**, and so on. To get the full benefit from this book, an understanding of these common .NET technologies will help and enhance your reading experience and appreciation for the migration scenarios.

What this book covers

Chapter 1, Introducing .NET 5 Features and Capabilities, provides a brief history of .NET technology and how .NET 5 fits into the picture. It covers the main new .NET 5 features and different types of applications that can be built using this platform. This chapter compares .NET 5 with its predecessors, which are .NET Framework and .NET Core. It discusses the merits of each of these frameworks and then provides comprehensive coverage of the performance enhancements in the .NET 5 platform.

Chapter 2, What's New in C# 9?, covers all the new C# language features, including those that have been improved from the recent C# 7 and C# 8 versions, such as pattern matching and text processing. Code-based examples have been provided for all the discussed features.

Chapter 3, Design and Architectural Patterns, discusses application design strategies using design patterns such as **SOLID**, messaging protocols, and architectural patterns such as **microservices**, **serverless**, and **distributed processing**.

Chapter 4, Containerized Microservices Architecture, is full of practical exercises to build microservices-based containerized applications on .NET 5 using technologies such as **gRPC**, **Tye**, **WSL 2**, and **Kubernetes**.

Chapter 5, Upgrading Existing .NET Apps to .NET 5, discusses migration approaches to transform .NET Framework applications to the.NET 5 platform. It provides a sample application migration exercise that upgrades a .NET Framework 4.7 application with **WPF**, **Entity Framework**, **ASP.NET**, and third-party libraries such as **AutoFac** to its .NET 5 equivalents.

Chapter 6, Upgrading On-Premises Applications to the Cloud with .NET 5, introduces the reader to the cloud services such as **Azure SQL Database**, **Azure Web Apps**, **Azure Functions**, and **Azure Container Instances**. It provides a practical example to transform an on-premises application and deploy it to the aforementioned cloud services.

Chapter 7, Integrating Machine Learning in .NET 5 Code, is written for .NET developers who wish to integrate machine learning services into their .NET apps. The chapter covers the **ML.NET** library along with **ML.NET Model Builder** and provides an exercise to build an **Azure function** that integrates with ML.NET.

To get the most out of this book

It is assumed that you have some prior experience with any version of .NET technology and the C# language.

You do not need to read this book from cover to cover. The contents of each chapter are fairly self-contained and refer to the appropriate sections in other chapters where prior reading is assumed.

The example exercises have been tested on **Windows 10** machines with **Visual Studio 2019 v16.8** installed. Each chapter has its own specific technical requirements. The instructions to download and install these technologies have been provided in the *Technical requirements* sections of the relevant chapters.

If you are using the digital version of this book, we advise you to type the code yourself or access the code via the GitHub repository (link available in the next section). Doing so will help you avoid any potential errors related to the copying and pasting of code.

Download the example code files

You can download the example code files for this book from your account at www. packt.com. If you purchased this book elsewhere, you can visit www.packtpub.com/ support and register to have the files emailed directly to you.

You can download the code files by following these steps:

1. Log in or register at www.packt.com.
2. Select the **Support** tab.
3. Click on **Code Downloads**.
4. Enter the name of the book in the **Search** box and follow the onscreen instructions.

Once the file is downloaded, please make sure that you unzip or extract the folder using the latest version of:

- WinRAR/7-Zip for Windows

- Zipeg/iZip/UnRarX for Mac

- 7-Zip/PeaZip for Linux

The code bundle for the book is also hosted on GitHub at `https://github.com/PacktPublishing/Adopting-.NET-5--Architecture-Migration-Best-Practices-and-New-Features`. In case there's an update to the code, it will be updated on the existing GitHub repository.

We also have other code bundles from our rich catalog of books and videos available at `https://github.com/PacktPublishing/`. Check them out!

Download the color images

We also provide a PDF file that has color images of the screenshots/diagrams used in this book. You can download it here: `https://static.packt-cdn.com/downloads/9781800560567_ColorImages.pdf`.

Conventions used

There are a number of text conventions used throughout this book.

`Code in text`: Indicates code words in text, database table names, folder names, filenames, file extensions, pathnames, dummy URLs, user input, and Twitter handles. Here is an example: "The main service here is called `Primecalculator`; you can see it in the top left. The other three consumers are `Primeclienta`, `Primeclientb`, and `Primeclientc`."

A block of code is set as follows:

```
syntax = "proto3";
option csharp_namespace = "microservicesapp";
package prime;
```

When we wish to draw your attention to a particular part of a code block, the relevant lines or items are set in bold:

```
syntax = "proto3";
option csharp_namespace = "microservicesapp";
package prime;
```

Any command-line input or output is written as follows:

```
wsl --set-default-version 2
```

Bold: Indicates a new term, an important word, or words that you see onscreen. For example, words in menus or dialog boxes appear in the text like this. Here is an example: "If you are using Visual Studio 2019, you can right-click on **Connected Services**, add a gRPC service reference, and point it to the Proto file created before in the server service."

> **Tips or important notes**
> Appear like this.

Get in touch

Feedback from our readers is always welcome.

General feedback: If you have questions about any aspect of this book, mention the book title in the subject of your message and email us at customercare@packtpub.com.

Errata: Although we have taken every care to ensure the accuracy of our content, mistakes do happen. If you have found a mistake in this book, we would be grateful if you would report this to us. Please visit www.packtpub.com/support/errata, selecting your book, clicking on the Errata Submission Form link, and entering the details.

Piracy: If you come across any illegal copies of our works in any form on the Internet, we would be grateful if you would provide us with the location address or website name. Please contact us at copyright@packt.com with a link to the material.

If you are interested in becoming an author: If there is a topic that you have expertise in and you are interested in either writing or contributing to a book, please visit authors.packtpub.com.

Reviews

Please leave a review. Once you have read and used this book, why not leave a review on the site that you purchased it from? Potential readers can then see and use your unbiased opinion to make purchase decisions, we at Packt can understand what you think about our products, and our authors can see your feedback on their book. Thank you!

For more information about Packt, please visit `packt.com`.

Section 1: Features and Capabilities

The first section is about focusing on the grand picture. It introduces the .NET 5 technology and talks about its differentiating factors by comparing it with the previous .NET versions and technologies. It presents the .NET 5 feature set and examines its usability across different types of applications and platforms, such as web, desktop, mobile, cloud, and IoT.

It then highlights the performance improvements that have been one of the cornerstones of the new .NET platform. Finally, there is a chapter dedicated to C# developers, covering all the exciting language enhancements in **C# 9** that help us write concise yet readable code.

This section comprises the following chapters:

- *Chapter 1, Introducing .NET 5 Features and Capabilities*
- *Chapter 2, What's New in C# 9?*

1
Introducing .NET 5 Features and Capabilities

This book, as its title suggests, mainly features .NET 5 and all the related best practices that surround any major development processes for professional and enterprise applications. In this first chapter, I will summarize it for you to a great extent so that you get a top-level view at a glance.

We will take a look at how it all started with .NET historically, and through this, we will reflect on why .NET matters and what benefits we can obtain easily when choosing .NET as our primary development platform. Finally, we will see how long its technical support mechanism works for when we adopt .NET 5 as our main development platform.

While we will visit cloud-native apps topics later in this book in *Chapter 4, Containerized Microservices Architecture*, and *Chapter 6, Upgrading On-Prem Applications to the Cloud with .NET 5*, in this chapter, we will go deeper into .NET 5 features and the most useful performance improvements that we can leverage in all of our new applications and services. Since .NET 5 has been built on .NET 3.1, we will be revisiting some of the most significant capabilities offered from the previous version that are also still delivered perfectly and, in some cases, with enhanced performance by .NET 5.

In this chapter, we will be looking at the following major topics:

- Evolution of .NET
- Discovering the distinguishing factors in .NET versions
- What is the outlook for jumping to .NET 5?
- Types of applications developed using .NET
- What are .NET 5 headliners?
- Performance improvements
- .NET release schedule
- .NET support life cycle

By the end of this chapter, you will be able to see the history, the types of applications that are best built by .NET in certain environments for standalone as well as enterprise products. You will also be able to see and utilize the latest features of .NET and use the performance-oriented improvements directly in your new .NET 5-based applications and services.

Technical requirements

This chapter has two examples of code. In order to run them, the following are prerequisites:

- .NET 5 SDK
- .NET Framework 4.8
- .NET Core 3.1
- .NET 5
- ab – Apache HTTP server benchmarking tool

More information on Apache Bench can be found here: `http://httpd.apache.org/docs/current/programs/ab.html`.

Online code for examples can be found at the following GitHub URL: `https://github.com/PacktPublishing/Adopting-.NET-5--Architecture-Migration-Best-Practices-and-New-Features/tree/master/Chapter01`

Evolution of .NET

Microsoft first started working on .NET at the turn of the century and released the first version of .NET around 18 years ago, in 2002. Then, it released its version 1.1 in 2003, version 2.0 in 2005, and so on. It is worth noting that there was no consistency in the release cycle.

Back then, it used to be known as **Microsoft .NET Framework**, but later, they commonly referred to it as **.NET Framework**. four years ago, in 2016, it emerged with a big shift vis-à-vis the open source world and with its primary focus on performance and backend applications, going by the name of **.NET Core**.

.NET Framework initially was a Windows-only platform and, not long after, there were non-Microsoft public domain ports to other Unix-based platforms with the name of **Mono**. Over time, Mono saw a lot of success with the general .NET Framework. In due course, we saw the emergence and popularity of Xamarin as a .NET-based platform for smartphone app development. Xamarin was based on Mono and was actually developed by the same engineers.

In 2016, Microsoft acquired Xamarin and, in the same year, it also introduced .NET Core as a free, open source, and managed framework for Windows, Linux, and macOS. It was a cross-platform and slim version of .NET Framework. With .NET Core, Microsoft's focus shifted toward open source technologies, embracing the advent of cloud-native development and container-based architecture in platforms other than just Windows. .NET Core 2.0 was released in August 2017, and .NET Core 3.0 in May 2019.

In 2020, Microsoft's vision is One.NET. What this means is that they want to avoid confusion and go fully open source with support for all platforms across all feature sets, in other words, merge .NET Framework and .NET Core. Hence, the next major release after .NET Core 3.1 will be **.NET 5**. From a developer's perspective, .NET is a cross-platform runtime with a huge class library that contains all the essential elements required to code web, desktop, or mobile applications; platform-specific as well as cloud-native across various tech verticals.

Programs in .NET can be developed with a variety of programming languages such as C++, Visual Basic, and Fortran (as F#), with C# being the most popular. C# is a feature-rich, object-oriented programming language initially based on the syntax of C/C++ and Java.

Any language used for programming in .NET meets a set of minimum requirements in terms of using the .NET class libraries. These requirements are called the **Common Language Specification (CLS)**. They share a **Common Type System (CTS)**, such as basic data types (integers and strings). CLS and CTS are also a part of the **Common Language Infrastructure (CLI)**. CLI is an open specification that was actually developed by Microsoft and then standardized by ISO as well as ECMA.

.NET programs are compiled to a processor-independent **intermediate language (IL)**. When .NET-based apps run on a particular platform, IL is compiled into a native code of the processor by a **just-in-time (JIT)** compiler. JIT compilation is implemented by the platform-specific **Common Language Runtime (CLR)**. Code written in .NET is known as **managed code** since the actual machine language is translated by the CLR.

In every .NET program, CLR provides garbage collection services. It determines whether a memory block is no longer referenced by any variable in the application and will free up that fragment of memory as and when required.

.NET Core uses consistent and well-defined API models, written in what is called **.NET Standard**, which makes it portable and usable to many .NET applications. In this way, the same .NET library can be used in multiple platforms and in multiple languages. If you build the .NET Standard version as the target for the assembly of your .NET library instead of .NET Framework or .NET Core, then your library will be able to use both .NET Framework and .NET Core.

Now that we have covered a bit of the history regarding .NET Framework and .NET Core, let's look at the last big part of this chapter – learning about the distinguishing factors in .NET versions.

Discovering the distinguishing factors in .NET versions

First of all, the biggest positive point for **.NET Core** over **.NET Framework** is that *.NET Core is open source*. Being open source is a huge plus point as it gets a look-over from critics all over the world as well as providing a lot of valuable feedback and improvements to the open source code. On other hand, .NET Core is newer and was rewritten for cross-platform intentions from the outset, which implies that it is meant to be portable, faster, scalable, and more performant with a lesser memory footprint.

Let's see the core advantages of .NET Framework and .NET Core over one another.

Understanding the advantages of one over the other

Remember that with the advent of .NET Core, .NET Framework is not dead. In the first chapter, we saw the support life cycle for both runtimes and that .NET Framework will still be supported for many years to come. Since it is going to stay, it does have some important aspects that render it preferable to .NET Core under certain conditions.

.NET Core has a heavy focus on microservices and cloud-native application development, and therefore is better in terms of memory and performance when using a containerized form, especially with Docker. .NET Core enables much simpler and smoother usage of side-by-side execution of the same code with different .NET Core versions in addition to its popular self-contained deployment feature.

Let's now have a quick and concise look at the benefits of one runtime over another.

Benefits of using .NET Framework as the main part of your technology stack

Although it sounds odd talking about .NET Framework, version 4.8 was released in 2019, the same year as .NET Core 3.1. Highlighting this reminds us that the tech is new and not irrelevant. Here, therefore, we see the benefits offered by .NET Framework over the other versions:

- .NET Framework has a very long support cycle compared to .NET Core. As a big enterprise that is not a software company, you do not upgrade your tech stack every 2 or 3 years, which is the case for .NET Core to remain in support.

- .NET Framework is shipped with Windows and is supported as long as the Windows OS version is supported. This means that the applications do not need to worry about the runtime installations and losing support.

- If your application is stable and does not require big changes, you are better off upgrading to the latest .NET Framework version and to the latest patch level, as it could be costly to catch up and stay up to date with .NET Core versions.

- If your existing app or services are using extensive and exclusive features (such as hosting WCF) of .NET Framework, then it is suggested to stay with .NET Framework but upgrade to the latest version. This may lead to a lot of efforts due to the number of changes required.

- You would need to stay with .NET Framework if your app has a heavy dependency on the use of third-party components or it uses certain NuGet packages that are only available for .NET Framework.

- If your app uses certain platform-specific features that are not available with .NET Core, then you have no choice to switch until you migrate those platform specific features; or wait until those become available with the latest .NET version.

- If your app's code is dependent on **Code Access Security** (**CAS**), then it will have to stay with .NET Framework because .NET Core does not support it. The CAS feature is not even supported after C# 7.0.

- There are more and more reference implementations, technical documentation, and resources available for .NET Framework compared to .NET Core.

- .NET Core often has breaking changes or changes that render previous .NET Core versions obsolete, which means that it would require code changes in order to stay with the latest version, so staying with .NET Framework means fewer code changes.

Benefits of using .NET Core as the main part of your technology stack

Here, we see the benefits of .NET Core compared with other versions:

- It is a cross-platform technology.
- It is a container-aware technology.
- It is rewritten instead of modifying.NET Framework, is built for performance, and has a smaller memory footprint, thereby making it more suited to containers.
- With this, Entity Framework Core was also introduced, which is better than Entity Framework as it has better support for mappings and query-level performance.
- .NET Core is shipped independently of Windows and has a clearer and more consistent release cycle.

Initially, .NET Core was built with a focus on server-side applications, but later it evolved into all popular types of applications. However, .NET Core increased its popularity and became a widely adopted framework from .NET Core 3.0. We will now see the additional aspects incorporated by .NET Core 3.0, up to .NET 5, on top of .NET Core.

Benefits of using .NET 5 onward as the main part of your technology stack

Here, we examine the benefits of .NET 5 over other versions:

- Starting with .NET Core 3, support for **WinForms** and **WPF** was included so that the modern Windows desktop apps can be built using .NET Core and .NET 5 has further improved its support.

- Starting with .NET 5, **Xamarin** evolved into **.NET MAUI**, and so now Android, as well as the iOS app, can also be built with the consistent platform and tooling.

- .NET 5 supports ARM64 Linux flavors, hence the extended support of edge computing for IoT.

- .NET 5 reduced the memory footprint even further, as well as the disc size, with improvements in app trimming, which has been furthered with container size optimization.

- .NET 5 introduced C# 9, which added a lot of new features (which we will talk more about in the next chapter).

- .NET 5 has introduced further performance improvements on top of the already world-class performance by .NET Core 3 in many areas.

In this section, we learned about the main offerings of the specific .NET platform as well as saw the benefits of one over the other and, in particular, what value we can add when we adopt the .NET 5 technology stack. In the next section, we will see why we are working with .NET 5.

What is the outlook for jumping to .NET 5?

It is not just the case that .NET 5 is the latest tech in the Microsoft and open source world. We see that adopting .NET 5 adds a lot of value as well. .NET 5 has many features that are forward-looking, such as not being tied just to the Windows platform, being container-aware, and supporting lots of cloud-native workloads. It has even added the superior support of technologies from .NET Framework, including WinForms, yet .NET 5 still does not support a number of technologies, including **WebForms**, **WCF** hosting, and **Windows Workflow (WF)**.

This means that if you are not starting a new application, but instead, are thinking about upgrading your existing applications or services, then it could also be the case that your application depends on some libraries or NuGet packages that are not yet available on .NET Core 3.1 or .NET 5. As a strategy, you may look for alternative technologies or wait until the vendor releases the newer versions specifically for .NET 5.

In all such cases, we will dive deeper in the later chapters of this book, where we will focus on the migration topics along with the relevant situations and the example codes that will help you in making better decisions on migration topics.

> **Tip for WCF and WF applications**
>
> Around May 2019, there was a kick-off for two community-based **open source software (OSS)** projects on GitHub that are intended to bring **WCF** and **WF** support to .NET Core.
>
> Check out Scott Hunter's blog post to see where **Core WCF** and **Core WF** fits in with the .NET 5 roadmap: *Supporting the community with WF and WCF OSS projects*:
> ```
> https://devblogs.microsoft.com/dotnet/supporting-
> the-community-with-wf-and-wcf-oss-projects/.
> ```

Now that we've understood the history and the advantages of .NET 5, let's check out the type of applications it can create.

Types of applications developed using .NET

.NET Core is a versatile framework that can be used to build many types of applications, including the following:

- Web apps
- Mobile apps
- Desktop apps
- IoT apps
- Cloud-native services
- Machine learning

Let's look at each one separately in this section.

Web applications

ASP.NET Core is the main framework for building web applications. It is a core component of the .NET Core ecosystem. Using the MVC architecture helps to build web apps as well as REST APIs. Razor is also a framework part of ASP.NET Core that assists in building dynamic web pages using C# and TypeScript.

> **Note**
>
> WebForms are no longer supported and the recommended alternative is ASP.
> NET Core Blazor.
>
> **Blazor** helps in building an interactive client-side web UI using C# instead of
> JavaScript. It is therefore sharing the server-side and the client-side app logic in
> .NET, which in certain instances may not be the ideal approach.

In the API domain, besides REST APIs, .NET Core dived deeper into the open source
world in communication protocols using a compact and performance-oriented RPC
mechanism with gRPC technology. gRPC support is also present in desktop applications,
Windows, Linux, and containers. .NET Core also still supports the capability to call the
SOAP services via WCF tech, but does not provide hosting as server-side SOAP services.
Note that gRPC is now a preferred technology over WCF.

Mobile development

.NET Core also offers mobile application development. The name of the feature set is
Xamarin, which is a set of tools and libraries, enabling you to build cross-platform mobile
apps. Developers can build native apps for iOS, Android, Windows, and even for macOS.

With .NET 5, Xamarin Forms are convoluted into .NET MAUI, which is open source
and present on GitHub at `https://github.com/dotnet/maui`. With .NET MAUI,
development is simplified by providing a single stack that supports all of these platforms:
Android, iOS, macOS, and Windows. It provides a single project developer experience
that can target multiple platforms and devices.

Desktop applications

With .NET Core 3.0, Microsoft made available the biggest improvements as regards
Windows desktop development using **Windows Forms** and **Windows Presentation
Foundation (WPF)**. It also supports the **Windows UI XAML Library (WinUI)**, which
was introduced back then along with the **Universal Windows Platform (UWP)**.

New boilerplate WPF or WinForms apps can be simply created using the CLI:

```
dotnet new wpf
dotnet new winforms p
```

Internet of Things

Edge computation is increasingly being utilized on a daily basis, from households and water pipes to cars, airplane engines, and what not. .NET Core also provides extensive support for IoT development via Azure infrastructure products, as well as via the UWP framework for IoT devices running Windows 10 IoT Core.

It also offers support for ARM64 on Linux, and ARM64 Docker images are also available. .NET Core has even added GPIO support for the Raspberry Pi.

Cloud-native development and microservices

All of the application deployment types available on Azure are achievable via .NET Core technologies. Various serverless, event streaming, containerization, and many other applications besides are directly supported in cross-platform flavors.

.NET Core fully supports and promotes microservice architecture-based development. It has full support for Windows, as well as Linux Docker containers, to implement microservices and fully adapts Kubernetes as a *container orchestrator*. It supports and promotes point-to-point communication via the *gRPC protocol*, as well as out-of-sync communication via various messaging patterns. We will dive deep into these topics in later chapters.

Machine learning

.NET Core provides support to execute machine learning via **ML.NET**, which is an open source and cross-platform machine learning framework. ML.NET allows you to create custom machine learning models, and train and build them using C# or F# for a number of machine learning scenarios. We will visit this interesting technology in more depth later in this book.

Visual Studio solution templates for .NET

Visual Studio 2019 provides some useful solution templates that generate the boilerplate code for some of the most common application development. They are shown here basically to highlight how straightforward it is to start .NET based development. Note that these solution templates are applicable to both .NET Core and .NET 5.

Here, I will provide you with a quick glimpse into the most popular solution templates for .NET Core-based projects that are readily available with Visual Studio 2019. Note that for all of these solutions, we can easily change the .NET SDK version by going into the project properties. It can be changed for any version of .NET Core and .NET 5 and so on.

Following are the solution templates for the web applications:

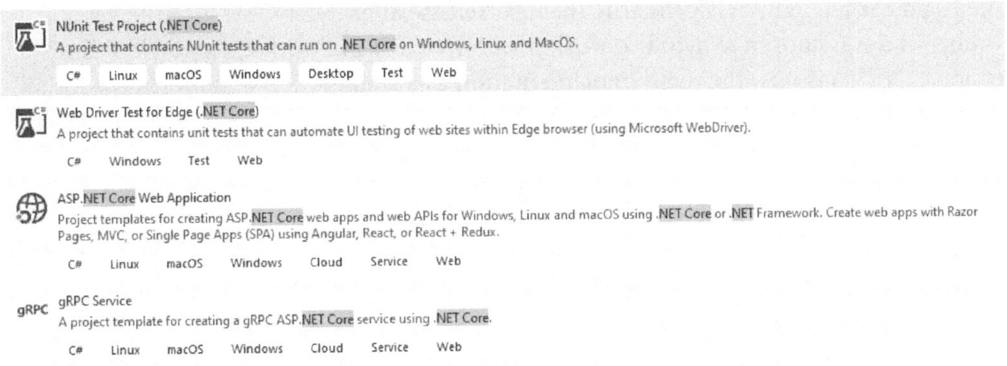

Figure 1.1 – Solution templates for web applications

For desktop applications, we have the following templates:

Figure 1.2 – Solution templates for desktop applications

With this, we can see how easy it is to generate the most popular application types from Visual Studio using .NET Core both for desktop and web application types. Note that in the project properties, you have the option to change the runtime to .NET 5, but the templates still name them as .NET Core.

Next, we will look at the major highlights of the single .NET, in other words, .NET 5.

What are the .NET 5 headliners?

Like I said earlier, .NET 5 is primarily the next release after .NET Core 3.1. The version number of 5 was chosen to avoid confusion with .NET Framework 4.x and .NET Core versions. .NET 5 is now the main implementation as a single .NET version stream for all the future releases of .NET. It will be released as .NET 5, .NET 6, .NET 7, and so on, since it has merged the two streams of .NET Framework and .NET Core into one. Therefore, .NET 5 supports more types of apps and platforms than .NET Core or .NET Framework.

Having an edge over .NET Core 3.1 and .NET Framework, .NET 5 has made considerable improvements in many areas, including the following:

- **Single-file, self-contained app**: This feature has been improved further, as provided earlier by .NET 3.1.

- **App trimming and container size optimization**: The size of the app has been reduced by trimming the types used inside the .NET libraries and reducing the size of the runtime binaries for containers just to what is essential.

- **C# compiler enhancements and C# 9 as well as F# 5.0**: Various new features have been added and performance improved further.

- **Windows ARM64**: ARM64 platform-specific optimizations in the .NET libraries.

- **Performance improvements**: Applied in many areas, including text, JSON, tasks, and more.

We have now learned the purpose of .NET and seen its main headliners. We will dive deep into various performance improvements and C# 9 features to further increase our knowledge and command over .NET 5 in the next main section. For now, let's get to know some more about some of its major features.

Discovering self-contained applications

To run .NET programs on a certain setup (such as a bare metal machine, VM, or container), .NET runtime is required. Prior to .NET Core 3.0, all the previous versions were dependent on the runtime pre-present in the setup in which it executes. .NET Core 3.0 comes with support known as **self-contained executables**, which enable you to publish applications as a single executable for a given supported platform such as Linux, Windows, 32-bit, or 64-bit.

In order to simulate the creation of a self-contained app, I will use the .NET 5 SDK. To see the version of dotnet SDK, we run the following command:

```
C:\Users\Habib\source\repos\Adopting-.NET-5--Architecture-
Migration-Best-Practices-and-New-Features\code\Chapter01>dotnet
-version
5.0.100-rc.2.20479.15
```

For demonstration purposes, I will create a sample console app via the command line:

```
C:\Users\Habib\source\repos\Adopting-.NET-5--Architecture-
Migration-Best-Practices-and-New-Features\code\Chapter01>dotnet
new console -o myscapp
```

Then, the command to generate the self-contained executable (for Linux 64-bit) would look like this:

```
C:\Users\Habib\source\repos\Adopting-.NET-5--Architecture-
Migration-Best-Practices-and-New-Features\code\Chapter01>dotnet
publish -c release --self-contained --runtime linux-x64 -o c:\
apps\myscapp_lx
```

Executing `dir C:\apps\myscapp_lx` shows me something in terms of which end part is something like this, with 186 files and around 75 MB of disk space:

```
...
25/09/2020   23:06                16.776 WindowsBase.dll
             186 File(s)       75.306.803 bytes
               2 Dir(s)   709.082.009.600 bytes free
```

In order to generate a self-contained executable in a *single* .exe file (for a Windows 64-bit platform), the command would be as follows:

```
C:\Users\Habib\source\repos\Adopting-.NET-5--Architecture-
Migration-Best-Practices-and-New-Features\code\Chapter01\
myscapp>dotnet publish -c release --self-contained --runtime
win-x64 /p:PublishSingleFile=true -o c:\apps\myscapp_win
Microsoft (R) Build Engine version 16.8.0-preview-20475-
05+aed5e7ed0 for .NET
Copyright (C) Microsoft Corporation. All rights reserved.

  Determining projects to restore...
  Restored C:\Users\Habib\source\repos\Adopting-.NET-5--
Architecture-Migration-Best-Practices-and-New-Features\code\
Chapter01\myscapp\myscapp.csproj (in 36,23 sec).
```

```
    You are using a preview version of .NET. See: https://aka.ms/
dotnet-core-preview

    myscapp -> C:\Users\Habib\source\repos\Adopting-.NET-5--
Architecture-Migration-Best-Practices-and-New-Features\code\
Chapter01\myscapp\bin\release\net5.0\win-x64\myscapp.dll
    myscapp -> c:\apps\myscapp_win\
```

I have the following output after running this command with the .NET 5 SDK:

Name	Type	Size
> This PC > Local Disk (C:) > apps > myscapp_win		
clrcompression.dll	Application exten...	731 KB
clrjit.dll	Application exten...	1.294 KB
coreclr.dll	Application exten...	5.034 KB
mscordaccore.dll	Application exten...	1.019 KB
myscapp.exe	Application	52.041 KB
myscapp.pdb	Program Debug D...	10 KB

Figure 1.3 – .NET 5 generating a self-contained app in a single .exe file

This generated six files instead of 180 plus files, and the main .exe file is around 50 MB on my machine using the .NET 5 RC2 SDK, and this file contains within itself all the required libraries from the framework and the runtime.

Additionally, .NET also provides a feature to generate the trimmed version of the self-contained executables. What this means is that the output will only contain the required assemblies that are used by the application code and avoid including any other runtime libraries that are not used. If the code is using reflection, the .NET assembly linker does not know about this dynamic behavior and therefore it could not include those types and the libraries that are required and expected by the code that uses the reflection at runtime. Therefore, you need to indicate the linker in relation to any of the types needed by reflection in the specified libraries.

A simple command line to generate the trimmed self-contained version would look like this:

```
C:\Users\Habib\source\repos\Adopting-.NET-5--Architecture-
Migration-Best-Practices-and-New-Features\code\Chapter01\
myscapp>dotnet publish -c release --self-contained --runtime
win-x64 /p:PublishSingleFile=true /p:PublishTrimmed=true -o c:\
apps\myscapp_win_2t
```

Running this command will generate the following output:

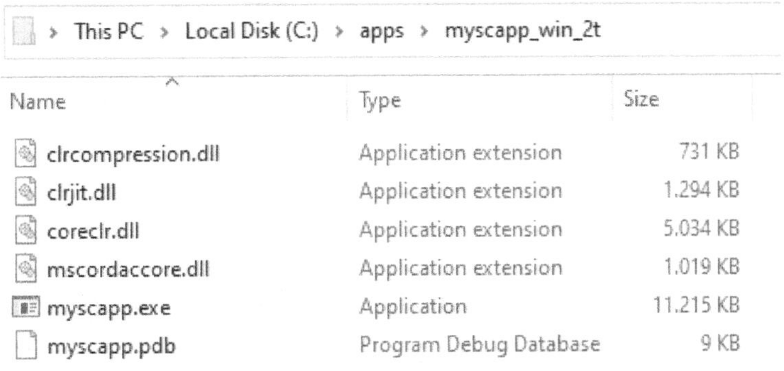

Figure 1.4 – .NET 5 generating a self-contained trimmed app in a single .exe file

Comparing the generated output files with our previous command line without using the trim option, which generated around 50 MB, this one generated around 11 MB of `.exe` files, and this contained all of the *required* .NET 5 runtime and framework libraries!

While single file and trimming might be regarded as a cosmetic change, the self-contained option is really a safeguarding boundary for your application so that it can run safely and in a stable manner with other applications using any other .NET runtime, especially when your app is not running in the container but in a shared environment.

.NET 5 app trimming optimizations

In .NET 5, trimming has been further optimized where the assembly linker goes deep inside the assemblies and removes even the types and members that are not used in all of the referenced assemblies. This is known as **member-level trimming**.

Member-level trimming can be enabled by passing `-p:PublishTrimmed=True` and `-p:TrimMode=Link` to the dotnet `publish` command.

In .NET 5, in order to give hints to the trimmer (known as the **ILLink**) for dynamic code such as reflection, a set of attributes has been added that enables the code to be annotated, and so should be included by the ILLink.

One more feature that is being added to .NET 5 allows us to conditionally remove code from applications using the feature switches. Feature switches remove the features provided by the framework, which even reduces the size of the .NET runtime.

> **Tip**
>
> Remember, when you trim your app, that it is necessary to perform exhaustive end-to-end testing of the published version of the application. The testing of a trimmed app should be carried out externally rather than by unit tests or code within the app, as the published code is only the trimmed output.

ReadyToRun

Another feature that has been introduced, starting with .NET Core 3.0 and above, is **ReadyToRun (R2R)**. R2R is a kind of **ahead-of-time (AOT)** compilation. It improves the startup time of your application by natively compiling your application assemblies in R2R format at build time so that JIT is not required to be done when assemblies are executed the first time.

R2R has the most significant effect in terms of startup time. Later, there should be little difference once the process is already warmed up.

Developing programs for .NET

To develop .NET programs, a fully fledged IDE is not required. The CLI tools provided, specifically the *dotnet command,* are enough to compile and build the programs. You can also use free, open source, and cross-platform Visual Studio Code, or Express, which is a free version of Visual Studio. For .NET Core 3 and .NET 5, you will at least require Visual Studio 2019.

You can also use *Visual Studio Code Remote Development,* which enables you to use a container, VM, remote machine, or the **Windows Subsystem for Linux (WSL)** as a fully fledged development environment. This allows your development machine to be different to your deployment machine. Your remote host (container, VM), which is used for building the application, is fully configured and streamlined according to the app requirements, and hence you would no longer want to modify your development machine. Binaries resulting from the source code are not even required on your local machine, which is why you can perform remote debugging on your remote host.

From May 2019, Microsoft introduced *Visual Studio Codespaces,* which provides Azure-powered, managed, on-demand development environments. You can work in these environments, which differ from your development machines, via *Visual Studio Code* or *Visual Studio 2019,* with certain extensions installed in your IDE.

You would need to use codespaces in these situations, where you may like to try out new tech, a new tool, or a different technology stack, without disrupting your own primary development environment, or setting these development environments locally would simply take too much time before you can even try it out. Unless we are ready to brick our fine-tuned development machine, we would mostly hesitate trying out a new stack, such as Node.js, Android development, or Python. This is where codespaces come in.

> **Head on over to the following link for more information:**
>
> ```
> https://code.visualstudio.com/blogs/2019/05/02/
> remote-development.
> ```

Next, we will be understanding performance improvements and checking how does it work in different .NET versions.

Performance improvements

Starting from .NET Core, since it was rewritten separately to .NET Framework, the main focus of .NET was performance, meaning performance was one of the most important features of the platform and, ever since then, each .NET version has enhanced performance further in every aspect of the platform.

Why performance is so important?

For any sizeable application, naturally, performance is a major area where non-functional improvements take place. Once all the processes and algorithms specific to the applications have been enhanced, there is not so much left to change that can add further performance enhancements. In such situations, analysis is required for every bit of code in minute detail. If performance improves by even just 0.001%, this may have a significant impact.

Let's have a few examples to build the context of how important performance improvements are that automatically affect the business and, hence, impact the functional part of the application.

According to independent statistics accumulated, as well as our own years of experience related to our online digital life that has become so normal these days, we can make the following general observations:

- More than 70% of customers who are dissatisfied with the performance of the web store are less likely to buy again and would rather seek alternatives next time.

- 1 out of 5 customers are likely to forego a purchase if the shopping cart and checkout process are very slow; some may even have a mistrust of the process.

- If a website is performing poorly, then no matter what type of services it provides, 30% of users would have a negative impression.

- Half of users expect the website to load in 2 seconds, especially on smartphones, and would leave the site if it takes more than 5 seconds to load.

- Amazon calculated that they would lose $1.6 billion every year if they slowed down by even just 1 second.

- Customers have a general perception that if it is fast, it must be professional!

- The rise of cloud computing means per-second billing of on-demand compute and memory resource consumption.

> **Performance stats by Skilled**
>
> Look here for stats from Skilled on how page speed affects e-commerce: `https://skilled.co/resources/speed-affects-website-infographic/`.

Seeing these real-world examples, we realize how vital performance improvements are for any online business presence. Even a second's improvement in the response time of a web application can generate significant profit!

These are the kinds of use cases as to why Microsoft has taken .NET to another level by focusing on improvements in every area and to every bit of code.

This means that if the underlying engine of the application code is supercharged, the application automatically reaps the performance benefits and, hence, the **return on investments (ROI)** gets increased as the company invests time and money in migrating to .NET 5.

Let's now see what are the main areas that have been improved in various versions of .NET, up to .NET 5, that are key to a faster application!

Performance improvements in .NET versions

Let's now look in depth at where .NET has improved performance, starting with .NET Core and going through to .NET 5. What we will do is examine the key focal points as regards improvements in .NET Core version by version. This will give us a good picture of how and where core performance improvements take place and how we automatically accrue the benefit of it in our applications.

By way of a general understanding based on the work of Microsoft and open source developers, all the newer versions of .NET Core (and now .NET from version 5.0) are built on top of previous versions, which means either they improve on top of existing performance tweaks or they even go back and increase performance gains, which, in the previous version, were improved in a slightly different manner. Further improvements in a newer version of an already improved feature are made possible due to the two main components:

- The first is following the availability of new C# language features (from C# version 7.3+), along with its improved **compiler**, which generates better code, for example, by utilizing techniques that take into account the best use case and also common scenarios.

- The second is owing to improvements in **JITTER**, which generates more efficient machine code by reducing the total number of instructions and using intrinsic instructions.

From the very first version of .NET Core, performance started to improve, and this held true for each version that followed. Let's visit the major improvement areas in order of the released versions.

Performance improvements in .NET Core

Performance improvements in .NET Core (for versions 1.0–2.1) initially focused on the following areas:

- Collections are faster as well as LINQ.

- Compression (specifically, `Deflate Stream`).

- Cryptography and math (specially `BigInteger`).

- Serialization (`BinaryFormatter` improved in .NET Core 2.0, but generally it is recommended to use other types of serialization).

- Text processing (improvement in `RegEx`, `UrlDecoding` – a minimum of 50% faster).

- Improvements in strings (`Equals`, `IndexOf`, `IndexOfAny`, `Split`, and `Concat`).

- Asynchronous file streaming (`CopyToAsync` is 46% faster).

- Networking (especially sockets, improvements in asynchronous read, write, and copy operations in `NetworkStream` operations as well as `SslStream`).

- Concurrency (threadpool, synchronization, especially `SpinLock` and `Lazy<T>`).

- JIT (devirtualization and often method inlining)

Performance improvements in .NET Core 3

Now, let's check major improvement areas in .NET Core version 3:

- Various improvements associated with manipulating data in memory, especially with span and memory.

- Improvements in arrays and strings (based on the use of spans and their vectorization optimizations).

- Collections are faster (`Dictionary`, `Queue`, `BitArray`, and `SortedSet` are around 50% faster than in .NET Core 2.1).

- `System.Decimal` has been overhauled and is much faster compared with .NET Core 2.0.

- Threading (tasks and async are faster, timers are optimized).

- Networking (an even faster `SslSteam`, **HttpClient**: a larger buffer size, thereby reducing system calls to transfer data).

- JIT's direct access to newer and compound CPU instructions.

- Many I/O improvements that are at least 25% faster than .NET Core 2.1.

- Improvements in the interop, which itself is used by .NET (`SafeHandle` 50% faster).

- Improvements in the **Garbage Collector (GC)** (set memory limits, and more container-aware).

Performance improvements in .NET 5

Finally let's overview the major performance improvements areas in .NET 5 that are on top of .NET Core's aforementioned improvements:

- **Garabage Collection (GC)**: GC has a process of marking the items that are in use. *Server GC* allocates one thread per core for the collection process. When one thread has finished marking all the items, it will continue to work on marking the items that have not yet been completed by other threads. In this way, it speeds up the overall collection process.

  GC is optimized to decommit the Gen0 and Gen1 segments upon which it can return the allocated memory pages back to the operating system.

  Improvements in the GC's scalability on machines with a higher number of cores reduces memory resets in low-memory situations.

  Movement in some of the code, such as sorting primitives from C code into C#, also helped in managing the runtime and in the further development of APIs, as well as in helping to reduce the **GC Pause**, which ultimately improved the performance of the GC as well as the application. GC Pause is a pause time, which means how long the GC must pause the runtime in order to perform its work.

- **Hardware Intrinsics**: .NET Core 3.0 added lots of hardware intrinsics that allow JIT to enable C# code to directly target CPU instructions, such as SSE4 AVX. .NET 5.0 also added a lot more intrinsics specific to ARM64.

- **Text Processing**: `char.IsWhiteSpace` has been improved, thereby requiring a smaller number of CPU instructions and less branching. Improvements in this area have also facilitated improvements in lots of string methods, such as `Trim()`.

  `char.ToUpperInvariant` is 50% faster than .NET 3.1, while `Int.ToString` is also 50% faster.

  Further improvements have been made in terms of encoding, for example, `Encoding.UTF8.GetString`.

- **Regular Expressions**: `RegEx` has seen more than a 70% performance improvement compared to .NET Core 3.1 in various cases.

- **Collections**: Lots of improvements have been made to `Dictionary`, especially in the lookups and utilizing the `ref` returns to avoid a second lookup, as the user would pick up the value when obtaining the keys with the computed hash.

  Similar upgrades applied to `ConcurrentDictionary` as well.

`Hashset` wasn't optimized previously, as was `Dictionary`, but now it is optimized on a similar algorithm to `Dictionary`, meaning it is much faster than .NET FW 4.8 and even .NET Core 3.1.

Iteration on `ImmutableArray` is optimized by inlining the `GetEnumerator` and further JIT optimization, and hence the iteration in .NET 5 is almost 4 times faster than 3.1.

`BitArray` is a specialized collection that was also optimized by the open source non-Microsoft developer by utilizing the hardware intrinsics using AVX2 and SSE2 advanced CPU instructions.

- **LINQ**: Improvements in .NET 5 for LINQ made `OrderBy` 15% and `SkipLast` 50% faster than 3.1.

- **Networking**: Socket improvements were made to the Linux platform for faster asynchronous I/O with `epoll` and a smaller number of threads. A number of improvements to the `Socket Connect` and `Bind` methods, along with underlying improvements, made them even faster than .NET Core 3.1.

  `SocketsHttpHandler` and `Date` format validation in the header is optimized, giving us more performance gains.

  HTTP/2 code is optimized as it was mostly functional in 3.1, but performance improvements took place in 5.0, which makes it perform twice as fast and consume almost half of the memory in certain scenarios.

- **JSON**: A number of improvements have been made to the `System.Text.JSON` library for .NET 5, especially for `JsonSerializer`, which makes it more than 50% faster than 3.1 and means it consumes much less memory.

- **Kestrel**: Kestrel is a web server included with .NET SDK. This web server is specifically designed to serve APIs built on .NET Core and .NET 5. It should be noted that as a result of performance improvements in the areas of reduced allocations in HTTP/2, along with the higher use of `Span` and improvements in GC, this has given a significant boost to the Kestrel implementation, which is included with .NET 5. These especially have a direct impact when serving gRPC-based APIs as well as REST APIs.

Wow! That was quite an impressive number of performance improvements and these, too, applied version by version to every level of the code. This many optimizations applied to such types of projects across this time duration is not something normally observed. All of this is the result of a number of expert Microsoft and other developers working on an open source project and we all reap the benefits from this in terms of our individual productivity.

Let's now look at a couple of examples to run the code and compare performance.

Let's do some benchmarking

In the previous section, we have seen a number of improvements applied to a plethora of feature sets. We have also seen that so far; .NET 5 is a superset of all the performance improvements and is the fastest .NET version out there.

At the end of this chapter, I have placed the links to the article where Microsoft has specified a number of benchmarks for each of the aspects they talked about. Like me, you can also run them very easily. Out of those, I will pick one and present it here, as well as the complete code, so that you can repeat the experiment on your own machine.

Benchmarking API performance between .NET versions

In the first benchmarking program, I will pick one of the benchmarking examples similar to the **Microsoft Blog post** for demonstration purposes and will also show the results as they ran on my machine. We will benchmark this with .NET Framework 4.8, .NET Core 3.1, and .NET 5.0:

1. To begin, first of all, this is a tiny project setup with only one `Program.cs` file required as a console application. In this, we use the NuGet package used for all types of .NET benchmarking: `benchmarkdotnet`. At the time of writing, I used version `0.12.1`.

2. To execute the benchmark, just use this simple `.csproj` file:

```
Benchmarks.csproj
1    <Project Sdk="Microsoft.NET.Sdk">
2
3      <PropertyGroup>
4        <OutputType>Exe</OutputType>
5        <TargetFrameworks>net5.0;netcoreapp3.1;net48</TargetFrameworks>
6      </PropertyGroup>
7
8      <ItemGroup>
9        <PackageReference Include="benchmarkdotnet" Version="0.12.1" />
10     </ItemGroup>
11
12     <ItemGroup Condition=" '$(TargetFramework)' == 'net48' ">
13       <PackageReference Include="System.Memory" Version="4.5.4" />
14       <PackageReference Include="System.Text.Json" Version="4.7.2" />
15       <Reference Include="System.Net.Http" />
16     </ItemGroup>
17
18   </Project>
```

Figure 1.5 – The csproj file for the benchmark project

For our example, I am using here this `Program.cs` file, while in the code repository for this book, I have included a couple more that you can also use to test out quickly:

```
C# Program.cs > ...
  1  ∨ using BenchmarkDotNet.Attributes;
  2    using BenchmarkDotNet.Diagnosers;
  3    using BenchmarkDotNet.Running;
  4    using System;
  5    using System.Text;
  6
  7    [MemoryDiagnoser]
       1 reference
  8  ∨ public class Program
  9    {
         0 references
 10      static void Main(string[] args) => BenchmarkSwitcher.FromAssemblies(new[] { typeof(Program).Assembly }).Run(args);
 11
         1 reference
 12      private byte[] _arr = Encoding.UTF8.GetBytes("Test to see improvements to IndexOfAny.. how are they?");
         0 references
 13      [Benchmark] public int IndexOf() => new Span<byte>(_arr).IndexOfAny((byte)'.', (byte)'?');
 14    }
```

Figure 1.6 – The Program.cs file for the benchmark project

On my machine, I have .NET Framework 4.8, .NET Core 3.1, and .NET 5 RC2 installed. So, in order to run these benchmarks successfully on your machine, please ensure that you install them too.

3. Typing this command generates the following output:

```
C:\>dotnet -version
5.0.100-rc.2.20479.15
```

This confirms that .NET 5.0 is the dominant SDK on my machine and which, if required, is changeable via the `global.json` file.

> **Tip**
>
> Placing this `global.json` file on the directory changes the default dotnet SDK for all of the sub-directories. For example, I place the following content in my `global.json` file to change the default SDK/compiler for all subprojects to .NET Core 3.1:
>
> ```
> {
>     "sdk": {
>         "version": "3.1.402"
>     }
> }
> ```

4. I placed the two files as mentioned earlier into the following folder: `C:\Users\Habib\source\repos\Benchmarks`.
5. Then, I run the following command to execute the benchmark:

```
dotnet run -c Release -f net48 --runtimes net48
netcoreapp3.1 netcoreapp5.0 --filter *Program*
```

The command is giving an instruction to build and run the code in the current directory using the entry point from `Program` and generate and execute three `.exe` files, one each for .NET Framework 4.8, .NET Core 3.1, and .NET 5.0.

6. Running this command on my machine now, I get the following result, which I will paste here for our reference. Remember that results may vary depending on the kind of machine on which we execute our benchmark. I am including here only the last part of the execution output, which is the summary of the benchmarking execution:

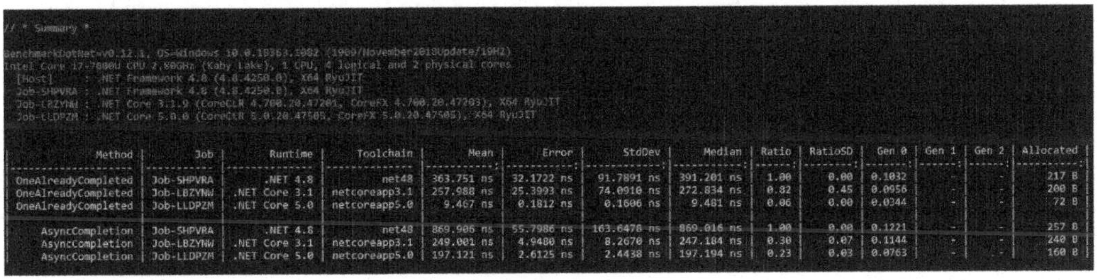

```
// * Summary *

BenchmarkDotNet=v0.12.1, OS=Windows 10.0.18363.1082 (1909/November2019Update/19H2)
Intel Core i7-7600U CPU 2.80GHz (Kaby Lake), 1 CPU, 4 logical and 2 physical cores
  [Host]     : .NET Framework 4.8 (4.8.4250.0), X64 RyuJIT
  Job-SHPVRA : .NET Framework 4.8 (4.8.4250.0), X64 RyuJIT
  Job-LBZYNW : .NET Core 3.1.9 (CoreCLR 4.700.20.47201, CoreFX 4.700.20.47203), X64 RyuJIT
  Job-LLDPZM : .NET Core 5.0.0 (CoreCLR 5.0.20.47505, CoreFX 5.0.20.47505), X64 RyuJIT
```

Method	Job	Runtime	Toolchain	Mean	Error	StdDev	Median	Ratio	RatioSD	Gen 0	Gen 1	Gen 2	Allocated
OneAlreadyCompleted	Job-SHPVRA	.NET 4.8	net48	363.751 ns	32.1722 ns	91.7891 ns	391.201 ns	1.00	0.00	0.1032	-	-	217 B
OneAlreadyCompleted	Job-LBZYNW	.NET Core 3.1	netcoreapp3.1	257.988 ns	25.3993 ns	74.0910 ns	272.834 ns	0.82	0.45	0.0956	-	-	200 B
OneAlreadyCompleted	Job-LLDPZM	.NET Core 5.0	netcoreapp5.0	9.467 ns	0.1812 ns	0.1606 ns	9.481 ns	0.06	0.00	0.0344	-	-	72 B
AsyncCompletion	Job-SHPVRA	.NET 4.8	net48	869.906 ns	55.7986 ns	163.6478 ns	869.016 ns	1.00	0.00	0.1221	-	-	257 B
AsyncCompletion	Job-LBZYNW	.NET Core 3.1	netcoreapp3.1	249.001 ns	4.9480 ns	8.2670 ns	247.184 ns	0.30	0.07	0.1144	-	-	240 B
AsyncCompletion	Job-LLDPZM	.NET Core 5.0	netcoreapp5.0	197.121 ns	2.6125 ns	2.4438 ns	197.194 ns	0.23	0.03	0.0763	-	-	160 B

Figure 1.7 – Output of the benchmark project

Notice here the mean execution time in nanoseconds and, in the last column, the number of bytes allocated to each execution of the test case.

From the final output, it can be clearly seen that .NET 5 outperforms both .NET Core 3.1 and .NET Framework 4.8 by a wide margin. With this, let's now move on to our second benchmarking program.

Benchmarking a tiny Web API using .NET Core 3.1 and .NET 5.0

In the first benchmarking example, we saw a performance comparison of one .NET API: `IndexOfAny` on the byte array, and how .NET 5 was the best of all. In this second example, we will create a very tiny Web API project, in fact, a default one from the dotnet scaffolding. We are then going to run it on localhost and call it 50,000 times and see the performance statistics in a manner that is almost akin to blackbox performance testing.

Note that this is not a realistic test in terms of a practical application, but it can give us an overall impression of the general performance of the same code using .NET Core 3.1 versus .NET 5.0 without applying any tweaks.

Setting up the benchmark

To begin our tiny benchmark, we first need to set up a few things. Here, I am listing them in short and easy steps:

1. First, we set up our project structure so that the instructions run perfectly for all readers. So, first of all, my directory hierarchy looks like this:

   ```
   C:\Users\Habib\source\repos\Adopting-.NET-5--
   Architecture-Migration-Best-Practices-and-New-Features\
   code\Chapter01
   ```

2. Now, using the `global.json` file as mentioned in the previous tip, I set my dotnet SDK version to be .NET Core 3.1 by placing the `global.json` file in the `Chapter01` folder.

3. Then, I execute the following commands:

   ```
   dotnet -version
   ```
   ```
   dotnet new webapi -o dummyapi31
   ```

   The first command is just to verify that the SDK is .NET Core 3.1, and the second command creates the default Web API project.

4. After that, just edit this file on Notepad++:

   ```
   C:\Users\Habib\source\repos\Adopting-.NET-5--
   Architecture-Migration-Best-Practices-and-New-
   Features/blob/master/Chapter01/dummyapi31/Controllers/
   WeatherForecastController.cs
   ```

5. Then, add the following lines to the Get() method:

```
[HttpGet]
public IEnumerable<WeatherForecast> Get()
{
    string src = "This is a source string that needs to be capitalized.";
    char[] dst = new char[1024];

    _logger.LogInformation(dst.ToString());
    src.AsSpan().ToUpperInvariant(dst);
    _logger.LogInformation(dst.ToString());
    Array.Reverse(dst);
    _logger.LogInformation(dst.ToString());

    var rng = new Random();
    return Enumerable.Range(1, 5).Select(index => new WeatherForecast
    {
        Date = DateTime.Now.AddDays(index),
        TemperatureC = rng.Next(-20, 55),
        Summary = Summaries[rng.Next(Summaries.Length)]
    })
    .ToArray();
}
```

Figure 1.8 – Code fragment to change in the default Web API project

6. After this, execute the following commands to run the Web API project:

```
cd dummyapi31
dotnet run
```

And I have the following output:

```
info: Microsoft.Hosting.Lifetime[0]
      Now listening on: https://localhost:5001
info: Microsoft.Hosting.Lifetime[0]
      Now listening on: http://localhost:5000
info: Microsoft.Hosting.Lifetime[0]
      Application started. Press Ctrl+C to shut down.
info: Microsoft.Hosting.Lifetime[0]
      Hosting environment: Development
info: Microsoft.Hosting.Lifetime[0]
      Content root path: C:\Users\Habib\source\repos\
Adopting-.NET-5--Architecture-Migration-Best-Practices-
and-New-Features\code\Chapter01\dummyapi31
```

7. Similarly, I do the same thing for the executable based on .NET 5.0. First, I disable the `global.json` file by renaming it, then I execute `dotnet -version` to verify that the active SDK is now .NET 5.0, and then I run the same command to create the Web API project with the name `dotnet new webapi -o dummyapi50`. I then edit `WeatherForecastController` in exactly the same way and then execute `dotnet run` to get the following output:

```
C:\Users\Habib\source\repos\Adopting-.NET-5--
Architecture-Migration-Best-Practices-and-New-Features\
code\Chapter01\dummyapi50>dotnet run
Building...
info: Microsoft.Hosting.Lifetime[0]
      Now listening on: https://localhost:5001
info: Microsoft.Hosting.Lifetime[0]
      Now listening on: http://localhost:5000
info: Microsoft.Hosting.Lifetime[0]
      Application started. Press Ctrl+C to shut down.
info: Microsoft.Hosting.Lifetime[0]
      Hosting environment: Development
info: Microsoft.Hosting.Lifetime[0]
      Content root path:
C:\Users\Habib\source\repos\Adopting-.NET-5--
Architecture-Migration-Best-Practices-and-New-Features\
code\Chapter01\dummyapi50
```

Now that we've set up the benchmark correctly, let's see how to execute it.

Executing the benchmark

Since our Web API projects are now set up, we are going to use the simple benchmarking application named **Apache Bench**. This is free and open source and the binary is available from within the Apache installer package:

1. I use Windows, so I downloaded the ZIP file installation via the following link: `http://httpd.apache.org/docs/current/platform/windows.html#down`. This downloaded the `httpd-2.4.46-o111h-x86-vc15.zip` file to my machine and, from this ZIP file, I just extracted one file, `ab.exe`, which is all I need.

2. I use the following configuration with Apache Bench to send the requests to our Web API project with 10 concurrent threads and a total of 50,000 requests:

```
ab -n 50000 -c 10 http://localhost:5000/WeatherForecast
```

3. Now, executing this against our `dummyapi31` project, which is .NET Core
    3.1-based, generates the following output:

```
Concurrency Level:      10
Time taken for tests:   12.358 seconds
Complete requests:      50000
Failed requests:        0
Non-2xx responses:      50000
Total transferred:      8850000 bytes
HTML transferred:       0 bytes
Requests per second:    4046.04 [#/sec] (mean)
Time per request:       2.472 [ms] (mean)
Time per request:       0.247 [ms] (mean, across all concurrent requests)
Transfer rate:          699.36 [Kbytes/sec] received

Connection Times (ms)
              min  mean[+/-sd] median   max
Connect:        0     0    0.4      0      5
Processing:     0     2    0.6      2     13
Waiting:        0     2    0.7      2     12
Total:          0     2    0.6      2     13
```

Figure 1.9 – Apache Bench output for the .NET Core 3.1-based Web API

And executing the same `ab` command against our `dummyapi50` project, which is .NET
5.0-based, generates the following output:

```
Concurrency Level:      10
Time taken for tests:   12.290 seconds
Complete requests:      50000
Failed requests:        0
Non-2xx responses:      50000
Total transferred:      8850000 bytes
HTML transferred:       0 bytes
Requests per second:    4068.38 [#/sec] (mean)
Time per request:       2.458 [ms] (mean)
Time per request:       0.246 [ms] (mean, across all concurrent requests)
Transfer rate:          703.23 [Kbytes/sec] received

Connection Times (ms)
              min  mean[+/-sd] median   max
Connect:        0     0    0.4      0      3
Processing:     0     2    0.6      2     33
Waiting:        0     2    0.8      2     33
Total:          0     2    0.7      2     33
```

Figure 1.10 – Apache Bench output for the .NET Core 5.0-based Web API

Note that I run the Apache Bench for each .NET version 5 times with no gaps, or say with
a gap of a maximum of 1 second in between the calls, and obtained the statistics from the
fifth run, meaning I ran 50,000 requests 5 times and got the results just from the fifth run.
This was done in order to also see whether there is some kind of caching that is applied as
well as a GC function that might happen in between as well.

From the results, we can definitely see the result that .NET 5.0 is faster than .NET Core 3.1. Even though the improvement is marginal, 0.2 to 0.5% faster, this tiny Web API is not meant to indicate a huge difference, but for a sizeable project, it demonstrates the capabilities in a very simple way that you can benchmark your own project against the two runtimes almost without modifying the code and see the performance gains by yourself in the real application.

Here, we can see that although the difference in performance is small, .NET 5 still performs faster in a tiny application with the very few APIs and features used.

Ending with these two benchmarking examples, we finalize the .NET performance topic. We have observed the performance improvements from various .NET versions down to the latest .NET 5 and noticed how .NET 5 encompasses all the improvements achieved by the previous .NET versions already baked into it.

The fact that the use of .NET 5 automatically improves the performance of the application without the need to change the code ought to be appreciated. For example, if the application was built using .NET Core 3.1 and is now compiled using .NET 5, it receives an additional performance boost.

The version of Kestrel that is included with .NET 5 already exhibits a significant performance improvement in terms of serving the APIs. Therefore, the same application code that was previously compiled with the older .NET version and is now compiled with .NET 5 and served by Kestrel does automatically get the better performance.

Hence, the effort of migrating the application to .NET 5 automatically adds a performance boost as an additional benefit without having to change the code with the purpose of improving performance.

Now that we have covered performance improvements and understood how it works in different .NET versions, let's look at the release schedule for .NET.

.NET release schedule

From now on, as well as in the future, .NET will be the only name carried forward by Microsoft when talking about .NET Core or .NET 5, so we will now use the dominant name from here on, .NET, when talking in general terms. We will highlight .NET 5 when the topic is specifically related to .NET 5.

We learned earlier that .NET has a consistent schedule and is independent of Windows release cycles and Windows updates. Let's have a quick look at what the schedule looks like:

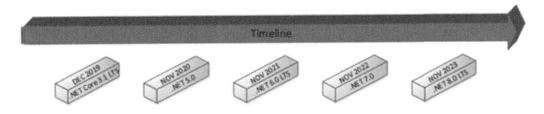

Figure 1.11 – .NET release schedule

With this, we realize that .NET has a very predictable schedule that a company can rely on. We see that .NET 5 gets released in November 2020, and .NET 6 in November 2021 – meaning that every year there is a new major release in November, and that every even-numbered release is a **long-term support (LTS)** where it is supported for 3 years.

What does industry highlight in relation to .NET?

With all the features and forward-looking technologies provided by .NET with full cloud-based modern application support, we have some really promising statistics from the industry side. Let's see what some of the top stats say:

- On GitHub, .NET Core is one of the highest velocity open source projects.

- On GitHub, C# is the fifth most popular language.

- In 2019/2020, .NET Core was the most loved framework on StackOverFlow.

- In terms of professional careers, .NET is the second most popular technology skill required by the hot jobs on LinkedIn.

We learned that it is with .NET 5 that the .NET Framework and .NET Core worlds are merged into a single .NET offering. We also realized that each technology platform's distinguishing factors are made clearly visible, meaning that it helps technology leaders make well-informed decisions. We also see now that the single version of .NET has consistent release dates provided in advance that enterprises can depend on. Next, we will visit the .NET Support policies for both .NET Framework and .NET Core.

.NET support life cycle

The support life cycle starts when a product is released and ends when it is no longer supported. End of support means that from this date, Microsoft will no longer provide fixes, updates, or online technical assistance. It is vital to keep your release updated before you reach this date. If Microsoft support is ended, you do not receive any security or critical updates, which may make your system vulnerable and open to malicious software.

.NET Framework support

.NET Framework is defined as a core component of the Windows OS, meaning its support is tied to the Windows life cycle. Every Windows OS as a product has a life cycle that starts when a product is released and ends when it is no longer supported.

For example, Windows 10 March feature updates are supported for the next 18 months, and September feature updates are supported for the next 30 months from the date of the release.

At the time of writing of this book,.NET Framework 4.8 is the latest version of .NET Framework that will continue to be distributed with future releases of Windows.

It will continue to be supported as long as it is installed on a supported version of Windows OS.

> **Tip**
> Support dates for all of the Microsoft products can be seen here:
> `https://docs.microsoft.com/en-us/lifecycle/`
> `products/`.

With this, we learned that there will be no newer versions of .NET Framework, but that it will be continuously supported as long as the underlying Windows OS is supported by Microsoft.

.NET Core support

Talking about .NET Core support includes .NET Core, ASP.NET Core, and Entity Framework Core. The .NET Core support life cycle offers support for each release. It has two kinds of release and, hence, two basic support models:

- **Long-term support (LTS) releases**: These are designed for long-term support. They include the most stable features and components and require fewer updates. These releases could be regarded as a preferred choice for big enterprises, where stability while staying up to date is the first choice.

    LTS releases are supported for 3 years following initial release.

- **Current releases**: These include the latest features, but they could change in the future and would potentially make your application unstable. These could be considered a good choice for active application development, but you need to upgrade more often to a later .NET Core release to stay in support.

    Current releases are supported for 3 months after each subsequent release.

Although both types of release receive critical fixes for security and reliability throughout their entire life cycle, you must stay up to date with the latest patches to remain qualified for support.

There is also a support case known as a **maintenance cycle**, offered in the last stage of the life cycle. During this cycle, a given release will only receive security updates. The maintenance time length is just 3 months for the current release, and 1 year for the LTS release.

> **.NET Core release life cycles**
>
> The following link has a table that keeps track of release dates and end-of-support dates for .NET Core versions: `https://dotnet.microsoft.com/platform/support/policy/dotnet-core`.

Summary

We have covered a brief introduction to the history of .NET Framework and .NET Core and now know the fundamentals of the framework, which are the essential first steps for a solid development foundation and architecture. We also learned the main features and capabilities of .NET 5 by comparing them directly with the capabilities of .NET Framework and .NET Core and we understood the benefits of one over the other. We also learned what the release schedule for .NET looks like from now on and what information is provided to us in the form of industry statistics, all of this designed to enable us to adopt the right technology at the right time and with the planned landscape already inline with our own application architecture and life cycle.

We saw the different types of applications that can be quickly and easily developed with it. We visited the support life cycle for both .NET Framework and .NET Core, which envisage us to architect and design the application software well in advance, with a better and long-term view of our own application product life cycle.

Lastly, we dived into performance improvements and some of the statistics by again doing a comparison with some of the previous versions of .NET. Since .NET 5 is a superset of all of the previous .NET Core versions with added features, it therefore already incorporates all of the previous performance gains applied to the earlier versions, which is why we also overviewed the performance improvements of the previous .NET Core versions and, finally, the specific improvements in relation to .NET 5.

I hope you have enjoyed learning the features of .NET Core and .NET 5 as much as I did and are now looking forward to the next portion of the book, which focuses on design and architecture.

2
What's New in C# 9?

Since its first release in 2002, C# has come a long way. While C#'s first iteration had a striking resemblance to C and Java, its subsequent evolutions outpaced other languages in introducing industry-leading features (LINQ, async-await, and lambdas, to name a few) and still continue to do so.

In this chapter, we'll learn about the new language enhancements offered by C# 9 using the .NET 5 runtime. Some of these enhancements are a continuation of features introduced in C# 7 and C# 8. We'll discuss the design philosophy of these features, and then with coding examples, we'll learn when, why, and how to best leverage the new features.

The main goal of this chapter is to provide code-based examples, keeping the theory minimal, and show the distinct advantages that these new language constructs have over existing ones. Some major goals of C# enhancements (simplifying the code intent and empowering immutability) are explained in more detail so you can appreciate the decisions made by the design team responsible for maintaining the language.

We are going to cover the following main topics:

- Learning about the .NET Framework requirements to use C# 9
- Understanding what's new in C# 9
- Immutable records
- Automatic type inference with the new keyword

- Productivity enhancements
- Leveraging performance improvements

By the end of this chapter, you will know how to take advantage of the new C# 9 features to write less boilerplate and less verbose code. Your code will be more readable with clearer intent and you will be able to understand C# 9 code, and its new features, written by your fellow developers.

Technical requirements

All code examples from this chapter can be downloaded from the GitHub repository: `https://github.com/PacktPublishing/Adopting-.NET-5--Architecture-Migration-Best-Practices-and-New-Features/tree/master/Chapter02`.

The sample code for the performance benchmark project discussed in the *Performance improvements* section and the player value calculator service from *Writing less code with pattern matching* are provided as a working solution. As other examples are short code snippets, these don't require the creation of a full C# solution to explore and execute. You can instead use a tool named **LINQPad 6** (explained further in the next section).

Having prior knowledge of C#

Basic familiarity with C# is a pre requisite for this chapter. It is not necessary (though it's helpful) for you to be aware of C# 7 and C# 8 features, but a working knowledge of C# up to version 6 is essential to understand the differentiating features of C# 9 described in this chapter.

Before going ahead, we will first see what we need to use C# 9.

The .NET Framework requirements to use C# 9

Generally, new C# versions have been released in conjunction with .NET Framework versions, as some of the language improvements are dependent on underlying .NET runtime support. Starting with C# 8, which was released with .NET Core 3.0/.NET Standard 2.1, Microsoft has announced tightly coupled C# and .NET version releases. So, C# 9 will be the default and latest language version for .NET 5.

In the future, we can expect a new C# major version release with each annual update of .NET Framework.

To develop programs in C# 9, you'll need the following:

- The .NET 5.0 SDK for the platform of your choice, be it Windows, Mac, or Linux. It can be downloaded from `https://dotnet.microsoft.com/download/dotnet/5.0`.

- If you use Visual Studio, you'll need Visual Studio 2019 16.7 or higher. You can use Visual Studio Code with the latest version of the C# extension installed. The extension can be downloaded from Visual Studio Marketplace: `https://marketplace.visualstudio.com/items?itemName=ms-dotnettools.csharp`.

- When writing C# 9 programs, in the `.csproj` files, ensure that the target framework moniker is specified as `net5.0`:

```
<TargetFramework>net5.0</TargetFramework>
```

When developing new C# programs in Visual Studio 16.7, Visual Studio will do this automatically for you.

> **Tip**
>
> When experimenting with or learning the syntax of new code, we don't have to configure a full C# 9 project and execute it. A simpler and convenient way is to use a tool named LINQPad 6 (`https://www.LINQPad.NET/LINQPad6.aspx`).
>
> LINQPad allows us to directly evaluate C# expressions and statements without creating solutions and projects. The basic edition of LINQPad is free for personal use.

Configuring LINQPad 6 for .NET 5 and C# 9

LINQPad 6 allows the user to choose any of the .NET Core or .NET 5 SDKs installed on the user machine to run C# code. By default, it picks the latest version of.NET, so as long you have the .NET 5 SDK installed, you should be able to run C# 9 code in LINQPad.

To ensure that all C# 9 features are available to be used, do the following:

1. Launch LINQPad 6 on your computer.

2. Select **Edit | Preferences | Query | Enable C# 9 preview features - including records and relational patterns (LangVersion=preview)**.

    This option can be seen at the bottom section of the screen:

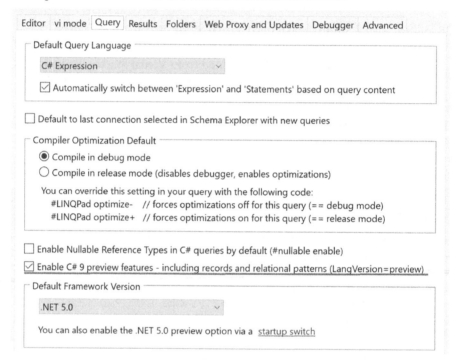

Figure 2.1 – Configuring LINQPad 6 for C# 9 preview features

3. Also, ensure that .NET 5.0 is selected as the option for **Default Framework Version** on the same screen.

4. Once LINQPad is configured, you can open the provided .linq files directly and execute the programs from its query window. As shown in the following screenshot, a program written in the **Query** window can be executed by clicking the play button:

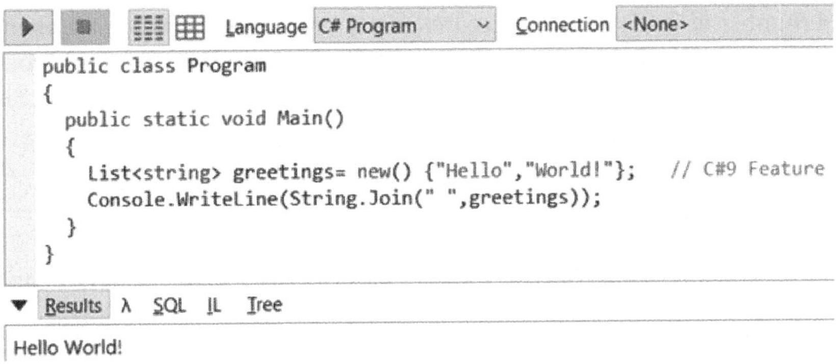

```
public class Program
{
  public static void Main()
  {
    List<string> greetings= new() {"Hello","World!"};    // C#9 Feature
    Console.WriteLine(String.Join(" ",greetings));
  }
}
```

```
▼  Results  λ  SQL  IL  Tree
```

Hello World!

Figure 2.2 – The Query window in LINQPad 6 showing hello-world.linq

The preceding `Hello World!` code explores one of the new C# 9 features where the `new` keyword automatically infers the variable type. We'll learn a lot more about this feature later in this chapter.

So essentially, a .NET 5 SDK for the target platform and our favorite code editor is all we need to get started with C# 9. In the next section, we'll learn about the language enhancements made in C# 9.

Understanding what's new in C# 9

With the development environment set up to run C# 9 code, it's now time to wear our adventurer hat and explore what goodies C# 9 has got for us.

Listening to the developer community feedback, C# 9 has implemented quite a few productivity-focused enhancements. In addition, there are features such as *immutable records*, which will be appreciated by programmers who are familiar with functional languages, such as F#.

> **Participating in C# language design**
>
> C#'s **language design team** (**LDT**) has developed C# 9 in collaboration with the community in an open source repository on GitHub.
>
> You too can participate, provide proposals, raise issues, and even contribute fixes in that repository.
>
> Even if you are just interested in keeping abreast of the latest C# language developments and its future direction, browsing this repository (`https://github.com/dotnet/csharplang`) will provide excellent first-hand knowledge.

Let's first start with features that have evolved through recent C# versions.

There are a number of C# 7 and C# 8 features that serve as a basis for more enhancements in C# 9. In particular, the C# 7 Span type, which enabled developers to avoid some memory allocations, saw significant performance improvements in .NET Core 3.0 and was then leveraged by C# 8 developers.

Similarly, switch expression-based pattern matching in C# 7 improved code readability and helped in writing bug-free code.

For developers who are new to the .NET Core platform, even C# 8 is a new language. We've seen in the *Technical requirements* section that we need .NET Core 3.0/.NET Standard 2.1 or higher to use all features of C# 8. As this chapter is about C# 9, there will not be exhaustive coverage of all C# 8 features, but I want to specifically introduce the pattern matching feature and its journey, from its simple implementation in C# 7 to its major enhancements in C# 8 and then its further evolution in C# 9.

Writing concise code with pattern matching

Designers of most programming languages strive to support features that improve code readability. Specifying the intent of code in a clear way is very important to developers. Pattern matching allows us to write expressions in a concise yet clear manner, which would otherwise require longer, nested, and somewhat error-prone techniques to achieve the same result.

C# 7 introduced patterns for type matching. So, you don't need to compare a variable type using this:

```
if(animal.GetType() == typeof(Lion)) { // Do something }
```

You can instead write the following:

```
If (animal is Lion) { // Do something }
```

Or, instead of switching on values, you can switch on the variable type directly. Here is a snippet of code that demonstrates this concept. In this example, we are taking different actions based on the type of the shape variable:

switch-on-type.linq

```
public static bool HasFourSides<T>(this T shape) where T :Shape
        {
            switch (shape)
            {
                case Square: return true;
```

```
            case Circle: return false;
            case Rectangle: return true;
            default: throw new
            ApplicationException("Unknown Shape Type");
        }
    }
```

C# 8 took this concept further and supported many more expressions that are typically seen in functional languages, such as F#. In modern application development, we often have to integrate with disparate systems and data sources where we can't control the shape of the data messages. This C# feature helps in programming paradigms where data and functionality live apart. Pattern matching simplifies making decisions based on the type and/or values of the incoming data.

Pattern matching can used for any of the following:

- Taking decisions based on the variable type
- Taking decisions based on property value
- Taking decisions based on logical and relational operators
- Taking decisions based on tuples

We'll demonstrate all of the aforementioned techniques in the sample scenario covered in the next section using an example service named Player Value Calculator.

Example service – Player Value Calculator

Learning by doing is a very effective way to grasp new concepts. To explore the pattern matching feature, we'll develop a small application to calculate the worth of a sports player based on their career statistics. In the real world, this could be implemented as a microservice that ingests players' career data from different sources and then calculates how much a sportsperson should be paid to represent a brand for brand endorsement.

The career statistics for different sports are calculated based on different criteria.

Let's start with a simple one: for soccer, let's say that the more goals a player has scored, the more valuable they are. For tennis, it is about the number of sets won, and for cricket, we'll use the number of runs scored as the value predictor.

The following classes will form the base of this service:

```
public class CricketStats
{
    public int RunsScored { get; set; }
    public int WicketsTaken { get; set; }
    public int MatchesPlayed { get; set; }
}

public class TennisStats
{
    public int SetsWon { get; set; }
}

public class SoccerStats
{
    public int GoalsScored { get; set; }
    public bool HasPlayedWorldCup { get; set; }
}
```

Using the classes defined to hold the player statistics, we'll now explore the power of switch expressions by implementing requirements that will gradually become complex with each iteration.

Iteration 1 – Taking decisions based on the variable type

In the first iteration, the service will assess the worth of the player as $100 per run scored, set won, or goal scored, depending on the sport:

```
public decimal GetPlayerValue_1(object stats)
{
    return stats switch
    {
        CricketStats cr => cr.RunsScored * 100,
        TennisStats t => t.SetsWon * 100,
        SoccerStats s => s.GoalsScored * 100,
        { } => throw new ArgumentException(message:
        "Not a known sports statistics", paramName:
        nameof(stats)),
```

```
                null => throw new
         ArgumentNullException(nameof(stats))
      };
   }
```

There are a few noteworthy points here if you are new to pattern matching:

- The variable name appears before the `switch` keyword. This indicates the fact that we are using the `switch` expression and not the traditional `switch` statement.

- The bodies on the right-hand side of `=>` are also expressions, not statements. This keeps the code concise, yet it is flexible enough to incorporate a statement block, if needed.

- The expressions will be evaluated in the same order as provided in the code. When the first matching case is found, subsequent expressions will not be evaluated.

- The second-to-last check, `{ }`, represents the case where the `stats` variable is of a type that doesn't match any of the types in the preceding expressions.

- We could also use the discard operator, `_`, for default processing when none of the other expressions evaluate to `true`.

In the preceding code, we saw that we can evaluate the player value based on the object properties, even if the object can have different types. In the next example, we will see how object property values can be taken into account for decision making as well.

Iteration 2 – Taking decisions based on property value

Let's say we want to improve on the criteria for soccer players. A soccer player is 50% more valuable if they have played in a world cup tournament. We can combine type matching with property value matching in this case:

```
public decimal GetPlayerValue_2(object stats)
{
   return stats switch
   {
      CricketStats cr => cr.RunsScored * 100,
      TennisStats t => t.SetsWon * 100,
      SoccerStats { HasPlayedWorldCup:true } s=>
      s.GoalsScored*150,
      SoccerStats { HasPlayedWorldCup: false } s =>
      s.GoalsScored * 100,
      { } => throw new ArgumentException(message:
```

```
        "Not a known sports statistics", paramName:
        nameof(stats)),

        null => throw new
        ArgumentNullException(nameof(stats))
    };
}
```

In the highlighted lines, we are comparing the value of the `HasPlayedWorldCup` property with constant values (`true` and `false`), but we will write more complex expressions with dynamic values in subsequent examples.

Iteration 3 – Taking decisions based on logical and relational operators (C# 9 only)

In C# 9, we can use relational operators (> , <=, <, and so on) as well as logical operators (and, or, and not) to write more involved expressions.

In the following example, we want to increase a cricket player's worth if they have played 100 or more matches and reduce it by 20% if they have played fewer than 50 matches:

```
public decimal GetPlayerValue_3(object stats)
{
    return stats switch
    {
        CricketStats cr => cr.MatchesPlayed switch
        {
            >=100 => cr.RunsScored*150,
            >=50 and <100  =>cr.RunsScored*100,
            < 50 =>cr.RunsScored*80
        },
        TennisStats t => t.SetsWon * 100,
        SoccerStats { HasPlayedWorldCup: true } s =>
        s.GoalsScored * 150,
        SoccerStats { HasPlayedWorldCup: false } s =>
        s.GoalsScored * 100,
        { } => throw new ArgumentException(message:
        "Not a known sports statistics", paramName:
        nameof(stats)),
        null => throw new
        ArgumentNullException(nameof(stats))
```

```
        };
    }
```

Notice how we've used a nested `switch` expression for the `MatchesPlayed` property inside the case of the `CricketStats` type. Compared to the practice of nesting `if` checks inside other `if-else` checks, the nesting of `switch` expressions is clearer in its intent.

Lastly, we'll go through one more iteration to make decisions based on multiple variables at the same time.

Iteration 4 – Making decisions based on tuples

In the final example, we'll use a different variable that is independent of player statistics. Let's say a company could afford to pay more for sponsorship if the brand is large enough in size. We want only cricket and tennis endorsements to be impacted by this new criterion as expressed in the table:

Sport	Achievements	Brand Size	Value
Cricket	Any	Large	150*runs scored
Cricket	Any	Medium	100*runs scored
Cricket	Any	Small	80*runs scored
Tennis	Any	Large	150*sets won
Tennis	Any	Medium	100*sets won
Tennis	Any	Small	100*sets won
Soccer	Has played in the World Cup	Any	150*goals scored
Soccer	Hasn't played in the World Cup	Any	100*goals scored

Table 2.1 – Player value calculation criteria

So, the value of the players is impacted by career stats as well as brand size. We'll define a new enum type named `BrandSize` and then translate the required criteria into code as follows:

```
Public enum BrandSize {Small,Medium,Large}
        public decimal GetPlayerValue_4(object stats,
        BrandSize brandSize)
    {
        return (stats, brandSize) switch
        {
            (CricketStats cr,BrandSize.Large) =>
            cr.RunsScored * 150,
            (CricketStats cr, BrandSize.Medium) =>
```

```
            cr.RunsScored * 100,
        (CricketStats cr, BrandSize.Small) =>
        cr.RunsScored * 80,
        (TennisStats t , BrandSize.Large) => t.SetsWon
        * 150,
        (TennisStats t, _) => t.SetsWon * 100,
        (SoccerStats s,_) => s.HasPlayedWorldCup
        switch
        {
            true => s.GoalsScored * 150,
            false => s.GoalsScored * 100
        },
        ({ },_) => throw new
        ArgumentException(message: "Not a known sports
        statistics", paramName: nameof(stats)),
        (null,_) => throw new
        ArgumentNullException(nameof(stats))
    };
}
```

Notice how we use the discard operator (_) where we don't care about the second parameter, brandSize.

We've now learned that switch expressions are quite powerful despite their syntax concision. In the next section, we'll talk about cases where they have a clear advantage over if statements.

The distinct advantage of pattern matching expressions

Apart from concision, there are two other advantages of using switch expressions over a series of if statements.

Not only does the intent become clearer to any reader of the code, but the compiler also understands code intent better. So, it can warn you in the case of the following:

- You've not covered all possible cases.
- You have expressions where criteria overlap.

Have a look at this example. If you omit the last check from this `MatchesPlayed` expression, the compiler will warn you with a message: **The switch expression does not handle all possible inputs**:

```
CricketStats cr => cr.MatchesPlayed switch
    {
        >=100 => cr.RunsScored*150,
        >=50 and <100  =>cr.RunsScored*100,
    },
```

This is because we have not specified what to do with cases where players have played fewer than 50 matches. Similarly, if you change >= to = in either expression, the compiler will complain because the case for when the value is exactly 100 (or 50) is not specified.

On the other hand, let's say you write the code where the criteria overlaps with the previous expression, as shown in the highlighted line of the following code:

```
CricketStats cr => cr.MatchesPlayed switch
    {
        >100 => cr.RunsScored*150,
        >50 and <100  =>cr.RunsScored*100,
        >50 and <70  =>cr.RunsScored*90,
        _  =>cr.RunsScored*80
    },
```

You'll get the following compiler error: **The pattern is unreachable. It has already been handled by a previous arm of the switch expression or it is impossible to match**.

When the expression tree evolves and gets complicated, these compiler checks become quite handy to discover unintentional code usage.

We have learned the importance of writing code with clear intent using `switch` expressions. It's now time to explore another feature in C# 9, immutable records, that also helps us in avoiding runtime errors by specifying the intent of code more clearly.

Keeping track of changes – immutable records

Immutable records are a new feature in C# 9, but the concept of immutability isn't. Let's first understand what immutability is and why and when it is useful.

Immutability is a programming concept (more popular in functional paradigms) in which by using language constructs, we restrict an object to change its state. Any changes to object values must be done by creating a copy of the object first and then applying the desired changes.

At first, it may sound like we are deliberately making our lives harder. But there are several benefits of this approach. The biggest of them is that we avoid unintended changes to our objects.

This is a common issue in multi-threaded programming where the same object is accessed by multiple threads in parallel and sometimes it's hard to predict the state of the object, as it could be modified in any order.

Even in single-threaded code, it gets very hard to trace the changes in an object if potentially any accessing function can change it.

The ownership of the object also gets muddled when there are multiple functions capable of changing its state.

To summarize, immutability helps in the following ways:

- Immutable objects are made thread-safe.

- In collections that use the value of the key to determine the position of the value, such as `Dictionary` or `HashSet`, keys must be immutable. This is because if the key itself changes, the corresponding value could be lost.

- It is easier to understand and trace code that uses immutable objects.

Immutability is not a silver bullet. There are ways in which it can be detrimental too:

- It could be far more efficient to make in-place changes to large or frequently changing objects rather than copying them every time. In the *Performance improvements* section of this chapter, we'll talk about `Span<T>`, which allows us to directly modify memory contents and provides significant performance benefits.

- Without proper language support, it could require a lot of boilerplate code to achieve immutability.

Before diving deeper into immutable records, let's also learn about the related feature of `init-only` properties.

Setting class properties as init-only

In C# 9, we can now mark properties with the `init` accessor. This prevents the consuming code from changing the value of the object property after initialization (initialization can either occur through constructor or object initialization syntax).

For example, let's say a `Player` class is defined as follows:

init-only-properties.linq

```
public class Player
    {
        public int PlayerId { get; init; }
        public string FirstName { get; set; }
        public string LastName { get; set; }
    }
```

We can then initialize an object using this:

```
var p1 = new Player { PlayerId = 10, FirstName= "John" };
```

But, the following code will throw an error as `PlayerId` can't be modified once the object is initialized:

```
var player2 = new Player();
    player2.PlayerId  = 10; // Error
```

This error is useful as it prevents the consuming objects from inadvertently modifying the object properties. Effectively, we are making the properties immutable as they can't be changed once initialized. So, can we easily apply the same concept to the whole object? Using the new `record` keyword in C# 9, the answer is a resounding yes.

Introducing the record keyword

`record` is the new member of the C# family. It is quite like `struct`, in the sense that it is also a value type. However, as we'll see in this section, it's pretty painless with records to achieve immutability in the code.

Let's define `Player` as a record this time:

records-with.linq

```
public record Player
    {
        public int PlayerId { get; init; }
        public string FirstName { get; init; }
        public string LastName { get; init; }
    }
```

Let's define a `player` object as follows:

```
var player = new Player { PlayerId =10,FirstName = "John",
LastName = "Citizen" };
```

Now if we want to change the name from John to Ron, we can't do so unless we create another object. But we can still copy the other properties from the original player, thanks to the new `with` keyword in C# 9:

```
var player2= player with { FirstName = "Ron" };
```

Even if it was the same player who later changed their name, we can track this change in the states of the `player` and `player2` variables, respectively.

When a `record` object is created from another one, a copy constructor is called and copies all the values from the original object to the new one. And then if we've used the `with` keyword, we can specify which values will be different in the new object.

It is possible to override the default copy constructor behavior. So, for example, we can modify it to not copy the player's age to a new object.

There are a number of convenience shortcuts introduced in C# to deal with records. Let's explore them now.

Autogenerating the constructor and deconstructor

We can avoid the need to define a verbose class definition and its constructor when defining records. As an example, let's define a `Player` class as follows:

records-positional-parameters.linq

```
public record Player(string FirstName, string LastName);
```

Note the following:

- Property accessors are not specified. For records, C# will assume it to be `{get;init;}`, by default. Unlike regular classes, the properties are assumed to be `public` by default.

- A constructor will be autogenerated, which will take `FirstName` and `LastName` as parameter values and initialize the properties.

So, we can initialize the object using constructor syntax, as follows:

```
var player = new Player("John", "Citizen"); // both properties
will initialize
```

Similarly, we can use an auto-generated deconstructor to assign object properties to tuples:

```
var (name1,name2) = player;  // name1 = John, name2= Citizen
```

In this example, the position of the `FirstName` and `LastName` parameters was used by the C# compiler to automatically generate the constructor and deconstructor expecting these parameters. This phenomenon is called positional construction or deconstruction.

Comparing records for equality

If two different records have the same values for all members, they are considered to be value-equal but not reference-equal (as the two variables do not refer to the same object).

To compare two different records for equality, we can use the `Equals` method as shown here:

records-equality.linq

```
var p1 = new Player ("John", "Citizen");
var p2 = new Player ("John", "Citizen");
Console.WriteLine(p1.Equals(p2)); // true, same values
Console.WriteLine(p1 == p2);      // false, different objects
Console.WriteLine(ReferenceEquals(p1,p2)); // false
```

Applying inheritance

With records and inheritance, C# 9 has provided a very sensible hidden cloning method that makes inheritance work with records.

Extending our player example, let's define another record type specifically for tennis players:

records-inheritance.linq

```
public record Player {public string FirstName; public string
LastName;};
public record TennisPlayer : Player { public int age; }
```

If we then create a TennisPlayer instance and assign it to a generic Player object, it will still hold the tennis player properties:

```
Player tennisPlayer1 = new TennisPlayer {
age=39,FirstName="Roger",LastName="Federrer" };
Console.WriteLine((tennisPlayer1 as TennisPlayer).age);   // 39
```

Moreover, if we create another Player object named tennisPlayer2 from the original tennisPlayer1 object, the clone method will magically create a true copy of the tennisPlayer1 object including the age property as well:

```
Player tennisPlayer2 = tennisPlayer1 with { FirstName="Rafael",
LastName = "Nadal" };
Console.WriteLine((tennisPlayer2 as TennisPlayer).age);      //
39
```

Comparing records with inheritance

So, when do we consider two objects to be equal when inheritance is involved?
If two Player objects have the same values, but one of the objects' underlying type is a derived type with additional properties, the two objects will not be considered value-equal.

Continuing with our `Player` and `TennisPlayer` example, the output of the following code will be `false` for both comparisons. This is because even when the `Player` equality comparison function thinks that both objects have all the properties, the `TennisPlayer` equality comparison method will take precedence (being the derived class) and will return `false` because the `player2` object is missing its `age` property:

records-equality-inheritance.linq

```
Player tennisPlayer1 = new TennisPlayer {
age=39, FirstName="Roger", LastName="Federrer" };
Player player2 = new Player { FirstName = "Roger", LastName =
"Federrer" };
Console.WriteLine(tennisPlayer1.Equals(player2) );   // false
Console.WriteLine(player2.Equals(tennisPlayer1));     // false
```

As we saw, support for defining immutable records is quite comprehensive in C# 9, with equality, inheritance, and cloning supported.

There is one more exciting feature of automatic type inference for the C# compiler. Let's learn how this could help us in writing concise code.

Letting the new keyword infer the type for us

The `var` variable has been a great timesaving keyword for C# developers that eliminates the need to specify the target type of a variable twice. The following two lines are functionally equivalent:

```
List<int> numbers = new List<int>();
var numbers = new List<int>();
```

In the preceding example, the compiler can automatically infer the type from the new expression. In C# 9, the new keyword has been enhanced to infer type automatically if it is specified on the left-hand side. So, the following is equivalent to the preceding two lines:

```
List<int> numbers = new ();
```

You might wonder, if `var` was already inferring the type on one side of the equation, what additional benefit this enhancement brings with it. Here are a few examples where type inference using `new` can be more convenient:

- When there are multiple `new` initializations in a single statement:

```
Dictionary < string,List<string> >
citiesInCountries = new()
    {
        { "USA", new() { "New York", "Los
        Angeles", "Chicago", "Houston" } },
        {"Australia", new() { "Sydney",
        "Melbourne", "Brisbane"} },
        { "Canada", new() {
        "Ottawa","Toronto","Edmonton" } }
    };
```

- When a method parameter's type can automatically be inferred. We can directly initialize the parameter without specifying the type. In the following code block, specifying the `Person` type name is redundant:

```
CloneThisPerson ( new Person("FirstName","LastName"))
```

We can instead let the `new` keyword figure out the type from the method signature:

```
CloneThisPerson(new ("FirstName","LastName"))
```

- When doing a field declaration in a class, we can't use `var` instead of the variable type. But we can now eliminate the type name after the `new` keyword:

```
public class MyClass
    {
        public List<string> myfield { get; set; } = new()
        { };
    }
```

You'd still need to declare the type where it can't be automatically inferred.

So, if a `foo` function has two signatures with one expecting `T1 bar` and the other expecting `T2 bar` as a parameter, then `foo (new ())` won't work.

Non-supported types

There are some non-supported types where type inference from new won't work, primarily because they don't have the constructor or the constructor syntax is special. These types include the following:

- Enums
- Function pointers
- Array types
- Interface types
- Tuples
- Dynamic
- Exceptions

> **Tip**
>
> A note on the last non-supported type mentioned, exceptions. It is generally bad practice to directly throw the base exception type, `System.Exception`, from our own code. The following Microsoft article provides guidance about when to create and throw exceptions: `https://docs.microsoft.com/en-us/dotnet/csharp/programming-guide/exceptions/creating-and-throwing-exceptions#things-to-avoid-when-throwing-exceptions`.

We've covered the major C# 9 enhancements so far, but that's not all there is. There are a number of other language tweaks that will make your life easier when writing C# code. Let's get an understanding of these enhancements.

Embracing other productivity enhancements

The following features are not groundbreaking per se but will help developers to improve their productivity and focus more on business features than on writing boilerplate code.

Type inference for the ?? and ?: operators

Prior to C# 9, both sides of a ?? expression or ? : condition were required to be of the same type. C# 9 improves this by allowing different types as long as both share the same base type. In the following example, the ?? and ? : operators will work fine because a shared base type can be inferred from types on both sides of the operator:

type-inference-from-shared-base.linq

```
        Animal someAnimal = animal ?? tiger; // Both share
Animal type
```

This feature will eliminate the unnecessary typecasting that was previously required to make the types on both sides compatible. Let's have a look at another time and memory saver: the discard parameter feature.

Discarding parameters in lambdas

C# 7 introduced a discard feature that allowed callers to ignore an out variable from a method if it is not needed and hence saved memory allocation. In the following example, we are ignoring the timeTook value as we are not concerned with telemetry information:

discard-lambdas.linq

```
        private void MakeHttpCall(string url, out long timeTook)
=>
            timeTook = 100;


    private void MakeCallToPackt()
    {
        MakeHttpCall("www.packt.com",out _);
    }
```

In C# 9, this concept has been extended to lambdas and function delegates. So, the implementation of these delegates can discard the parameters that they don't need to use:

```
    var items = new List<string>{"Item1","Item2","Item3"};
    items.ForEach(_ => Console.WriteLine("Another item
        processed"));
```

The C# compiler may avoid allocating the variable in this case, which could be particularly helpful in event handlers where we don't always need to use all parameters. Note that for backward compatibility, if there is only one parameter to a delegate and it's named _, then the compiler will treat it as the name of the variable.

Writing programs using top-level statements

The following is a complete C# 9 program:

top-level-programs\hello-world\program.cs

```
using System;
Console.WriteLine("Hello World from C# 9");
```

Yes, you read it right! There is no `Program` class. There is no `Main` method. Just a `using` statement and the actual code. The compiler will do its magic to automatically generate the `Main` method for you. All you need to ensure is the following:

- The `using` statements are still needed (this might be simplified in future C# versions).

- Your statements should appear after `using` but before any `namespace` declarations.

- In a given C# project, only one file can contain top-level statements, which will then be treated by the C# compiler as an entry point.

This could be quite intuitive for beginners to learn C# as we don't have to start with classes and methods and can focus on simpler statements.

Another use case is when you want to explore the sample code quickly or write a small service without making a full-fledged program.

The beauty of top-level statements for C# beginners is that we can still gradually introduce more complex features without fully diving into boilerplate code.

As an example, we can add local methods to top-level statements:

top-level-programs\hello-world-with-method\program.cs

```
using System;
Console.WriteLine(SayHello("John"));

string SayHello(string name)
```

```
{
    return $"Hello {name}";
}
```

We can also use classes and other C# statements such as `for` loops in top-level programs, as shown in the extended hello-world example here:

top-level-programs\hello-world-with-classes\program.cs

```
using System;

for (int i=0;i<10;i++)
    Console.WriteLine(GreetingsProvider.SayHello("John"));

internal class GreetingsProvider
{
    public static string SayHello(string name)
    {
        return $"Hello {name}";
    }
}
```

You can also return values from your program, which is useful for shell scripting. You can write asynchronous code using `async/await`. However, at that point, it might make more sense to add more structure to your program and have a `Main` method defined as an entry point.

Executing startup code with module initializers

In C# 9, we can run application startup code in a method using the `[ModuleInitializer]` attribute on that method. Think of it as if these methods are module constructors. It might not be that useful for executable applications because such applications have a defined entry point (typically a `Main()` method), but library developers will find it pretty useful to put their library initialization code in such methods.

The method must be `static`, must not take any parameters, should return `void`, and should be `internal` or `public`.

It is possible to run the method asynchronously; however, there is no guarantee that the method will complete before the `Main()` method begins its execution.

Let's have a look at an example:

module-intializer\Program.cs

```
public static string ConnectionString;
static void Main(string[] args)
{
    Console.WriteLine($"ConnectionString =
    {ConnectionString}");
}

[ModuleInitializer]
public static void Initialize()
{
    ConnectionString = "DB Connection String";
}
```

In the preceding example, the code in the `Initialize()` method will run before the `Main()` method, so any module-specific initialization can be performed there.

Before we wrap this section up, we'll cover some other convenience features introduced in the language.

Convenience features

These convenience features have been added based on C# community feedback. They support the overarching goal of reducing the code verbosity and catch more errors at compile time:

- Previously, the `GetEnumerator()` public method was required on a collection for it to be used in a `foreach` loop. In C# 9, implementing a `GetEnumerator()` extension method on a collection will also make it enumerable in a `foreach` loop.

- Lambdas can be declared `static`, which will ensure at compile time that no non-static capturing variables are used.

- Method attributes are now also supported on local functions.

- A function in a derived type can override the return type of the same method from the parent class so long as the overriding method's returned type is derived from the overridden method's return type.

- Partial methods now support `out` parameters, non-void return types, and an access modifier such as `public` or `internal`.

We'll now see how C# 9 helps developers to write more performant code by making trivial or no changes to the code.

Leveraging performance improvements

How nice it is to get better performance without changing our code! Yes, that's what the .NET Core team has been doing for us. There are a number of performance improvements in the .NET 5 runtime that will make your code run faster without changing a single line (except for targeting the framework at .NET 5).

Most performance improvements are a continuation of the language and runtime features introduced in prior .NET Core versions. The .NET team is now incorporating these features in widely used methods and classes for developers to benefit from. I'll provide some notable examples of these enhancements later in the chapter.

One critical consideration for performance-oriented C# developers is to reduce the number of times that garbage collection has to kick in. In C# 7.2 and .NET Core 2.1, a new system type, Span<T>, was added that helps developers to access contiguous memory without creating additional memory allocations. It's worth looking at Span<T> before we talk about other performance improvements as many of these improvements are built on top of this.

Introducing Span<T>

Span<T> provides safe access to a contiguous region of allocated memory. A Span instance of type T holds elements of the T array:

```
var intArray = new int[4];
Span<int> span = new Span<int>(intArray);
Console.WriteLine(span.Length); // 4
intArray[0] = 40;
Console.WriteLine(span[0]); // 40
```

Span is quite versatile as it can point to heap, stack, or even unmanaged memory. A related type, ReadOnlySpan<T>, allows read-only access to underlying content.

As you know, `string` in C# can be represented as an array of `char`; C# provides an implicit casting mechanism so that `string` can be used where `ReadonlySpan<char>` is expected:

```
ReadOnlySpan<char> myText = "Hello world";
```

From a performance perspective, one of the great strengths of `Span` is its ability to provide access to a subset of an array using the `slice` method without duplicating the contents first:

```
ReadOnlySpan<char> myTextAsSpan = "Hello world";
string myTextAsString = "Hello world";
var helloAsSpan = myTextAsSpan.Slice(0, 5);   // No new string
allocated
var helloAsString = myTextAsString.Substring(0, 5);   // New
string allocated on heap
```

Less memory allocation means less garbage collection, which results in faster, more predictable performance.

Let's demonstrate this by benchmarking a full example.

Choosing the winner – Substring versus Slice showdown

In this example, we'll count occurrences of a substring within a larger text by using `Span<T>.Slice()` and the traditional `String.Substring()` method. Note that in this example, we do not need to modify the contents of the substring. So, `ReadOnlySpan<T>` would work just fine for us. This is quite clear from the word `ReadOnly` in the name of the type itself.

It is a hard job to write precise and reliable benchmarking code. So, I've used `BenchmarkDotNet` NuGet, which was introduced in the previous chapter. It is fast becoming standard to measure and compare the performance of .NET methods.

You can download the full example from the book's GitHub code repository: `https://github.com/PacktPublishing/Adopting-.NET-5--Architecture-Migration-Best-Practices-and-New-Features/tree/master/Chapter02`.

Most of the code is pretty self-explanatory. Apart from setting up the benchmarking code, we've written two methods, `CountOccurencesBySlice()` and `CountOccurencesBySubstring()`, which differ by only one line.

`CountOccurencesBySubstring` uses the `Substring` method:

```
if (text.Substring(i, searchString.Length) == searchString)
```

`CountOccurencesBySlice` uses the `Slice` method to get the same substring:

```
if (text.Slice(i,searchString.Length).
SequenceEqual(searchString))
```

In the method signatures, you will notice one more difference. `CountOccurencesBySlice()` expects `ReadOnlySpan<char>` as a parameter, whereas `CountOccurencesBySubstring()` expects `string`. The calling code doesn't have to be aware of this as C# does the implicit casting for us.

> **Tip**
> Before you run the project, ensure that your solution configuration is set to run in **release** mode. This eliminates one factor (that is, the attached debugger) that can cause variance in performance in different environments.

In this example, **Benchmark DotNet** is set up to run as a C# console app; it will run many iterations of both methods to get reliable comparison results. Here are the results when I ran this project. Your results might vary a little based on processor speed and other processes running at the same time:

Method	Mean	Error	StdDev	Gen 0	Gen 1	Gen 2	Allocated
Substring	60.63 us	68.115 us	3.734 us	15.2588	-		62.45 KB
Slice	15.35 us	4.545 us	0.249 us	0.3052	-	-	1.33 KB

Figure 2.3 – Substring versus Slice benchmark results

The results show that the `Slice` method is a clear winner, for the following reasons:

- The execution time is faster (as shown by the **Mean** column).
- The performance is a lot more consistent (as shown by the **StdDev** column).
- Memory allocation is significantly lower (as shown by the **Allocated** column).
- A small fraction of garbage collection occurred compared to with the `Substring` method (as shown by the **Gen 0** column).

The preceding example shows the dramatic performance improvement that results from avoiding unnecessary memory allocations. In the next section, we will have a quick recap of the .NET library method improvements (many of which use the `Span` type) and then summarize what we learned in this chapter.

Utilizing .NET library performance improvements

A lot of C# 9 code that uses .NET 5 library methods for text processing, collections processing using LINQ, multi-threading, and JSON processing will run faster just because of the performance improvements made at the underlying library function and runtime levels. If you have not read it already, you can review the *Performance improvements* section of *Chapter 1, Introducing .NET 5 Features and Capabilities*, of this book, which provides details about these .NET 5 improvements.

> **Future improvements**
>
> The .NET team will continue to improve upon runtime performance even after the .NET 5 release. The most significant of these improvements will be ported back to .NET 5 as service updates, whereas others will be released as part of .NET 6 / C # 10.

Improving your own library code

Do you have your own utility functions library for .NET? If you do, try creating the overloaded versions of functions that operate on the `string` type using `ReadOnlySpan<char>` instead and see whether you get any performance improvement. Remember not to over-optimize, though. A best practice is to benchmark your code and find the hot path for improvement and only optimize code that has the biggest impact on the overall performance of your solution.

So, folks, that was the grand tour of C# 9's new features. Let's summarize what we have learned in this chapter.

Summary

In this chapter, we've learned about the core goal of the C# design team: to enable C# developers to write code that focuses on core business problems and eliminate some verbosity from the code using the improved `switch` expression.

We've learned about the benefits of using immutable records for better traceability and how we can take advantage of performance improvements in the .NET runtime to write more performant code ourselves.

The cool thing about C# is its backward compatibility, which lets you jump on to the .NET 5 bandwagon with a code base written using prior C# versions. Even so, I hope this chapter has given you enough encouragement to start taking advantage of the new and cleaner C# 9.

With knowledge of the .NET 5 new features under our belt, in the next section, we will learn about architectural best practices and design patterns that can be leveraged in the .NET 5 world.

Further reading

This was a brief introduction to C# 9's new features. The following links provide more specific information on related topics and consolidate the reference links provided elsewhere in the chapter:

- Source generators are a new C# compiler feature that allows developers to dynamically generate code. You can read about them at `https://devblogs.microsoft.com/dotnet/introducing-c-source-generators/`.

- The complete C# language reference can be found at `https://docs.microsoft.com/en-us/dotnet/csharp/language-reference/`.

- C#'s design and its future direction are discussed at the following GitHub repository: `https://github.com/dotnet/csharplang`.

- The best practices for creating and throwing exceptions in C# code are documented in this Microsoft article: `https://docs.microsoft.com/en-us/dotnet/csharp/programming-guide/exceptions/creating-and-throwing-exceptions#things-to-avoid-when-throwing-exceptions`.

Section 2: Design and Architecture

This section covers the evergreen concepts of the solution design and architectural patterns in light of the modern application development landscape. It first equips the reader with the requisite knowledge of the popular application and solution patterns for the containerized and distributed applications. After that, it puts these concepts into practice with hands-on exercises. It shows how to build modern microservices-based applications using the .NET 5 technology stack, including **gRPC**, **Windows Subsystem for Linux** (**WSL 2**), **Tye**, and **Kubernetes**.

This section comprises the following chapters:

- *Chapter 3, Design and Architectural Patterns*
- *Chapter 4, Containerized Microservices Architecture*

3
Design and Architectural Patterns

In this chapter, we will now focus on application design and architecture, taking a holistic approach. We will first look at an application with a few typical modules or layers and then also look at when an application runs in a distributed environment, be it on-premises or in the cloud.

As we look inside the application, we will talk about design patterns, and when we look beyond the application code, we will check for architectural patterns in an enterprise setup, considering various system boundaries. The knowledge gained in this chapter will prepare us for the deep dive we'll take into building applications with microservices based architecture in the next chapter.

We will be talking about the following topics:

- Why should we follow design strategies?
- Application design patterns
- Communication styles and protocols

- Architectural patterns
- Some popular architectures

By the end of this chapter, you will have a fundamental understanding of design and architectural patterns as well as event-driven enterprise architectures.

Technical requirements

This chapter contains tiny pieces of code that are used to show the workings of two popular design patterns. In order to run these examples, you will need the .NET 5 SDK installed. The .NET 5 SDK can be downloaded from `https://dotnet.microsoft.com/download/dotnet/5.0`.

The code for the examples can be found online at the following GitHub page: `https://github.com/PacktPublishing/Adopting-.NET-5--Architecture-Migration-Best-Practices-and-New-Features/tree/master/Chapter03`.

Why should we follow design strategies?

Nobody wants their software product or service to be difficult to build, change, maintain, and scale. As in any aspect of a business, if you want to build something, you must have a clear strategy for making a profit and continuing to make a profit by remaining competitive and adding value.

On the software side, we always want products, code, and their environments to be stable, flexible, robust, reusable, and scalable. To enable this, we come up with strategies at different levels that create our enterprise architecture landscape. Within the landscape, we consider each decisive attribute of the company and how the digital software products or services can enable and support them, and also how new features and growth in the future can be enabled with the desired amounts of stability, scalability, and predictability.

Quite often, we do not need to reinvent the wheel as we can identify recurring patterns even in seemingly different problem domains. Therefore, we look for well-established, market-proven methods that succeed in the relevant industry and in certain contexts. We look for successful patterns and we follow them. So, we have patterns in code, patterns in application design areas, and patterns in architecture. For an application or system, we start with the reference architecture that most closely matches our industry and area.

Such patterns are proven by years of testing and trial and therefore are expected to fulfill the promises they make. That means if you choose the right patterns in architecture and design with the correct implementation, keeping the constraints intact and building upon them with the right choices, then this strategy is bound to be successful in the long run and enable and support growth.

We can see that the need for a strategy is evident before commencing a project build; and for us in IT (for the applications and services fields, in particular), our strategy should be to have an architecture landscape with architectural patterns and design patterns. Going forward, we will look at some of the most-used design and architecture patterns.

Application design patterns

Application design patterns, which will henceforth be referred to as **design patterns** for brevity, provide solutions to common problems related to software development using a historically proven method so that you do not have to reinvent the wheel, as the saying goes.

Here we will cover some of the most popular design patterns, which are known as the **Gang of Four (GoF)** design patterns. We will also explore some fundamental object-oriented programming and design principles, known as the **SOLID principles**, that also serve as a basis for some of the more modern design patterns.

The **GoF** design patterns are generally considered the foundation for all other design patterns in software development. When using these famous design patterns, it is not only easy to re-use the code and the logic as prescribed by the design pattern, but it is also easy for other developers to read your code; when another developer sees the code, they will be able to tell that you used a certain design pattern. As such, these design patterns provide another benefit in terms of code maintainability.

Let's quickly get an overview of the GoF design patterns, which will serve as a refresher for us to lay a strong foundation for your professional projects.

Refreshing the GoF design patterns

These GoF design patterns are also used throughout the source code of .NET. So, for our overview here, I will list 20 of the GoF object-oriented design patterns, giving them single-line definitions that can serve as a reference for you.

These fundamental GoF patterns are divided into three categories. Let's look at them one by one.

Creational design patterns

These deal with the object's creational mechanisms as best they can in a given context. The following are the creational design patterns:

- **Abstract Factory**: This pattern provides an interface that creates families of related classes or groups of similarly connected classes in a certain category.

- **Builder**: This pattern enables the separation of a complex object construction from how it is represented.

- **Factory Method**: A simple interface that is used to create an object without specifying the exact class to be created.

- **Prototype**: Enables you to create pre-initialized objects by cloning an existing internal object.

- **Singleton**: The most commonly used pattern, this lets you have a class that can only have a single instance across your application.

Structural design patterns

These help us to identify and establish a simple way to realize relationships between entities with some kind of structure:

- **Adapter**: The Adapter pattern allows us to convert an interface of a class into another interface that the client expects by wrapping its own interface around an existing class.

- **Bridge**: This pattern separates an object's interface from its implementation so that the two can work independently of each other and vary from each other.

- **Composite**: This pattern enables you to compose zero or more similar objects in a tree structure (parent/child) so that they can be manipulated as one container object to represent part or the whole of the hierarchies of the objects.

- **Decorator**: This pattern enables you to dynamically add or override behavior in an existing object.

- **Facade**: The Facade pattern lets you have a unified interface on top of a set of interfaces of a subsystem.

- **Flyweight**: This pattern enables the efficient sharing of a large number of similar objects; this can improve performance and also reduce memory usage.

- **Proxy**: This is an object that acts as a placeholder for another object and enables you to control access to it, thereby reducing complexity.

Behavioral design patterns

These help us identify the common communication patterns between objects and then increase the flexibility of communication between them. The following are the types of behavioral design patterns:

- **Chain of Responsibility**: This pattern decouples the request sender from the request receiver by chaining more than one receiver object in such a way that if one receiver object does not handle the request completely, then it passes on to the next until the request has been handled.

- **Command**: This pattern enables the encapsulation of a request or an action or an event along with other attributes as a command object.

- **Interpreter**: This pattern enables the specification of a way to interpret or evaluate sentences in a given language in order for there to be a meaningful interpretation.

- **Iterator**: This pattern enables the sequential access of the elements present in an aggregate object without exposing its underlying structure and storage.

- **Mediator**: This pattern promotes loose coupling by encapsulating the interactions between various objects so they can hook on to receive events dynamically.

- **Memento**: This design pattern enables snapshotting an object's internal state so that it can be restored to the same state at a later point in time.

- **Observer**: This pattern has two main entities: observables and observers. An observable object sends events to many listening objects known as observers, in a one-to-many fashion.

- **State**: This design pattern allows changes in an object's behavior based on a change to its internal state.

Having had this quick and dense summary of the GoF design patterns, we will now have a quick refresher of the **SOLID** design principles.

Refresher of the SOLID design principles

The SOLID principles are considered the baseline **Object-Oriented Design (OOD)** principles, helping you reach better and more maintainable code. They also relate to some of the classic design patterns as well as laying the foundation for some of the more modern design patterns. They were first published by Robert C. Martin, who is generally known as Uncle Bob.

Again, we will not dive deep into these principles but merely skim the surface, just as when we revised the fundamental design patterns previously:

- **Single Responsibility Principle (SRP)**: This principle says that a class should have only one reason to change, which means that a class should be purpose-built and should have only one primary job to do. Such a class can be extended, though, for example, via inheritance.

- **Open-Closed Principle (OCP)**: A class should be designed in a way that means it is open for extension but closed for any modification. This means it should strictly follow the interface it implements.

- **Liskov Substitution Principle (LSP)**: This principle states that all of the derived classes should be replaceable with their parent class. This means all of the derived classes must retain the existing behavior of the parent class. For example, when the client code is using pointers or references of the parent's class, then it must be able to use objects of derived classes without knowing about it.

- **Interface Segregation Principle (ISP)**: This principle states that the interfaces should be fine-grained and specific to the client's usage. This means that if the class has various use cases, then it should have a specific interface for each use case.

- **Dependency Inversion Principle (DIP)**: This is probably the most famous principle of this decade. It states the following: *Depend only on abstractions rather than on concretions.* For example, a class should not depend on the objects it contains and the contained objects should not depend on its container class; rather, both should only depend on their respective abstractions, that is, the interfaces they are supposed to fulfill. Conversely, interfaces should not depend on classes; rather, classes should depend on the interfaces they implement.

Having had this refresher on application design patterns and SOLID design principles, let's go through two brief examples of the popular design patterns. For these two examples, I chose dependency injection and the repository pattern, as they both are popular patterns and are designed on top of the fundamental design patterns.

Dependency injection

Dependency injection (**DI**) is achieved by providing (or injecting) dependencies into those objects that need them. The general pattern is known as **Inversion of Control** (**IoC**) and DI is its practical implementation. The principle explains that the classes having members inside them (which can also be classes of some types) are considered as **dependencies**; instead of a class creating the dependencies in its constructor, it has its dependencies injected into it.

Here is a simple class diagram that depicts this idea:

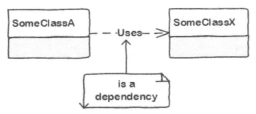

Figure 3.1 – A simple dependency of a class

Let's say that there is a class that fulfills a set of interfaces. When this class implements the functionality as declared by its interfaces, it will need some additional components in the form of other classes as a containment or association to help fulfill its work. Instead of this class creating the dependent objects by itself using, for example, the new keyword, we invert the control and let the dependencies be created and injected into the class. This functionality is implemented as a DI pattern.

The DI pattern is relatively modern pattern; previously, we used to achieve this kind of functionality via **Service Locator** or the **Abstract Factory** pattern, both of which have become a bit obsolete since the advent of the DI pattern.

For reference here, I will include the simple interfaces and the class to show a sample implementation of the DI pattern in the form of C# code:

```csharp
public class DependentClass : ISomeUsecase
{
    private IDependencyOne dependencyOne;
    public DependentClass(IDependencyOne dependencyOne)
    {
        this.dependencyOne = dependencyOne;
    }
    public void IDoSomeActivity() //From the interface
                                  //ISomeUsecase
    {
        //I do some activity using dependencyOne
    }
}
```

This is the main class, which is dependent on another dependency named
IDependencyOne. Notice that the dependency is on the abstraction (that is, an
interface) instead of a concrete class:

```
public interface IDependencyOne
{
    void DoSomething(string something);
}
```

This is the interface abstraction of the dependency or dependent object. Note that this
object itself is also dependent on another object:

```
public class DependencyOne : IDependencyOne
{
    private IDependencyTwo dependencyTwo;
    public DependencyOne(IDependencyTwo dependencyTwo)
    {
        this.dependencyTwo = dependencyTwo;
    }
    public void DoSomething(string something)
    {
        //Use dependencyTwo and DoSomething
    }
}
```

And this is a dependency that could be a simple implementation of IDependencyOne.

Note that DependentClass is dependent on IDependencyOne and
DependencyOne could itself be dependent on other dependencies.

The code example here shows that the dependency is injected but it does not tell us how it
is injected. Let's see the possibilities.

Methods to inject dependencies

Normally, there are two straightforward ways to inject dependencies without applying
any tricks. This means we inject the dependencies either via the *constructor* or via the
properties setters.

Once you start following this approach, you will have many classes that need dependencies to be resolved or injected into them. It then becomes tedious to set everything in the constructor or setters manually for each class. Here comes the need for something called the *DI container*. The container simply keeps a map of each interface and its implementing class, and when you get an instance from the container, it returns the implementing concrete class against the interface you requested it for. In a large application, injecting and resolving inner dependencies can become complex. This is where the DI container shines, as it can auto-resolve the underlying dependency tree for each of the dependent classes, which may also depend on other classes. The creation of all of the classes in an application will be handled smoothly by a DI container.

There are loads of fancy DI containers available on the market to make the developer's life easier by offering several features. With regards to .NET Core, the framework now includes a DI container by default in the `Microsoft.Extensions.DependencyInjection` namespace, which is more than sufficient for all general-purpose DI needs.

Consider the code example in the previous section about `DependentClass` and the other dependencies. You will have seen that none of the classes were created as an object using the `new` keyword. Instead, they are injected. And in general, even with the simplest .NET 5-based program, you have a DI container available by default, which is used to inject dependencies all over the application.

We've had our overview of DI; we will now look into a second modern and common design pattern known as the Repository pattern.

The Repository pattern

Many applications today use the Repository pattern, especially to uniformly access entities and objects stored in some type of datastore, such as a database. In the old days of monolithic applications, we used to have an *n-tier architecture*, where we would have a **business layer** and a **data access layer**. We may still use layers with modern and container-oriented applications, but inside the layers, we apply the Repository pattern to access stored entities consistently.

Here, I will present the simplest and fundamental form of the Repository pattern in the same way that I presented the DI pattern in the previous section.

With the Repository pattern, what you want to achieve is access to your stored objects in a consistent way, no matter where and how the actual data is stored. It can even be stored in one or more databases – after all, when you execute your test cases, you do not want to play with your normal datastore but would prefer to use a Mocked datastore or an in-memory temporary store that only exists during the lifetime of the test cases' execution.

To make things clearer, I depicted this concept in the following figure:

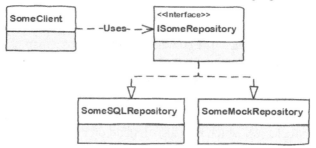

Figure 3.2 – Concept of the Repository pattern

> **Tip**
> When following the Repository pattern, remember that you can have more
> than one repository in your application that depends on your entities or
> the group of entities. How you would want to consider a set of entities as
> a repository depends on your context and domain design. It does not just have
> to depend on the type or number of datastores you use in your application.

Let's see a simple example of the Repository pattern in code. Suppose we have an object
or some other candidate for storage called `Student`. For its storage and retrieval, we
implement it as `IStudentRepository`.

A `Student` class might look something like this in its simplest form:

```
public class Student
{
    public int Id { get; set; }
    public string Name { get; set; }
    public string Email { get; set; }
}
```

This would result in a corresponding simple repository, like this:

```
public interface IStudentRepository
{
    IEnumerable<Student> GetAllStudents();
    Student Get(int Id);
    Student Add(Student student);
    Student Update(Student changedStudent);
    Student Delete(int Id);
}
```

Let's say we have a `MockStudentRepository` implementation to use with test cases; we might implement it in memory temporarily using `List` or `Hashset` of students. The implementation would look something like this:

```csharp
public class MockStudentRepository : IStudentRepository
{
    private HashSet<Student> students;
    public MockStudentRepository()
    {
        students = new HashSet<Student>()
        {
            new Student() { Id = 1, Name = "Student1",
            Email = "one@something.com" },
            new Student() { Id = 2, Name = "Student2",
            Email = "two@something.com" },
            new Student() { Id = 3, Name = "Student3",
            Email = "three@something.com" },
        };
    }

    public Student Add(Student Student)
    {
        Student.Id = students.Max(e => e.Id) + 1;
        students.Add(Student);
        return Student;
    }
    public Student Delete(int Id)
    {
        Student Student = students.FirstOrDefault(e => e.Id ==
        Id);
        if (Student != null)
        {
            students.Remove(Student);
        }
        return Student;
    }
    public IEnumerable<Student> GetAllStudents()
    {
```

```
            return students;
    }
    public Student Get(int Id)
    {
        return this.students.FirstOrDefault(e => e.Id == Id);
    }
    public Student Update(Student StudentChanges)
    {
        Student Student = students.FirstOrDefault(e => e.Id ==
        StudentChanges.Id);
        if (Student != null)
        {
            Student.Name = StudentChanges.Name;
            Student.Email = StudentChanges.Email;
        }
        return Student;
    }
}
```

In this code, we implemented IStudentRepository using MockStudentRepository, which uses a temporary in-memory store with HashSet. This implementation can be used, for example, during test case execution. Corresponding to MockStudentRepository, we would have a realistic repository implementation that would be something like this, using a SQL relational database as its storage medium:

```
public class SQLStudentRepository : IStudentRepository
{
    public Student Add(Student student)
    {
        ...
    }
    public Student Delete(int Id)
    {
        ...
    }
    ...
}
```

This was a very simple sample implementation of the Repository pattern. I hope that it has explained the concept well enough for you.

We have now covered all that we will cover regarding application design patterns and principles, along with examples of the DI and Repository patterns. I hope it was a good refresher for you.

Before jumping into architectural patterns, let's quickly get an overview of the protocols that are fundamental to communication in any type of architecture.

Communication styles and protocols

Communication protocols and the data formats carried by those protocols are not design patterns but they are things that need to be decided upon and followed as part of an application design strategy. Hence, they are a fundamental part of any architecture, especially if communication is required across process or the machine boundaries. They are to be considered even more carefully for modern cloud-based implementation architectures.

Before listing the communication protocols, let's look at the most widely used communication methods in the next sections.

Synchronous and asynchronous communication

In an enterprise application setup, there are two main types of communication mode: synchronous and asynchronous. In your C# code, when calling any web service via REST or an RPC method, you may use async calls to invoke the web service on the client-side code. This is basically asynchronous execution on the client side that is applied at the thread level to avoid waiting for the I/O completion of a network call. But in this case, essentially the call between the client and server is *synchronous* and is also limited by the send and receive timeouts, which usually have defaults of 60 seconds.

On the other hand, there could be a requirement where the server process needs to work on certain requests for a longer period of time, such as hours or even days. There are also some requirements that would entail having long-running background tasks. There could also be some requirements where work needs to be done in a push and pull manner and the consumer has to work on several event-based tasks and fulfill them via parallel execution on one or more machines.

This requires a different type of communication pattern that does not immediately expect a response but eventually gets the job done in a non-waiting, non-busy *asynchronous* manner.

Asynchronous communication patterns require a third party to dispatch calls between clients (or requestors) and servers (or fulfillers). This third party is considered middleware that takes care of decoupling. We will look at such middleware in the last part of this chapter. For now, let's look at various communication standards.

Standard communication protocols

Here we will list the protocols that are used as a common standard for certain types of communication pattern:

- **Synchronous Request/Response**: This type of communication is between one client and one server. In such a setup, the standard protocol is **HTTPS** and **WebSockets**. The popular data formats are XML, JSON, and now gRPC with protocol buffers.

- **Asynchronous Consumers/Producers**: A producer is an entity that produces or creates messages, while the consumer is an entity that consumes the messages created by the producer. This type of communication could be between one producer and many consumers or even between many producers and many consumers. Therefore, this is asynchronous by nature and requires an intermediary middleware entity between the producers and consumers. The standard protocols in these mechanisms are **Advanced Message Queuing Protocol** (**AMQP**) and **Java Message Service** (**JMS**). A protocol similar to the AMQP protocol but with very tiny payloads, specialized for IoT edge devices, is **Message Queuing Telemetry Transport** (**MQTT**). MQTT does not mandate a specific data format. Popular data formats for these protocols are XML, JSON, or binary.

- **CloudEvents**: CloudEvents are a modern offering for asynchronous eventing and, as the name suggests, fit with the cloud-based architecture. They describe event data in a common way. They simplify event declaration and delivery across services and cloud platforms. The specifications are under the **Cloud Native Computing Foundation** (**CNCF**). CloudEvents are generally processed on HTTPS binding with the JSON data format.

After having had a quick review of the communication mechanisms, we will now move on to the architecture side and check out some architectural patterns.

Architectural patterns

We have so far covered some design patterns along with some useful examples. We have also seen some standards for communication protocols that are vital to any integrated system or connected application. We will now look at the bigger picture by considering architectural patterns.

Since the architecture is essentially a macro-level view of the system and its development, we will focus on the entire development process and keep the sequence of activities in place. Let's begin with a full view of the general software development life cycle, setting aside any specific methodology for now.

A typical software development process has the following activities in this order, while still having iterations of all the activities or parts of certain activities:

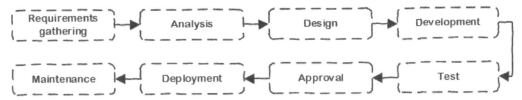

Figure 3.3 – The typical activities in a software development process

What we went through in the previous section applies to the development phase or the development activities. In the development phase, your activities are around design patterns, coding, scripting, and tooling. In the design phase, before that, your main activity is defining the architecture of the system or application under consideration as well as defining non-functional attributes. There are some components in the architecture that may come from an existing organizational architecture or an enterprise architecture; if none exists, it may come from an industry-standard reference architecture. Such components may include but are not limited to API gateways, web servers, API standards (such as SOAP/XML, REST/JSON, and HTTP/gRPC), messaging infrastructure, and so on.

An organization thus has something that can be called an **architecture repository**. In terms of the architecture repository, we will talk only about the *software solution architecture*.

The software solution architecture involves but is not limited to the quality of service, the system interfaces (that is, the API design and publishing mechanisms), the enterprise components, and the architectural patterns.

Architectural patterns define the components and define how they are organized and assembled. Therefore, architectural patterns have a higher-level scope than design patterns, as design patterns describe how to build those components.

Architectural patterns, for example, define patterns for the selected architecture, which could be an n-tier architecture, a microservices architecture, SOA, and so on. Let's get a quick overview of some of the more common application architectures.

Monolith application architecture

This architecture has become widely known in the industry as the "monolith" since the advent of the microservices architecture, but this kind of application was most commonly known as the **layered or n-tier architecture** back in the day.

In the layered architectural pattern, an application is broken down into layers, also known as **modules**, that are stacked on top of each other. These layers, while segregated, are fundamentally part of the same executable. This meant that all the layers would be built as separate library components and linked together to form a common executable application. Without going into much further detail, let's see a diagram of this pattern:

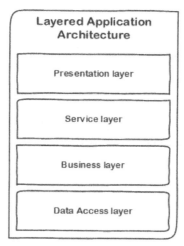

Figure 3.4 – Layered (monolith) application architecture

Though this architectural pattern provides some flexibility and separation of concerns, and you are able to manage code synchronization to allow multiple developers to work concurrently (with the dependency on the source control tool), this architecture resists scalability.

It can still be considered as a decent architecture for a desktop or a smartphone-native app, since those are client-side, single-instance applications, but for web applications, it is quite outdated and resists scalability, that limits the growth usage in case of the huge numbers of consumers.

However, this architecture can still easily enable horizontal scalability by the replication of services with the proper usage of a load balancer. Doing this does limit the proper utilization of the underlying infrastructure resources, though, and it is very difficult to improve the performance of any individual component or service that actually needs optimization to improve the overall system's performance. This means that bottlenecks cannot be improved, and the only way to improve the performance of the application is by replicating the whole application.

Without going into further implementation details and while staying away from design patterns, let's move on to the next architectural pattern.

Microservices architecture

This architectural pattern is the most-used application architecture of recent times, which is why we will cover it in detail along with a sample implementation in the next chapter. The microservices architecture, as opposed to the monolith architecture, not only provides separation of concerns but divides all the major service components into separate executables. So, in this architecture, an application is served by many services that are scalable both horizontally and vertically. This results in each service serving as an independent, complete, and stable component that could also be referred to as an API.

Without going into the design and implementation details, let's see a simple demonstrative diagram of this architectural pattern:

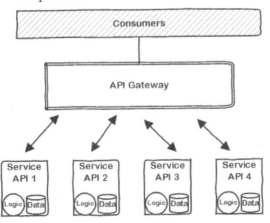

Figure 3.5 – Microservices architectural pattern

From the figure, it's quite clear that the application is broken down into several APIs that are behind an API gateway. Moreover, these are different services, where each of them can be individually scaled as per your needs and the load.

To have a clearer architectural view of this pattern, let's have a look at the architecture of an individual microservice service that serves a single API in a typical manner:

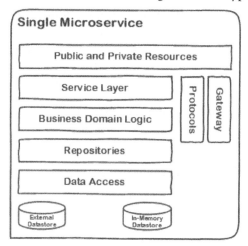

Figure 3.6 – Typical architecture of a single microservice

This architectural pattern represents the most common type of microservice, with all of its capabilities packed inside as a single serving executable, following the best practices of the container architecture. We will get into the details of the microservices architecture in the next chapter. For now, let's look at other architectural patterns.

Backend for Frontend (BFF)

BFF is not a full-fledged architecture on its own but is an architectural pattern. It is a commonly applied pattern, along with the microservices architecture, but it can also be glued together with other types of architectures.

It simplifies development for frontend teams by defining additional composite services or gateway services that perform the work of orchestration for the underlying services serving certain APIs. The frontend does not need to know or remember each and every API behind the scenes; instead, it interacts with the BFF in a façade-esque manner.

A common BFF implementation would look something like the following:

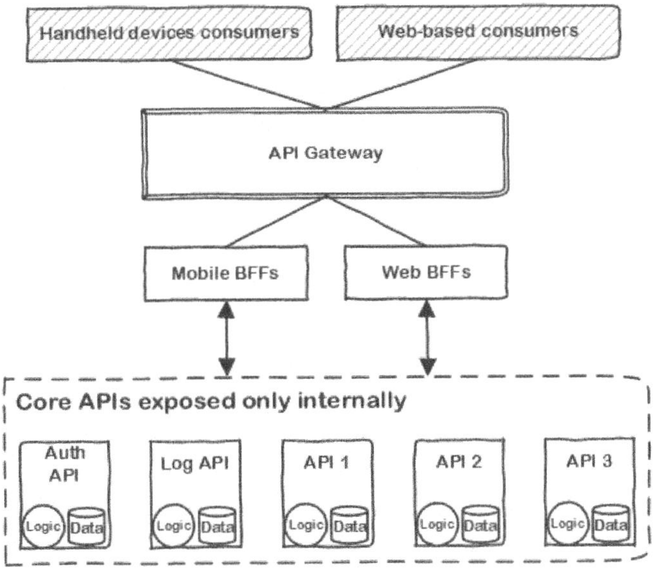

Figure 3.7 – Sample BFF architectural pattern

Tip

You may notice that there can be more than one BFF serving hundreds of different APIs behind the scenes. In some cases, it is also possible that the final implementation does not even have an API gateway. Rather, it treats the BFF services as the only gateway entry points to a whole set of APIs behind the scenes. In such cases, BFFs are typically exposed only behind the load balancer instead of behind a full-fledged commercial API gateway.

BFFs are client-specific, focusing on the composite API and reducing the clutter and complexity. With the BFF architectural pattern, frontend teams are more independent, being focused on their prime functionality and UX, and even helping build the BFF interface.

The BFF pattern also enables the smart devices development team to trim the payload size and request frequencies. And the frontends are protected against API changes for the underlying services. With that, we will now look at another architectural pattern.

Serverless architecture

The serverless architecture emerged with the advent of cloud-based offerings and the term was first coined by Amazon Web Services. In this architecture, application developers are freed from having to consider server machines, virtual machines, and containers, and they do not even need to consider hosting their services on any application server as such. These architectural patterns rely primarily on remotely hosted, scalable, invocable, triggered, and background-running micro APIs.

In this architecture, clients are usually rich clients with frontend logic APIs as **Function as a Service (FaaS)** solutions and storage, or third-party services, such as **Backend as a Service (BaaS)** providers.

Consider the following simplified high-level serverless architecture diagram:

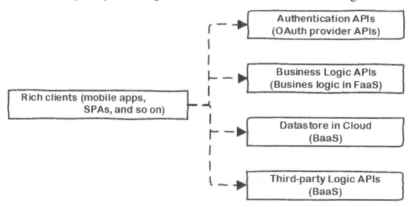

Figure 3.8 – High-level serverless architecture

Let's define a few terms and patterns that we used in this architecture:

- **OAuth**: OAuth is an open standard for authentication. There are OAuth provider APIs that help your application to take care of the authentication part. This mechanism is used by and provided by companies such as Facebook, Google, and Microsoft.

- **BaaS**: BaaS provides infrastructure-oriented software services, which may include storage as a service, database as a service, and messaging/notifications as a service. In the serverless architecture, the application uses a combination of BaaS services. Some BaaS examples include Google's Firebase, Amazon's DynamoDB, Auth0, and Azure Active Directory.

- **FaaS**: These provide server-side business logic as a hosted tiny service, usually serving only one functionality, and they are also considered as micro APIs. The developer need only focus on the functionality and is free from any other hosting and web infrastructure concerns. FaaS is the heart of the serverless architecture. Some FaaS examples include Azure Functions and AWS Lambda. These functions or APIs are short-lived, mostly event-driven, and utilize server-side resources hidden from developers that are provided by the cloud infrastructure as part of the ecosystem. These are usually charged for based on the number of invocations, network bandwidth, and CPU and memory usage.

In a serverless architecture, you only communicate via APIs or event-driven mechanisms. The architecture frees you from the hassle of server or operating system management and worrying about any application server hosting requirements. Thus, the serverless architecture enables quick development and fast time-to-market. It is not necessarily the most performant setup, but it is neat, quick, and stable.

Each of these architectural patterns could have a chapter or even a book dedicated to it, if we really wanted to cover it to its fullest extent. For now, let's continue and get just a taste of these wonderful architectural patterns.

Enterprise Service Bus (ESB)

To see where the ESB fits, we need to consider **Service-Oriented Architecture (SOA)**. SOA is not just a simple architecture or a bunch of architectural patterns but a whole methodology of architectural practices. SOA provides a complete set of architectural patterns as a middleware for enterprise IT applications, and the implementation of SOA revolves around an ESB.

An ESB is a collection of features and tools that is essential for any SOA implementation. An ESB provides the following components to fulfill the SOA needs:

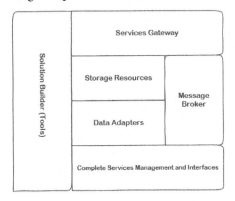

Figure 3.9 – Main components of an ESB

Let's have a brief overview of each major component in an ESB:

- **Services Gateway** entails the proxy, reverse proxy, protocols, and security. It enables the communication proxy in both directions, along with throttling and control.

- **Message Broker** entails distributed asynchronous communication. A message broker acts as an entity sitting in the middle of two or more communication parties, of which some are sending messages and others are receiving them.

- **Services Management Interface** entails setup, administration, management, and monitoring.

- **Solution Builder** entails the solution designer (IDE) and CLI tools.

- **Storage Resources** entails in-memory storage, persistency, logs, as well as audits.

- **Data Adapters** entails data and services plugins that connect to various resources, including third parties, to fetch or provide information.

> **Tip**
>
> You can learn more about SOA in practice with my previous book, *Enterprise Application Architecture with .NET Core*, published by Packt.

This was probably the shortest overview of what an ESB is and the main features it provides. I do hope that it has provided a fair amount of information to you to give you a good start in this direction, specifically to determine whether this is a kind of setup that your enterprise application may need. Let's jump to out-of-process, event-based message processing in the next section.

Distributed processing

Distributed processing is processing done across process boundaries or OS/machine boundaries and in some cases even network and data center boundaries. Distributed processing at scale takes place in many enterprise applications that do not communicate directly with each other in a one-to-one manner. They communicate asynchronously and their workloads are usually implemented across several services. These services could be working in parallel or in sequence. Some may take longer to finish, while others can complete their tasks in just a couple of seconds.

This kind of communication and processing requires intermediary middleware that takes care of acquiring and dispatching requests across one or thousands of services. The middleware component here is either a message broker or an event streaming engine. Let's see the standard distributed processing patterns in the following subsections. Please note that all these patterns follow asynchronous communication mechanisms.

Queuing

This is a common distributed pattern that is typically between a producer and a consumer, where they communicate via a queue that acts as a pipe with two ends. At one end, there is a producer, and at the other, there is a consumer. The producer produces a message and does not wait for the consumer to respond:

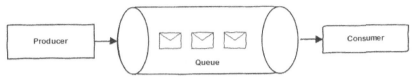

Figure 3.10 – Typical queue configuration

The preceding diagram shows the communication mechanism in a queue between a consumer and a producer. Let's look at more patterns for distributed processing.

The publish-subscribe pattern

This pattern is typically between a publisher and one or more subscribers who are interested in receiving messages or events from the publisher. The publisher is also referred to as a **producer** and the subscribers as **consumers**. The message brokers have a mechanism to fulfill this pattern, known as **topics**. Topics allow one message input to be pushed to one or more subscribers, and every subscriber gets a copy of the same message. It is also possible for subscribers to specify a filter that can then select a subset of published messages on a given topic. Refer to the following diagram:

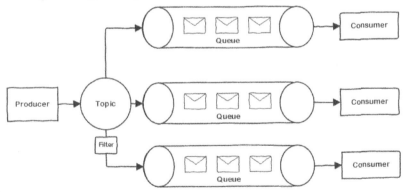

Figure 3.11 – Typical topic configuration

The preceding diagram depicts the workings of a publish-subscribe pattern using a topic created inside a message broker. Here a topic is connected to a queue, which in this case is acting as a subscriber to which certain consumers are connected. Note that one consumer connects to one queue, but ultimately many consumers get data from a single queue. Let's see some other patterns.

Stateful processing

In stateful processing, in the context of distributed processing, we usually pull messages from a stream or a queue in a sequential manner. All of these messages are directed to a process that works as a state aggregator, for example, a rolling average calculator.

In this kind of processing, message consumption can be suspended or interrupted and later resumed elsewhere as required. Typically, this can be achieved using a single consumer with single-threaded connectivity to the message queue as it aggregates the messages in a sequence.

Sparse connectivity

This distributed communication pattern is popular with wireless applications and IoT edge applications where connectivity can be intermittent. For example, mobile users may switch network or go out of range, or load may reach the bandwidth cap for edge devices. This pattern allows communication to be completely asynchronous through the use of local queues on the client side. The client first pushes the messages or events to the local queue, which later get forwarded to the actual queue on the server side somewhere in the cloud. In this way, even if there is sparse connectivity, the local queue preserves the messages until the connectivity is restored. Let's see it in a diagram:

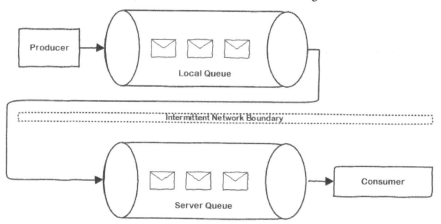

Figure 3.12 – Typical sparse connectivity

The preceding diagram depicts the concept of sparse connectivity using a mechanism between a local queue and a server queue. The producer in this case is a client and the consumer is a server-side process consuming the messages for a certain kind of processing.

Partitioning

Partitions are different from the publish-subscribe (**pubsub**) scheme; they allow a type of message (say, a topic) to be divided into multiple partitions. Each partition is read by a different consumer but they do not receive the same copies of messages. A producer puts the message uniquely into each partition using the *hashing criteria* so that the processing load is divided between more than one consumer. This mechanism is used in the processing of streams of billions of messages, with hundreds of thousands of consumers processing them.

Partitions are chosen when they are created, that is, before publishing, while for publish-subscribe scenarios, a new subscription can be added at any point and the new subscriber starts receiving published messages from that point.

Messages in partitions are processed with multiple consumers in parallel and without any overlapping. Messages are produced in event streaming topics in an append-only fashion and are read from beginning to end. A topic with multiple partitions does not provide a guarantee of the sequence of the messages across the entire topic, but it does for a single partition. Let's see a diagram of it here:

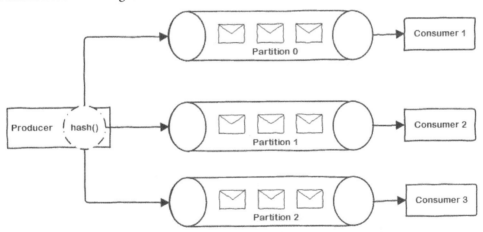

Figure 3.13 – Representation of message processing in partitions

With the distributed processing architectural pattern of partitions, we have come to the end of our quick overview of popular and standard architectural patterns. We hope you have learned a lot and enjoyed the process as well.

> **More info on messaging**
>
> Read more about various offerings from Azure Messaging Services that are supported using .NET 5 at `https://docs.microsoft.com/en-us/azure/messaging-services/`.

Summary

In this chapter, we learned about a lot of design and architectural patterns, just as a quick overview. These industry patterns are frequently implemented by modern applications developed using .NET 5, along with various types of message brokers.

We learned about many patterns as well as learning about the difference between design and architectural patterns. We also covered patterns that are applicable on desktop and web applications as well as applications of a distributed nature, which span across various machines, networks, and even a huge number of consumers in the cloud.

In the next chapter, we look at the microservices architecture and study a sample implementation using .NET 5.

4

Containerized Microservices Architecture

Microservices-based architecture is one of the most popular architectures to use when developing new products and services. Containerization has enabled us to achieve microservices development and deployment to perfection. .NET Core and .NET 5 support microservices majorly by providing a number of features that are very container aware and are strongly performant in cross-platform scenarios with best-in-class support for Linux-based .NET containerized apps.

In this chapter, we are going to build on the topics that we have learned about .NET features and design patterns in previous chapters, *Chapter 1, Introducing .NET 5 Features and Capabilities* and *Chapter 3, Design and Architectural Patterns*. We will make use of new tools and technologies that are available now, along with the .NET 5 echo system.

Therefore, when following this chapter, you should already be aware of .NET Core or .NET 5 and the common design patterns and popular architectures as a prerequisite. Adding on top of the main microservices architecture that we covered in the previous chapter, in this one, we will build a small set of services in a microservices-based architecture using containerized technologies and the latest tool offerings from Microsoft along with the release of .NET 5.

In this chapter, we will be looking at the following main topics:

- What is the gRPC communication protocol, and what are its benefits and its usages with .NET 5?

- What is WSL?

- What is Tye and how can we use it extensively in our demo microservices application?

- What are container orchestration and its concepts with regard to Kubernetes?

- Architecture and the implementation of the demo microservices application

By the end of this chapter, you will be able to understand and implement practical microservices architecture-based applications using the latest Microsoft tooling with much ease.

Technical requirements

In this chapter, we will code a tiny proof-of-concept containerized microservices application and use debugging techniques with Tye. In order to build and run them, we will need the following:

- Windows 10, **Windows Subsystem for Linux (WSL)** 2 (with Ubuntu distribution), Tye, .NET 5, .NET Core 3.1 (for Tye), and Docker Desktop.

- You can use **Visual Studio Code (VS Code)** or Visual Studio 2019 Community edition as an IDE.

- Online code for the examples can be found at the following GitHub URL:
  `https://github.com/PacktPublishing/Adopting-.NET-5--Architecture-Migration-Best-Practices-and-New-Features/tree/master/Chapter04.`

Let's move ahead and explore this interesting chapter!

Why overview other topics and not just microservices?

When talking about microservices applications, you might wonder, why not reveal the architecture and just implement it? This is natural and there is nothing wrong with doing this. We are learning about the other technologies in this context as they are going to help us in our journey toward the development of microservices-based applications. The surrounding technologies have been improved with the introduction of .NET 5, so you are encouraged as a developer to work in the modern architecture with modern technology with ease, from the development machine to the on-cloud clusters.

gRPC is going to help us to select the latest and fastest communication technology between the microservices. **WSL 2** makes our development life easier when developing and debugging the microservices .NET applications on Windows machines, and **Tye** will help us tie it all down within the local development machine and ease us to quickly move our process toward complex cloud-based infrastructure.

The gRPC communication protocol

gRPC is an open source framework that was originally developed by Google in 2015 and now is a part of the **Cloud Native Computing Foundation (CNCF)**, which provides the global standard for cloud-native offerings.

RPC stands for **remote procedure call**, meaning you make a method call over a network boundary either on the same machine, on a private network, or on a public network. gRPC is a modern, cross-platform, high-performance RPC that is available on almost all popular programming languages. A gRPC server exposes a remotely callable method, which a gRPC client calls via a local function that internally invokes a function on a remote machine serving some business operation.

There are similar RPC technologies, such as very old versions of Java's **RMI**, **Thrift**, **JSON-RPC**, **WCF**, and more. But the open source community and CNCF are more unified on gRPC, and it also has the widest level of cross-platform support.

gRPC uses HTTP/2 and Protobuf technologies. Let's learn about them in the next subsection.

HTTP/2 and Protobuf

HTTP/2 enables client/server communication in bi-directional mode as well as enabling streaming calls. It also enables multiplexing, which makes it possible to make several requests in parallel over the same connection. HTTP/2 also enables the binary framing for data transport, unlike HTTP/1.1, which was only text-based.

Protobuf, or **Protocol Buffers**, is a cross-platform technology that defines the **Interface Definition Language (IDL)** to declare the service interfaces that are called remotely. gRPC uses a contract-first approach whereby the contracts are defined in Protobuf format, usually in `*.proto` files. Protobuf defines the human-readable format and its machine-level representation and handles the translation between the two. gRPC libraries for each language/platform enable the definition of Protobuf's IDL into the language's own type format, for example, C# types to handle **requests** and **response** objects.

To communicate between services, we can use communication mechanisms other than RPC, such as REST and **Simple Object Access Protocol (SOAP)**, among others. Let's quickly see the major differences between the most popular options in the .NET world.

gRPC versus REST APIs versus SOAP

Before gRPC, the most popular communication options for .NET service developers were HTTP REST APIs and HTTP SOAP with Web API and WCF technologies. Let's have a look at the major differences between them:

gRPC	REST APIs	SOAP Methods
RPC principle.	Uses HTTP verbs.	XML-based protocol format.
Contract first.	Content first (based around resources identified by URLs).	Contract first.
Contract is managed via a proto file.	Contract is optionally managed via OpenAPI (Swagger). Contract schema specifications are not essential.	Contract is managed via Web Services Definition Language (WSDL)
Proto file uses Protobuf's IDL for interface definition.	Custom interface specifications as defined by OpenAPI format using JSON.	Interface specs are in WSDL format using SOAP via XML schemas.

gRPC	REST APIs	SOAP Methods
Point-to-point protocol generally between client and server but with a fixed contract.	Point-to-point protocol generally between client and server but with a flexible or even unknown contract (for example, in HATEOAS architecture).	Point-to-point protocol generally between client and server but with a fixed contract.
Content is in binary format and is meant for machines.	Content is in JSON text and is human-readable and very simple.	Content is highly structured, in XML text, and is human-readable.
Hides remoting complexities.	Enforces HTTP verbs around resources and APIs.	Highly structured format to follow between client and server.
Binary protocol, small size, Protobuf binary serialization, HTTP/2 header compression, low network usage.	Simple JSON text protocol, medium size, JSON-to-object serialization.	Complex XML text protocol, large size, slower XML-to-object serialization.
Focuses on high performance.	Focuses ease of use for the largest sets of consumers.	Focuses on structure. Tightly integrated consumers and producers, targets interoperability with a lot of conventions.
HTTP/2 streaming, HTTP/2 multiplexing allows multiple calls via the same TCP connection, low overhead, higher performance.	By standard, not specific to HTTP/2 improvements.	By standard, not specific to HTTP/2 improvements.

Table 4.1 – Comparison between web services communication protocols

From this comparison table, we can see why the gRPC protocol is a clear winner for high-performant, point-to-point communication between any two services. It is the protocol of choice for internal communication over a local network but it can be as popular for internet communication once the major web services gateway adds the support for handling the gRPC protocol. Until then, REST/JSON is the go-to protocol for all the public APIs, as it is widely supported on almost all platforms and API gateways, as well as directly supported by frontend technologies such as JavaScript within browsers.

Having covered the advantages of gRPC over other protocols, let's learn more about it.

What's new with gRPC in .NET 5?

gRPC was already available with .NET Core, but now with .NET 5, it has more features and improvements. Let's have a quick look at them:

- gRPC was implemented as a wrapper over its C++ implementation, but now with .NET 5, it has been completely re-written into managed C#. With this, it is producing more performance by avoiding the context switch of the safe to unsafe code courtesy also to improved C# compiler.

- Improvements in the Kestrel server that commonly hosts gRPC services are as follows:

    Reducing allocations

    Improving concurrency

    Response header compression

- gRPC hosting on Windows operating systems via the IIS server, thanks to the new version of HTTP.sys that enabled the feature set improvements for HTTP/2 at the operating system level that were not present before.

- **Inter-Process Communication (IPC)** can now use the gRPC protocol.

- gRPC-Web adds support for browsers so that JavaScript or Blazor WebAssembly-based client apps can communicate via the gRPC protocol.

Now that we know about gRPC and its support in .NET 5, let's have a look at a sample proto file to get a feel of a gRPC-based service.

Sample service proto file

In order to get the essence of gRPC, it is a good idea to have a view of what a proto file using Protocol Buffers IDL looks like.

The following is the proto file that we are actually going to use when developing the microservices application in this chapter. This is basically telling us about the interface for a service with the name **PrimeCalculator**. It has one method, namely IsItPrime, with a request and a response:

```
syntax = "proto3";
option csharp_namespace = "microservicesapp";
package prime;


//Service Interface
```

```
service PrimeCalculator {
   rpc IsItPrime (PrimeRequest) returns (PrimeReply);
}


//Request message
message PrimeRequest {
   int64 number = 1;
}


//Response message
message PrimeReply {
   bool isPrime = 1;
}
```

gRPC has four different types of RPC methods. IsItPrime in the preceding example is of the *unary* type.

The RPC method types are as follows:

- **Unary RPC**: These types of methods have a one-off method call with a single request and a single response.

- **Server streaming RPC**: In this mode, the client sends a single request and the server sends back a stream of messages.

- **Client streaming in RPC**: In this mode, the client opens up a stream and sends a sequence of messages to the server. The server reads all the messages and then returns the response to mark the end of the call.

- **Bidirectional streaming RPC**: In this mode, both the server and the client send streams of messages in sequence. In this case, both have two different read-write streams. The two streams are independent and can be read in any manner. For example, a server can decide to first read all the input stream and then write to the output stream, or read a single message and write a single response. It can also do any other combination of reading and writing the messages to the respective streams.

Now that we have covered sufficient ground for what gRPC is, we can use it in our microservices-based applications.

> **Pro tip**
>
> If you are debugging an ASP.NET application (whether REST or gRPC) on a Windows machine, you would need to accept and install the SSL certificate, which enables HTTPS for the development machine and enables successful debugging. Run this command on Windows to enable it: `dotnet dev-certs https -trust`.
>
> Visit this link for more information – *Enforce HTTPS in ASP.NET Core*: `https://docs.microsoft.com/en-us/aspnet/core/security/enforcing-ssl`.

Now, let's look further for features that support the debugging of Linux container-based .NET 5 C# code on Windows.

What is WSL?

WSL allows us to run a full-fledged Linux environment inside Windows without using a dual boot setup or running inside a virtual machine. Currently, there are two versions: WSL 1 and WSL 2. Naturally, WSL 2 is an improved version; it is recommended and we will be using it. WSL 2 has increased the filesystem performance and added full system call compatibility.

With WSL, for example, we can debug our .NET applications that are supposed to run in a Linux production environment somewhere on the cloud on our local Windows developer desktop. It can also speed up the debugging of a Linux-based container on a Windows machine.

In addition to that, with WSL, you can install a selected number of Linux distributions that are available on Microsoft Store, and you can use Linux command-line tools, such as `grep`, on the Windows filesystem, such as in your C drive. You can also run database services such as MySQL, MongoDB, and PostgreSQL inside your WSL. It is also possible to install more applications using your distribution's package manager, for example, Ubuntu's **Advanced Packaging Tool** (**APT**) and `dpkg` as a package manager for Debian-based systems.

For a detailed comparison of WSL 1 and WSL 2, please check out the following link: `https://docs.microsoft.com/en-us/windows/wsl/compare-versions`.

Let's now prepare WSL on our machine so that we are ready to debug our containerized applications when we need to.

Installing WSL on your development machine

In this section, we will install the WSL 2 version that will later be useful to actually do debugging if required. To install WSL and get it up and running, we will follow the steps that we will look at in the next subsections.

Step 1 – installing the WSL Windows feature

This can be installed from the Windows 10 features area in the Control Panel. You can also type the following in your Windows Explorer bar: `Control Panel\All Control Panel Items\Programs and Features`.

This will bring you to the features page, and from there, you can click on **Turn Windows features on or off** and then select **Windows Subsystem for Linux**:

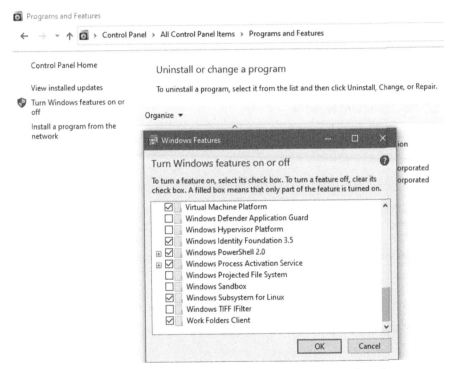

Figure 4.1 – Showing Windows Subsystem for Linux as a Windows feature

Installing the WSL feature from the Windows Control Panel would look like as in *Figure 4.1*.

Step 2 – installing the Linux kernel update package

You will need to download and install the Linux kernel update package on your Windows machine. It is available as **WSL2 Linux kernel update package for x64 machines** from `https://wslstorestorage.blob.core.windows.net/wslblob/wsl_update_x64.msi`.

Step 3 – making WSL 2 a default version

You may be required to do this but on my machine, it was already the default version. It can be set using the following command:

```
wsl --set-default-version 2
```

Step 4 – installing the Linux distribution of your choice

Head on to Microsoft Store and install the Linux distributions that you would like to try. For our purpose of building a microservices application, we will install the latest version of Ubuntu's distribution, which at the time of writing is *20.04 LTS*. The following screenshot shows what it looked like when I launched the Microsoft Store app on my Windows 10 machine and typed `WSL`:

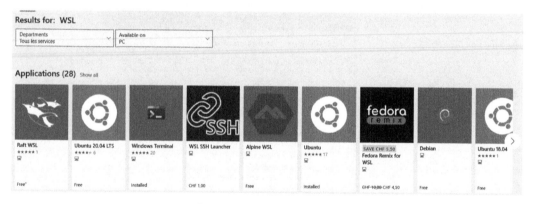

Figure 4.2 – View of Microsoft Store displaying Linux distributions

Selecting the Ubuntu distribution in Microsoft Store will show the following screen. Just click **Get** and let it install:

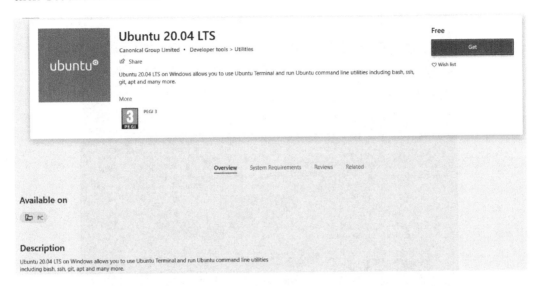

Figure 4.3 – Microsoft Store screen displaying Ubuntu 20.04 LTS ready to install

While you are at it, you may also install the **Windows Terminal** app from Microsoft Store; it can come in handy as it allows you to run multiple consoles as a tabbed view within this single app. For example, you can run cmd, WSL, and PowerShell all from within the tabs of the Windows Terminal app:

```
Ubuntu
Installing, this may take a few minutes...
Please create a default UNIX user account. The username does not need to match your Windows username.
For more information visit: https://aka.ms/wslusers
Enter new UNIX username: habib
New password:
Retype new password:
```

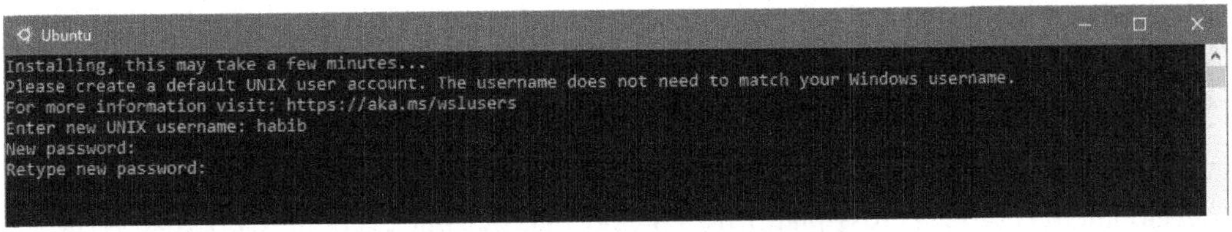

Figure 4.4 – The Ubuntu installation on WSL

Once Ubuntu is installed for WSL, it will look something like this, which you can invoke by typing `ubuntu` or `wsl` in the Windows Start menu:

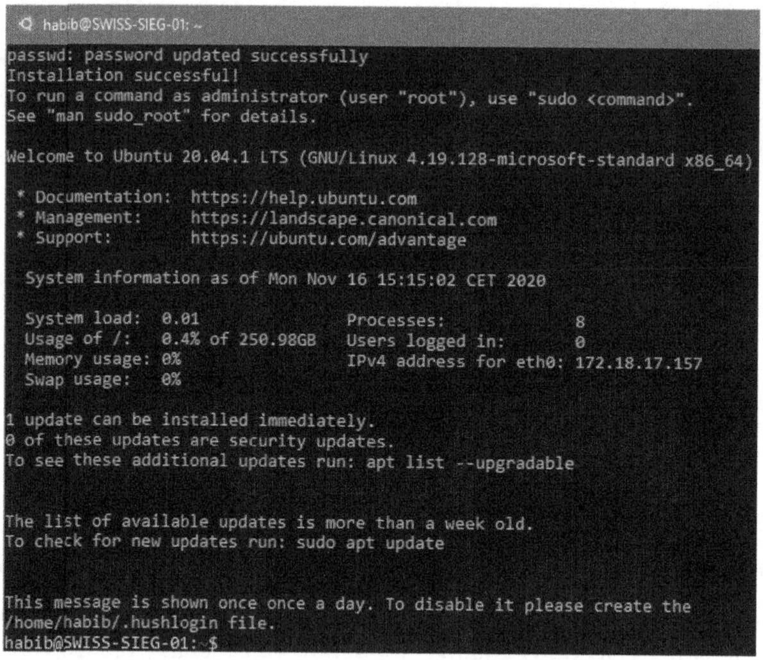

Figure 4.5 – The first run of Ubuntu on WSL

Now that we have WSL up and running, let's see two more tips that could make our development life easier.

Some useful VS Code-related extensions

VS Code is a very popular, lightweight, cross-platform editor. Since microservices-based development is usually cross-platform, VS Code has become even more popular as the editor of choice.

To increase the developer's productivity with VS Code, we suggest a couple of extensions within VS Code that make the microservices development journey more pleasant. These extensions are as follows:

- Remote WSL

- Remote Containers

- Kubernetes

I imagine that you already have extensions for C# and Docker. If not, go ahead and install them too. Let's install a new useful extension: **Remote WSL**.

These extensions are, of course, directly available to download from the *VS Code Extensions* button on the left sidebar.

The following is how it looks after installing the Remote WSL extension:

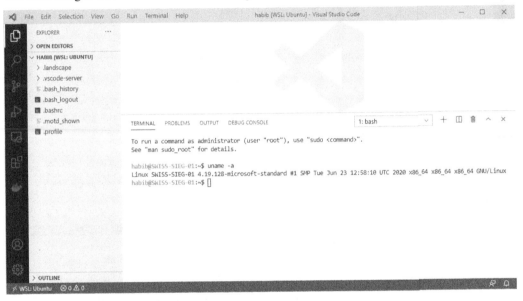

Figure 4.6 – The Remote WSL extension in VS Code

From the previous screenshot, you can see that VS Code is connected to **Ubuntu** via the Remote WSL extension. You can also note that now, Terminal within VS Code is running inside Ubuntu with Bash and not on Windows with **PowerShell**.

Let's also install the other two useful extensions that we previously mentioned:

- **Remote Containers**: With this extension, you can explore all the running Docker containers on your machine right inside VS Code!

- **Kubernetes**: With this extension, you can explore your Kubernetes clusters within VS Code:

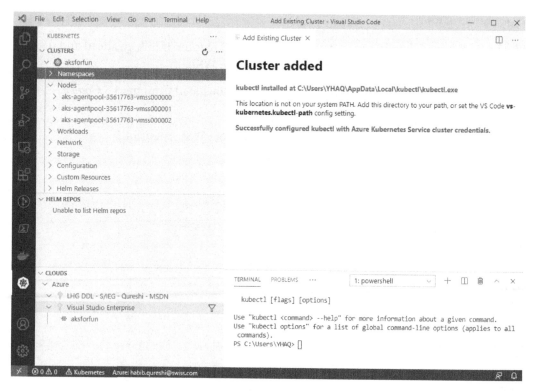

Figure 4.7 – Shows the Kubernetes extension in action in VS Code

In the previous figure, you can see the Kubernetes extension in action, which is connected to my Azure account and displays a Kubernetes cluster that is created inside **Azure Kubernetes Service**.

With all the useful extensions set up already, you would want to debug code too!

Things to check before you start debugging with WSL

Here, we have another piece of useful information that you should know before you start debugging your .NET 5 code in WSL. To be able to debug in WSL, which in our case is using Ubuntu, you will need to install the .NET 5 runtime to be able to execute the .NET code. For that, you need to follow these two steps:

1. Install Microsoft's Debian (compatible with Ubuntu)-based package:

    ```
    wget https://packages.microsoft.com/config/ubuntu/20.04/
    packages-microsoft-prod.deb -O packages-microsoft-prod.
    deb
    ```

    ```
    sudo dpkg -i packages-microsoft-prod.deb
    ```

2. Install the `dotnet` and ASP.NET runtimes:

    ```
    sudo apt-get update; \
        sudo apt-get install -y apt-transport-https && \
        sudo apt-get update && \
        sudo apt-get install -y dotnet-runtimeaspnetcore-
    runtime-5.0
    ```

    ```
    sudo apt-get install -y aspnetcore-runtime-5.0
    ```

Following these two steps, you are ready to execute your .NET 5-based services as well as debug them on Ubuntu with WSL, all while staying within your Windows 10 operating system.

For .NET 5 install instructions on platforms other than Ubuntu, look here for more information: `https://docs.microsoft.com/en-us/dotnet/core/install/linux-ubuntu`.

> **Visual Studio debugging with WSL**
>
> One more tip that we do not want you to miss is about debugging .NET code in Linux containers utilizing WSL and Visual Studio 2019.
>
> Head over to YouTube and watch this 4-minute video – *.NET Core Debugging with WSL 2 in Visual Studio 2019*: `https://www.youtube.com/watch?v=Skn8m8oCBoA`.

With these useful VS Code extensions and debugging tips with us, let's now jump into our last tip that is useful for microservices development utilizing WSL.

WSL as a Docker engine

We will now do an additional step that is not required for WSL but is an advantageous step for container-based development on our local development Windows machine.

You may already have a Docker Desktop version installed on your machine; if not, you may install it now as it is also a prerequisite for our sample project.

With the WSL 2 Linux distribution of choice installed, we can now configure Docker to use WSL 2 as its engine, which uses **Hyper-V** in a very optimized virtual machine to execute Linux containers on Windows, giving a better performance to the containers' execution on the Windows platform.

The following figure shows how to set WSL 2 as the engine for Docker Desktop on Windows:

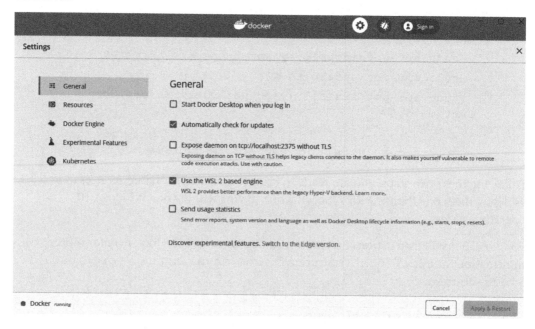

Figure 4.8 – Docker settings to select WSL 2 as the Docker engine

Finally, the installation of Ubuntu is completed on WSL using WSL 2 as the default version. I hope these steps were helpful to get your WSL up and running successfully and will later be useful in your microservices development journey. We will now go on to the next section and discover a new tool in the market, **Tye**.

What is Tye?

Microsoft is continuously taking developers' feedback, and even more so after going full open source mode, when they realized the pain of Microsoft .NET developers who were building microservices-based applications, debugging, and deploying them to test and production environments. So, they set up a team to build a tool that would help simplify all of this, and hence a new tool named **Tye** (also referred to as Project Tye) was born.

As of November 2020, they consider this tool as experimental and not yet complete or stable. The positive part is that for us as developers, we can already start using it!

Tye is a command-line tool that supports developers, especially during the development phase, whereby the developer can easily run, test, and debug the containerized application on their local development machine without worrying about other services and dependencies in other containers or Docker, or even a container orchestrator on their machine. Additionally, it even allows you to deploy your microservices to a Kubernetes cluster by automatically containerizing your .NET application, if you need to.

We now know what Tye is and what it is used for. Do not worry about an example with its CLI for now as we will look at its practical usage in the development of our sample microservices application in the last part of the chapter.

Now that we have covered some tips and tools with modern development, let's go ahead and touch base on some containerization concepts before we develop our microservices-based application.

> **Learn more**
>
> Learn more about Tye and its open source project located at `https://github.com/dotnet/tye`.
>
> A simple walkthrough Tye tutorial to quickly learn its features can be found here: `https://github.com/dotnet/tye/tree/master/docs/tutorials/hello-tye`.

Introduction to containerization and container orchestration

Containers provide processes isolation, meaning they run in an isolated space. They also provide effective control of I/O resources in a manner that is kind of like a sub-operating system hosted by an existing operating system with virtual boundaries.

The operating system that is hosting the container(s) can either be running on a physical machine or itself inside a virtual machine.

A container is an isolated place that is virtually boundary-walled using the process and namespace isolation technology provided by the host operating system so that an application running inside the container runs without affecting the rest of the system outside the container boundary.

The idea behind this kind of virtual environment was initially proposed by a MIPT professor in 1999. This was basically an improvement on the chroot model having three main components:

- Groups of processes isolated by namespaces
- A filesystem to share part of the code
- Provide isolation and management of key resources such as networks

Some of the containerization technologies from the past include **chroot** in the 80s, **FreeBSD Jails** in 2000, **Solaris Zones** in 2004, **OpenVZ** in 2005, **cgroups** in 2006, **LXC** in 2008, **lmctfy** in 2013, and **Docker** in 2013, as well as others.

Docker itself internally uses **containerd**, which is an industry-standard container runtime also chiefly used by Kubernetes. Introducing the basic concept and brief history, let's discover the fundamental concepts around a container.

What are some modern container fundamentals?

With containerization becoming so popular in this decade, it has matured into some fundamental concepts that go along with it. Let's take a short look at their definition:

- **Container host**: This is an operating system running on a physical machine or a virtual machine. This operating system actually hosts containers inside it.
- **Container operating system image**: Containers are deployed in the form of layers of images and they stack up. The base layer provides the basics of an operating system environment for the desired applications eventually inside the container.
- **Container image**: A container image is intended for applications. It contains the base operating system, application, and all application dependencies in the form of container layers along with all the required configurations to deploy and run the container.

- **Container registry**: A container registry is the place that keeps container images that can be downloaded on demand. Popular container registries include Docker Hub and Azure Container Registry. You can even have a container registry on-premises or temporarily on a local development machine.

  In our microservices app demo, we will set up a local container registry on our development machine.

- **Configuration**: The container configuration file is used to create container images. It can, for example, specify the required base images, directory mappings, networking, and required files before the given container is started. For Docker-based containers, it is a **Dockerfile**.

- **Container orchestration**: When you deploy many containers that make up an application, tracing, tracking, and managing, their deployment and execution require sophisticated management and orchestration.

  Container orchestrators assign a pool of servers (nodes) in a given cluster and the respective schedule to deploy containers onto those nodes. These orchestrators configure networking between containers, load balancing, rolling updates, extensibility, and more. Examples of popular container orchestrators include the following: Docker Compose/Docker Swarm, Kubernetes, and Mesos/DCOS. Kubernetes is the most popular container orchestrator and there are various Kubernetes-based implementations on the cloud as well as on-premises.

Talking about fundamental concepts and bringing Docker into the picture brings up a couple more supporting concepts. The most basic of them are discussed here.

What are the fundamental components of a Docker engine?

The Docker engine is a fundamental component in a Docker-based echo system. It is a core application that is deployed on the operating system and enables hosting the Docker containers.

It has three major components:

- **dockerd**: A daemon that is a long-running server program.
- **REST API**: Exposes the interface so that the programs can talk to this daemon.
- **CLI**: Enables us to interface with Docker using the `docker` command. It basically talks to the Docker engine via its REST APIs.

So far, we have covered the fundamentals of the containers. Let's now understand the basics of the container orchestrator. We chose Kubernetes as our orchestrator as it is the most popular and highly capable container orchestrator in the market.

Kubernetes basics

In this section, we will cover the basic concepts of Kubernetes, also known as **K8s**, container orchestrator. We are going to use the term Kubernetes and K8s interchangeably. Kubernetes is an extensible, open source container orchestration platform for configuring, managing, and automating container deployment, execution, and orchestration. It was originally developed by Google and was open sourced by them in 2014, and is now maintained by the CNCF.

Kubernetes itself is a huge subject that deserves its own book as well as training. Here, we will cover only the basics of some of its most commonly used components.

Kubernetes components

Some of the Kubernetes components are fundamental and are mostly required by all types of apps deployed to a K8s cluster using container images. We will learn about these essential components and you should understand them because they are vital for any containerized deployment, as well as used in a short demo of our microservices application later in this chapter.

The following figure depicts basic concepts on a very high-level basis:

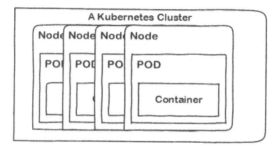

Figure 4.9 – Kubernetes basic concepts

This figure shows that in a Kubernetes cluster, we have nodes, and inside nodes, we have one or more pods, and inside pods, we have one or more containers:

- **Node**: A node is kind of a machine or a virtual machine that provides all the computation resources to underlying components.

- **Pod**: A Pod is a basic deployable component that is deployed in a given K8s cluster. It has a set of containers running inside it.

- **Container**: Any container image for our application that we want to deploy to a K8s cluster gets deployed and runs under a K8s managed entity that is a Pod.

The following is a typical setup of a three-node Kubernetes cluster:

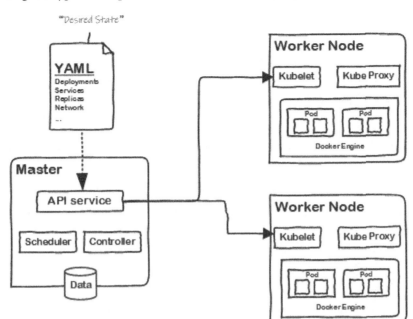

Figure 4.10 – Concept of a basic three-node Kubernetes cluster

Here, again, we depict and talk about the most essential components that are required for basic understanding while omitting other, more detailed concepts.

Deploying an application to a Kubernetes cluster is done by giving a *YAML*-based deployment description file, which basically tells K8s to enable and maintain a desired state of services. With this, if a service in a container image is down, or a pod or a node is down, K8s will automatically spin up a new, relevant instance and maintain the desired state as we requested via the YAML file.

Let's understand the preceding figure by learning the basic definitions of each component mentioned here:

- **Container runtime**: Kubernetes supports several container runtimes inside it to facilitate the application's container execution. This includes Docker, containerd, CRI-O, and any implementation of the Kubernetes **Container Runtime Interface (CRI)**.

- **Master**: A master node is a node with which we interact and provide the YAML-based deployment descriptor. This is a necessary component for a K8s cluster.

- **API service**: As the name suggests, it exposes the Kubernetes API.

- **Scheduler**: This is a component of a master that is responsible for assigning the best nodes to the given pods at the given point in time.

- **Controller**: This component has most of the control logic of a K8s cluster. It controls nodes, replication, endpoints, and secrets/tokens.

- **Data store**: This is basically an etcd-based storage that keeps configuration information.

- **Service**: This enables a way to expose a service running on a given pod or pods accessible outside of a container as a network service.

- **Kubelet**: This is an agent that runs on every node in a cluster. It ensures that the containers are running in their respective pods.

- **Kube proxy**: This is a network proxy that runs on each node of a cluster. It implements part of the Kubernetes service, enabling networking between various pods and containers in them as well as enabling accessibility outside of the K8s cluster.

- **kubectl**: Last but not least, `kubectl` is the command-line tool that lets you control Kubernetes clusters by using its API service. We will use `kubectl` to configure the K8s cluster.

> **Learn more**
>
> For more information on Kubernetes architectural concepts, please head on to `https://kubernetes.io/docs/concepts/`.

The basics of containerization concepts and Kubernetes as a whole that we have learned so far are enough for us to continue the development of .NET 5 microservices-based services. Let's now begin the design to implement our microservices demo application.

Let's build a demo microservices application

All of the topics covered in this chapter so far provide us with the solid foundation that we need to build out small but useful concepts to build a real-world microservices application. These are the concepts and the tools that we require in our modern development jobs, as well as what we are going to use in our demo application.

We have also now learned about good concepts of containerization as well as container orchestrations; they are going to come in handy from now onward in our day-to-day jobs in our professional careers.

Backend-focused applications are a more common scenario in enterprise applications or as a middleware for a set of commercial products and apps. So now, let's begin building our demo for the rest of the chapter.

What is the application?

We are not building a real-world application, although it has components that match any real-world scenario. It has tiny components, good enough to fit in a chapter and to understand the concepts of building microservices applications using the latest tools offered by Microsoft along with .NET 5. Our application is simply about prime number calculations.

There is a service that is capable of, let's say, calculating prime numbers. We have three other client services that request this service by giving a number and expect a result of whether the given number is prime or not. Each of the three services asks about a number in their own sequence so that the main service gets the requests in various orders. This is just to simulate a random load. Clients are sending requests one by one continuously with a delay of 10 milliseconds in between. You can, of course, adjust it when you want to execute code in your own development machine.

This is a basic idea of the application; in professional language, it is sort of a *business case* for a real-world application. With the basic purpose of the application known to us, let's now build the architecture.

Architecture for the demo application

Any application architecture is incomplete if it does not satisfy all the requirements and criteria. We also have certain constraints. First and foremost, that the application is short enough to fit in the context of a chapter and long enough to be able to touch on all the key concepts of a microservices application in the context of Microsoft's .NET 5 technology stack.

When building the architecture for this application, we already have certain known requirements. One already-known fact is that this has to be a microservices-based application architecture; others are that it has to use .NET 5-based technology and that we will use Tye to tie up this application together to build, debug, and also eventually deploy to a Kubernetes cluster and run from there.

Keeping these requirements and constraints in mind, here is the architecture that we have built. Following the architecture diagram, we will define all the components mentioned in it:

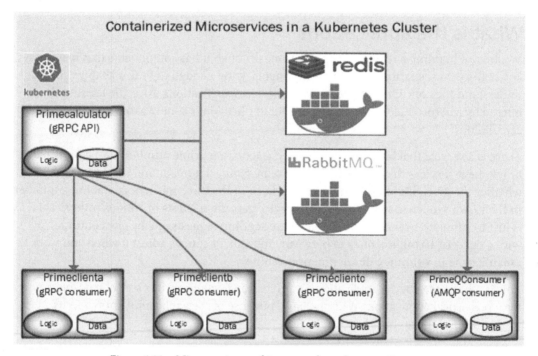

Figure 4.11 – Microservices architecture of our demo application

Microservices in our application do not have data as such but if there has to be some data stored in a service, that data should reside exclusively along with that microservice and should not be shared as such. In order for a microservice to be completely independent, it should carry all of its resources along with itself as it terminates, creates, or replicates itself.

In the preceding architecture diagram, you can see in total seven microservices while in our application statement, we talked mainly about four services, where the first one is primarily a server service doing the number crunching and the other three are basically its consumers.

The main service here is called `primecalculator`; you can see it at the top left. The other three consumers are `primeclienta`, `primeclientb`, and `primeclientc`. The names are chosen for simplicity.

Some points to note as we build further

Note that all of the services here are containerized using Docker as a container technology and are deployed as containers with the help of Tye. There are five custom services in the architecture; all of them are developed using .NET 5. We will deploy them to a simple Kubernetes cluster. We won't be creating a **Dockerfile** and Kubernetes **YAML** deployment files for our .NET 5 services; instead, we will utilize the power of Tye to do it for us. Tye does not create the deployment descriptor for external services/containers when deploying to the K8s cluster; therefore, we will be creating them and deploying them to the cluster by ourselves. When not using a K8s cluster, all the work will also be done for us by Tye using the Docker containers for external services on our machine, which is kind of acting as a development time containers orchestrator.

Let's now define the components we are using in this architecture.

What are the various components in this architecture?

With the architecture defined, let's list down the various components in this architecture:

- **Primecalculator**: This is a microservice that does the calculation to determine whether an input number is a prime or not. Therefore, it exposes an API callable via other services. It uses high-performance point-to-point gRPC as the communication protocol for its API.

- **Primeclienta**: This is a microservice that uses the `primecalculator` microservice's API to get its answers. It runs the code in an infinite loop starting from number 1 as an input and continuously asks for prime numbers. Naturally, it communicates using gRPC.

- **Primeclientb** and **Primeclientc**: These services are both similar to `primeclienta` except that they ask for prime numbers in a different sequence. For example, one of them asks for prime numbers only greater than 100,000.

- **Redis**: This is a well-known distributed cache. In our demo microservices application, it is used as cache in a Redis Docker container. `Primecalculator` calculates and writes its results into the cache as well for 30 minutes; so, if the same number is requested by any client, it returns the results from the cache instead of calculating it again. This is used here just as in similar certain real-world scenarios.

- **RabbitMQ**: This is a popular message broker. `Primecalculator` calculates a result and if it is a prime number, it puts that number into a message queue named as `primes`. RabbitMQ is used here in a Docker containerized version. We defined the concept of message brokers and queues in the previous chapter.

- **Primeqconsumer**: This is a service that is attached to a message queue named `primes` in RabbitMQ. Therefore, it just receives all the prime numbers generated by `primecalculator`. Again, here it is used just to replicate real-world scenarios. You may also note that this is the only asynchronous microservice in our architecture and it uses the **AMQP** protocol to receive messages from the message queue.

- **Cluster**: Finally, all the microservices in our architecture are present in a single **Kubernetes** cluster.

Our architecture is complete now; all the components are listed and defined and their functionality is clear. Communication mechanisms are also certain now as well as technologies. Primarily, we are going to use .NET 5-based code with Docker containers, using Tye to test as well as deploy to a Kubernetes cluster. Let's now move on to the implementation mode, that is, start the development!

Developing the microservices application

Before we start the development, we set up the key infrastructure items required. So far, we assume that you are on Windows 10 and have already installed Docker Desktop and the .NET 5 SDK, and enabled WSL 2 with Ubuntu. If not, you can find install instructions in the *Installing WSL on your development machine* section to install WSL 2. You either have VS Code or Visual Studio 2019 also installed, or you may be able to use any other editor, such as Notepad++, as well. We love and recommend VS 2019.

In addition to what you already have installed on your machine, you will need to set up a few more components. Let's set them up.

Infrastructure items you need to set up

We already have some of the required components installed on our development Windows machine, such as Docker Desktop. We will need to install some more essential components. Let's discover and install them.

Installing the tool – Tye

You will need to install the **Tye** tool. It requires .NET Core 3.1, so please have that installed too. Tye can be installed today by running the following command:

```
dotnet tool install -g Microsoft.Tye --version "0.5.0-
alpha.20555.1"
```

We will also need to have access to a **container registry**. It is required to publish the container images for five of our .NET 5-based services. Docker and Kubernetes are required to pull the images from the registry before they execute them. Luckily, we have Tye, which will have us automatically build the **Dockerfile** and push the images to the registry and will also automatically enable us to pull and deploy them to a Kubernetes cluster. Therefore, with this new tool, we need not worry about creating the Docker images of our services by ourselves.

Once Tye is installed, and when it publishes the artifacts to a K8s cluster, it will be publishing Docker container images. This requires a container registry where Tye will publish and then pull into the K8s cluster. Let's set it up.

Installing the Docker container registry

For development and local testing purposes, we are going to use a local container registry before we publish a releasable version of our microservices.

This will both avoid costs and speed up the deployments and testing multiple times. We will set up a temporary development time registry that is available on a local machine and is based on a local Docker container registry.

At a later point in time, when you want to release the completed version of your microservices, you can release them to any public or private container registry that is available over the desired public or private network.

We choose to install the Docker container-based container registry because it is quick to install and you are up and running within a minute. Additionally, it runs inside a Docker container, so we do not need to set up or configure anything else and need not worry about installing and removing it from the machine, which can be done anytime we like without making our machine dirty. We can install a local registry with the following command:

```
docker run -d -p 5000:5000 --restart=always --name registry
registry:2
```

The last infrastructure item remaining now is the *container orchestrator*. We have already decided to use Kubernetes for that purpose as it is by far the most popular in the market.

A developer can use the Kubernetes cluster on the cloud or can set up a simple single-node cluster on their development machine to enable faster development and debugging before going to the staging and production setup. Therefore, here we have decided to build our application on a development machine with a single-node K8s cluster.

Choosing the Kubernetes cluster for the development machine

Setting up the single-node cluster on a local development machine is also a task that requires some consideration as there is more than one implementation that exists for this type of setup. Here, we list down the most popular ones and then we will choose one from them:

- **Docker Desktop**: This is probably the easiest way to run Kubernetes on your local Windows-based development machine. It provides a single-node Kubernetes cluster that runs completely locally within the Docker instance.

- **KinD by Kubernetes**: **KinD** is **Kubernetes in Docker**. It lets you run the Kubernetes cluster on your local computer. This tool requires that you have Docker installed and configured. The Kubernetes team uses KinD to test Kubernetes itself. It also uses Docker to run a virtual machine inside it. It is a good setup for development and also enables you to set up a multi-node cluster but requires more settings than Docker Desktop.

- **Minikube by Kubernetes**: Like KinD, **Minikube** is a tool that lets you run Kubernetes locally. Minikube runs a single-node Kubernetes cluster on your personal computer (including Windows, macOS, and Linux PCs) so that you can try out Kubernetes, or for daily development work. It has a lot of customization, which makes it a bit more complex than Docker Desktop.

- **MicroK8s**: This enables micro-Kubernetes clusters. It is Kubernetes in Snaps (sandbox in Linux). However, the Snaps feature is strongly supported only in Ubuntu. If we use it, it has to be under WSL 2 with Ubuntu. It is still good but it creates unnecessary limitations for us and ties the development machine with Ubuntu, so we can try it some other day.

- **K3S**: K3S is a lightweight Kubernetes distribution by Rancher but it is mainly intended for IoT and Edge computing.

- **K3D**: KD3 is basically K3S in Docker; so that you can get it to run on a Windows platform. But then it would require additional steps to make the whole deployment chain run smoothly for our development machine; therefore, it is also going to take more time to configure than to actually get it up and running quickly.

Based on all the basic definitions of local Kubernetes clusters, we can see that Docker Desktop is the most straightforward and easy-to-set up single-node cluster. We can set it up quickly in a matter of minutes on Windows. This is perfect for the local development machine. Let's now install the Kubernetes that comes with Docker Desktop.

Installing Docker Desktop for Kubernetes

Assuming that we have already made Docker use the WSL-based engine as mentioned in the WSL section of this chapter, we will now similarly enable Kubernetes via the Docker Desktop settings. This can be seen in *Figure 4.12*:

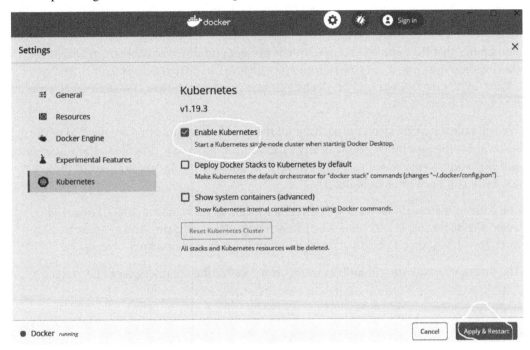

Figure 4.12 – Enabling Kubernetes in Docker Desktop

Once it is installed, you can verify it by executing the kubectl command line:

```
kubectl config current-context
```

This should show the following:

```
docker-desktop
```

So far, all of the required infrastructure components for our microservices implementation are decided and also, they should be installed by now and ready to be used. Let's start the development!

Starting the development!

By now, everything is set up and we are ready to implement the services. The code here is not complex; it is doing only a simple calculation for prime numbers. So, we do not need to explain it. While we do all the necessary steps for building the microservices here, we are not doing the actual coding, which anyway isn't much in the case of our demo application.

Remember that the complete source code is present and downloadable from GitHub at this location: `https://github.com/PacktPublishing/Adopting-.NET-5-`
`-Architecture-Migration-Best-Practices-and-New-Features/tree/`
`master/Chapter04`.

We will take a step-by-step approach for all the important points that we need to perform, so I will list them point by point. In any case, you can otherwise download the whole code and skip some steps related to .NET projects; all other steps that are not part of the source code will still need to be executed.

The code in my case is set up at this directory location: `C:\Users\YHAQ\source\`
`repos\Adopting-.NET-5--Architecture-Migration-Best-Practices-`
`and-New-Features\code\Chapter04\microservicesapp`.

The directory structure will look as in *Figure 4.13* after the completion of our project:

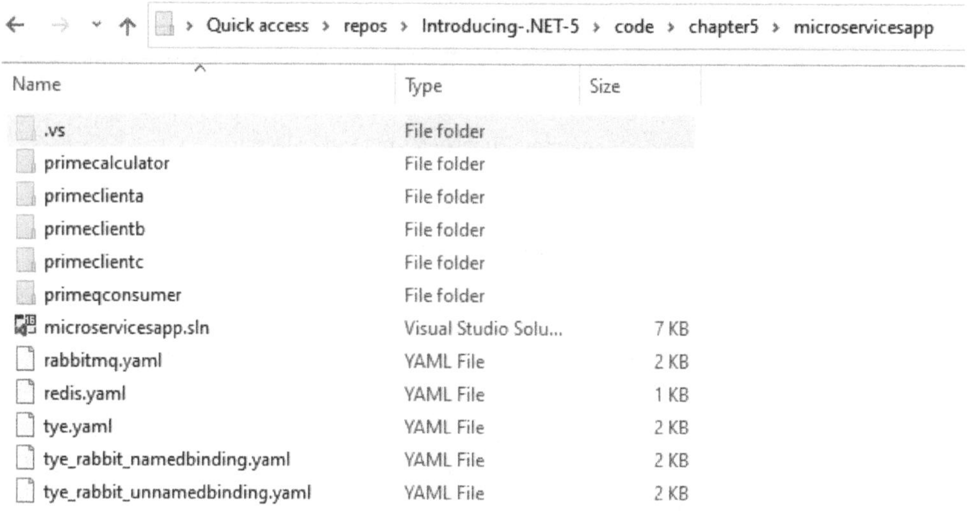

Name	Type	Size
.vs	File folder	
primecalculator	File folder	
primeclienta	File folder	
primeclientb	File folder	
primeclientc	File folder	
primeqconsumer	File folder	
microservicesapp.sln	Visual Studio Solu...	7 KB
rabbitmq.yaml	YAML File	2 KB
redis.yaml	YAML File	1 KB
tye.yaml	YAML File	2 KB
tye_rabbit_namedbinding.yaml	YAML File	2 KB
tye_rabbit_unnamedbinding.yaml	YAML File	2 KB

> Quick access > repos > Introducing-.NET-5 > code > chapter5 > microservicesapp

Figure 4.13 – Directory structure for the demo application

First of all, note that we have placed `nuget.config` at the root of our solution. This file is present at the top of all the chapters in the source code repository. It tells the compiler to use `nuget.org` to download all the publicly listed NuGet packages that we need in our projects.

Open cmd or PowerShell at the source code root directory for our application, at `microservicesapp`, and run the following command; expect to see the result given here:

```
PS C:\Users\YHAQ\source\repos\Adopting-.NET-5--Architecture-
Migration-Best-Practices-and-New-Features\code\Chapter04>
dotnet --version
```
```
5.0.100
```

This confirms that .NET 5 is active at this location, in case you have multiple .NET versions installed on your machine.

Imagine you are in PowerShell at the location up to `Chapter04\code`, and then you begin from there. I am doing most of the stuff via the command line in order to be least dependent on the graphical tools; in this way, the whole process can be applied to more or less any platform.

Let's continue setting up each component of our architecture one by one for its implementation!

Setting up the primecalculator and primeclienta services

The following are the steps required in the correct sequence in order to build our main server service, `primecalculator`, and its primary client service, `Primeclienta`:

1. Starting from the `Chapter04\code` location, we will be doing these steps:

    ```
    mkdir microservicesapp
    cd microservicesapp
    dotnet new grpc -n primecalculator
    dotnet new sln => microservicesapp.sln
    dotnet sln .\microservicesapp.sln add .\primecalculator\
    ```

    Here, we created a new project – `primecalculator` – which is a gRPC service using `grpc` as the project template. Then, we created an empty `microservicesapp.sln` solution and added the newly created project to our solution.

2. The `primecalculator` project contains a folder named `Protos` that contains the `proto` file, which is a Protobuf definition of a service that uses the gRPC protocol. This file can be edited using any editor; you can download the file from GitHub, while we will paste the content of the file here for your reference. The file is named `prime.proto` in this case:

```
syntax = "proto3";
option csharp_namespace = "microservicesapp";
package prime;


//Service definition for the microservice:
PrimeCalculator
service PrimeCalculator {
    //Sends a true false if the number is prime or not
    rpc IsItPrime (PrimeRequest) returns (PrimeReply);
}


//Request message
message PrimeRequest {
    int64 number = 1;
}


//Response message containing the result
message PrimeReply {
    bool isPrime = 1;
}
```

The proto file tells us that this is a unary gRPC operation where the client calls the server with the `IsItPrime` method by passing a request that contains a number and expects a response as a Boolean value to confirm whether the input number was a prime number or not.

`csharp_namespace` tells the code generator to use this name as the namespace for the generated C# code.

3. Now, implement the `IsItPrime` method in C#. The implementation of prime numbers is simple and I will skip over this part, but it can be seen in our source code on GitHub.

4. We will now set up our first client for this service, namely `primeclienta`. Run these commands in order to have them ready:

```
dotnet new worker -n primeclienta
dotnet sln .\microservicesapp.sln add .\primeclienta\
dotnet add .\primeclienta\primeclienta.csproj package
Grpc.Net.Client
```

Here, we added `Grpc.Net.Client` as a NuGet package reference to the `primeclienta` project. The output of this command would be similar to this:

```
Determining projects to restore...
  Writing C:\Users\YHAQ\AppData\Local\Temp\tmpBDD1.tmp
info : Adding PackageReference for package 'Grpc.Net.
Client' into project '.\primeclienta\primeclienta.
csproj'.
info :    GET https://api.nuget.org/v3/registration5-gz-
semver2/grpc.net.client/index.json
info :    OK https://api.nuget.org/v3/registration5-gz-
semver2/grpc.net.client/index.json 494ms
info : Restoring packages for C:\Users\YHAQ\source\repos\
Chapter04\microservicesapp\primeclienta\primeclienta.
csproj...
info : Package 'Grpc.Net.Client' is compatible with all
the specified frameworks in project '.\primeclienta\
primeclienta.csproj'.
info : PackageReference for package 'Grpc.Net.
Client' version '2.33.1' added to file 'C:\Users\YHAQ\
source\repos\Chapter04\microservicesapp\primeclienta\
primeclienta.csproj'.
info : Committing restore...
info : Writing assets file to disk. Path: C:\Users\YHAQ\
source\repos\Chapter04\microservicesapp\primeclienta\obj\
project.assets.json
log  : Restored C:\Users\YHAQ\source\repos\Chapter04\
microservicesapp\primeclienta\primeclienta.csproj (in 182
ms).
```

5. Similarly, we also add the following four packages to `primeclienta`:

```
dotnet add .\primeclienta\primeclienta.csproj package
Grpc.Net.ClientFactory
dotnet add .\primeclienta\primeclienta.csproj package
Google.Protobuf
dotnet add .\primeclienta\primeclienta.csproj package
Grpc.Tools
dotnet add .\primeclienta\primeclienta.csproj package
--prerelease Microsoft.Tye.Extensions.Configuration
```

6. If you are using Visual Studio 2019, you can right-click on **Connected Services** and add a gRPC service reference and point it to the proto file created before in the server service. The service reference screen would look like this:

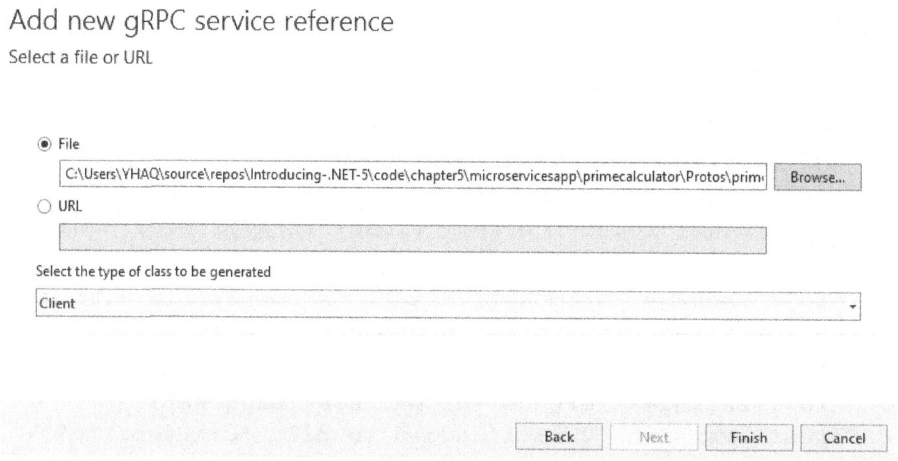

Add new gRPC service reference

Select a file or URL

⦿ File

`C:\Users\YHAQ\source\repos\Introducing-.NET-5\code\chapter5\microservicesapp\primecalculator\Protos\prim` Browse...

○ URL

Select the type of class to be generated

Client

Back   Next   Finish   Cancel

Figure 4.14 – The Add new gRPC service reference screen in Visual Studio 2019

Adding this will auto-generate the code behind C# for the gRPC client.

7. Update `Program.cs` and add the following lines to the `ConfigureServices` method:

```
services.AddGrpcClient<PrimeCalculator.
PrimeCalculatorClient>(o =>
{
    //primecalculator will be inject to configuration via
Tye
    o.Address = configurationFromHostBuilderContext.
GetServiceUri("primecalculator");
});
```

8. Now, update `Worker.cs` and add the logic to call the server service – that is, `primecalculator` – repeatedly, starting from 1 to infinity.

   The most important piece of code here is to make the gRPC call, and that looks like the following:

   ```
   var response = await _primeClient.IsItPrimeAsync(new
   PrimeRequest { Number = input });
   ```

9. Now, our gRPC service and its client are both ready. From the microservices directory, which is a root directory for this application and where the `sln` file resides, we will now execute Tye for the first time and see it launch both the services together:

   ```
   tye run
   ```

10. The output of this Tye command would be similar to this:

    ```
    Loading Application Details...
    Launching Tye Host...


    [13:02:16 INF] Executing application from C:\Users\YHAQ\
    source\repos\Chapter04\microservicesapp\microservicesapp.
    sln
    [13:02:16 INF] Dashboard running on http://127.0.0.1:8000
    [13:02:16 INF] Building projects
    [13:02:18 INF] Launching service primeclienta_e6134cc4-
    0: C:\Users\YHAQ\source\repos\Chapter04\microservicesapp\
    primeclienta\bin\Debug\net5.0\primeclienta.exe
    [13:02:18 INF] Launching service primecalculator_
    ed5ba94c-5: C:\Users\YHAQ\source\repos\Chapter04\
    microservicesapp\primecalculator\bin\Debug\net5.0\
    primecalculator.exe
    [13:02:18 INF] primecalculator_ed5ba94c-5 running on
    process id 20804 bound to http://localhost:53936,
    https://localhost:53937
    [13:02:18 INF] Replica primecalculator_ed5ba94c-5 is
    moving to a ready state
    [13:02:18 INF] primeclienta_e6134cc4-0 running on process
    id 20352
    [13:02:18 INF] Replica primeclienta_e6134cc4-0 is moving
    to a ready state
    ```

```
[13:02:19 INF] Selected process 20804.
[13:02:19 INF] Selected process 20352.
[13:02:19 INF] Listening for event pipe events for
primecalculator_ed5ba94c-5 on process id 20804
[13:02:19 INF] Listening for event pipe events for
primeclienta_e6134cc4-0 on process id 20352
```

11. Launching the `http://localhost:8000` URL, you will have the output as shown here:

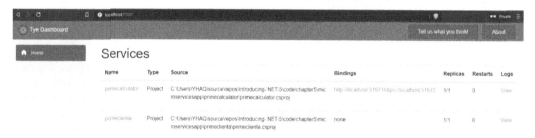

Figure 4.15 – The Tye dashboard

On this Tye dashboard, you can see the service logs on the right side. Since our microservices app is a backend app, we will see the execution output from the service logs.

12. Now, let's check the logs from the server service, which is `primecalculator`:

Logs for primecalculator

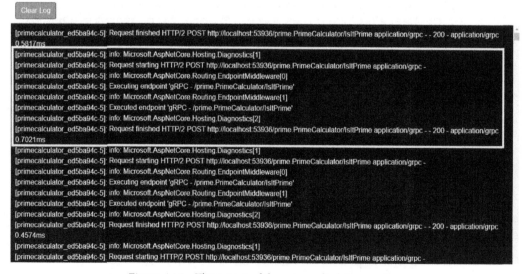

Figure 4.16 – The output of the primecalculator service

Note that in the output, the highlighted area shows the execution of a single gRPC call that took around 0.7 milliseconds.

13. Similarly, we check the logs from the client service, which is `primeclienta`:

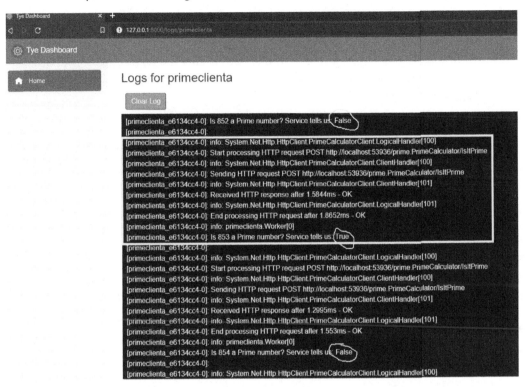

Figure 4.17 – The output of the primeclienta service

Note that in the output, the highlighted area shows the execution of a single gRPC call. In some cases, we received a `False` result when the input number wasn't prime and `True` in the other case.

14. In PowerShell, press *Ctrl + C* to indicate to Tye to terminate the services execution.

We have now successfully created two gRPC services, executed them via Tye, and seen their logs that show the services in action. Let's now move on to the next step.

Adding a Redis cache to the equation

We will now add a Redis cache to our demo application; not that we really need a cache in this case, but this is just to simulate a realistic application:

1. To add Redis as another containerized microservice to our application, we will need some help from Tye. We will ask Tye to generate an application descriptor file in a simplistic Tye YAML format. For that, we execute the `tye init` command, which generates the `tye.yaml` file. The contents of the generated `tye.yaml` file would look like this:

```
name: microservicesapp
services:
- name: primecalculator
  project: primecalculator/primecalculator.csproj
- name: primeclienta
  project: primeclienta/primeclienta.csproj
```

2. We are now going to add Redis to this file. Just add the following lines to your YAML file:

```
- name: redis
  tags:
    - be
  image: redis
  bindings:
  - port: 6379
    connectionString: "${host}:${port}"
- name: redis-cli
  tags:
    - be
  image: redis
  args: "redis-cli -h redis MONITOR"
```

Note that `redis-cli` will only add the service so that from its logs, you can see what is happening with the Redis cache. This component is optional, though.

3.   You can now go back to the command line and execute the following:

```
dotnet add .\primecalculator\primecalculator.csproj
package Microsoft.Extensions.Configuration
```

```
dotnet add .\primecalculator\primecalculator.csproj
package Microsoft.Extensions.Caching.StackExchangeRedis
```

This will add the required references to your code so that you can access Redis' distributed cache. After that, add the relevant code to `Startup.cs` and your `IsItPrime` method implementation, in the `PrimeCalculatorService` class. I chose to omit that piece of code to keep our focus on topic. Anyway, the code is tiny and you can see it in the code repository.

4.   If you want to test and debug the code while launching via Tye, you can still do so with a command such as this:

```
tye run --debug primecalculator primeclienta
```

With this command, Tye will launch everything in the YAML file and will wait to attach the debugger for the services mentioned in the parameters here. These services will only execute further after you attach the debugger successfully.

5.   After adding Redis, we will now want to add a message broker to our microservices application. For this purpose, we choose the popular RabbitMQ container version.

> **Tip**
>
> If you want to run a Redis cache in a container without Tye, you can do so with the following command line: `docker run --name redis_ container -p 6379:6379 -d redis`
>
> Note that you do not run Redis manually and also via Tye at the same time, as they are both using the same port.

Adding RabbitMQ to the application

We will now add RabbitMQ as a message broker to our demo application. Not that we really need a message queue in our application, but it is added to simulate a real-world scenario in the application as well as to show an event-driven microservice in modern architecture.

To add RabbitMQ to our microservices application, the first step is to add it to the YAML file just like we did with the Redis cache:

1. Add the following lines to the end of your YAML file to enable RabbitMQ via Tye:

```
- name: rabbitmq
  tags:
    - mw
  image: rabbitmq:3-management
  bindings:
  - port: 5672
    protocol: rabbitmq
```

2. At the same time, if you also want to enable the RabbitMQ user interface, called the **MUI**, then you can also add these lines to the YAML file:

```
- name: rabbitmq
  tags:
    - mw
  image: rabbitmq:3-management
  bindings:
  - name: mq_binding
    port: 5672
    protocol: rabbitmq
  - name: mui_binding
    port: 15672
```

If you have exposed the MUI, then it will be accessible from `http://localhost:15672/` and you can log in to the MUI using the default credentials, `guest/guest`.

Note that the YAML file with Tye does not work if you expose the MUI and also publish to Kubernetes; there seems to be some bug in Tye parsing, which, at the time of writing, I have notified the Tye team of. Therefore, I have copied two YAML files in the code repository: one that you can use with K8s and one that you can use directly with the `tye run` (that is, with a named binding) command.

3. We will now enable the RabbitMQ NuGet package to our server service by executing the following command:

```
dotnet add .\primecalculator\primecalculator.csproj
package RabbitMQ.Client
```

We are now required to add the code related to the message sending in the `primecalculator` service. Since the code is lengthy and not exactly relevant to this exercise, we chose to omit that part from here. We added the code using dependency injection and by adding some additional classes under `namespace Messaging` inside the service code.

4. You can now launch the application again with the `tye run` command. Then, going to the MUI in the browser, you can see a view that would be something as in *Figure 4.18*:

Figure 4.18 – The RabbitMQ MUI main screen

In *Figure 4.18*, you can see the RabbitMQ MUI's **Overview** screen. It is telling us that there is one queue present in the message broker and there are around 16 messages per second coming into the queue; currently, there are already 2,763 messages present in the queue.

What we have coded in `primecalculator` is that every prime number found that is sent as a result of an API call to the client is also sent to the message queue: `primes`. In this way, RabbitMQ's message queue carries all the calculated prime numbers. It does not carry all the numbers requested; therefore, it also does not show the total number of calls processed by the service at any point in time. But it does confirm that the whole flow between all the microservices is working perfectly as it is the last part of the microservices flow, which is getting the results successfully.

You may have also realized that message brokers enable asynchronous flow, hence our queue is running in a completely decoupled mode and in an asynchronous fashion, disconnected from all other microservices but connected only to a message broker.

We have so far added the Redis cache and RabbitMQ in the form of microservice containers, and we have successfully executed all of the service stacks specified in the YAML file using Tye and verified the execution of the full flow via the RabbitMQ MUI.

> **Tip**
>
> If you want to run RabbitMQ in a container without Tye, you can do so with the following command line: `docker run -d --hostname my-rabbit --name rabbitmq -p 5672:5672 -p 15672:15672 rabbitmq:3-management`
>
> You can then access the MUI from `http://localhost:15672`.
>
> Note that you do not run RabbitMQ manually and via Tye at the same time, as they both use the same port.

We are now going to add two more similar prime number clients to what we have already added and another client that is basically connected to the message broker and asynchronously reads the incoming data from the prime numbers message queue.

Adding the remaining microservices

We are going to add two more .NET services that act very similar to `primeclienta`; they request the numbers in sequence if it is a prime number or not. The difference is just that their sequences are different. We will call these services `primeclientb` and `primeclientc`, like `primeclienta` and so on.

Later, when we execute the complete collection of services, we are also going to add the replicas of the services in order to see how the service replication works and whether there is anything additional that needs to be done. Note that we can execute replicas of the service not just with a Kubernetes cluster but also using Tye. Here, I will show you an example of how a replication format in YAML with Tye would look like:

```
name: microservicesapp
services:
- name: primecalculator
  project: primecalculator/primecalculator.csproj
  replicas: 2
- name: primeclienta
```

```
project: primeclienta/primeclienta.csproj
replicas: 4
```

Let's begin to add new services:

1. Here, again, I will start by creating the services via the CLI.

    You can execute the following commands in sequence and it will prepare our service, with primeclientb as a gRPC client. Before executing the commands, ensure that you are at the solution directory level – microservicesapp:

    ```
    dotnet new worker -n primeclientb

    dotnet sln .\microservicesapp.sln add .\primeclientb\

    dotnet add .\primeclientb\primeclientb.csproj package
    Grpc.Net.Client

    dotnet add .\primeclientb\primeclientb.csproj package
    Grpc.Net.ClientFactory

    dotnet add .\primeclientb\primeclientb.csproj package
    Google.Protobuf

    dotnet add .\primeclientb\primeclientb.csproj package
    Grpc.Tools

    dotnet add .\primeclientb\primeclientb.csproj package
    --prerelease Microsoft.Tye.Extensions.Configuration
    ```

    These commands first create the project of the worker type. A worker or worker process template is a type of project that enables the application to be able to run in the background. It is a console application with configuration, logging, and dependency injection, with .NET fully available to it. Additionally, it can be executed as a web service as well as a Windows service. After creating the project, it adds the necessary libraries that are required to communicate with the services using the gRPC protocol.

    We have already mentioned, in *Chapter 1, Introducing .NET 5 Features and Capabilities*, that with .NET 5, the gRPC versions of libraries are compiled using C# and do not use existing C++ libraries, and hence do not require safe-to-unsafe execution switches on every call; this has resulted in performance gains with the latest version of the gRPC libraries.

2. Similar to `primeclientb`, please execute the same set of commands for `primeclientc`. Once you have both services ready, just copy the code from `primeclienta` and paste it into `Worker.cs` of both services inside the `ExecuteAsync` method. After that, just change the value of the input to start from `100000` instead of `1`. You will also need to add the gRPC service reference to the proto file similar to what we did with `primeclienta` in the *Setting up the primecalculator and primeclienta services* section.

3. We will now add our last client service, called `primeqconsumer`. As the name suggests, this .NET service is connected to the RabbitMQ queue to receive all the listed prime numbers one by one as they are being calculated.

4. Execute the following commands to prepare the new service:

```
dotnet new worker -n primeqconsumer
dotnet add .\primeqconsumer\primeqconsumer.csproj package
RabbitMQ.Client
dotnet add .\primeqconsumer\primeqconsumer.csproj package
--prerelease Microsoft.Tye.Extensions.Configuration
```

5. After that, we need to write the code inside the service that connects to RabbitMQ and start getting the data as it arrives in the queue. We chose to omit that piece of data but you can get it all from the source code repository. The main piece of code that we are mainly interested in here is the following:

```
var consumer = new EventingBasicConsumer(queue);
consumer.Received += (model, ea) =>
{
    var strPrime = Encoding.UTF8.GetString(ea.Body.Span);
    _logger.LogInformation("Received a new calculated
prime number: " + strPrime);
};
```

This code creates the queue consumer in an asynchronous eventing way instead of polling, and registers the anonymous method, which gets executed every time there is a new message coming from the queue. Upon receiving the message, it will consume the message just by logging it.

6. With this done, our two new gRPC clients, as well as our queue client, are ready to go. Just for visualization, if you want to know how the solution looks in Visual Studio 2019, it would be something like the following:

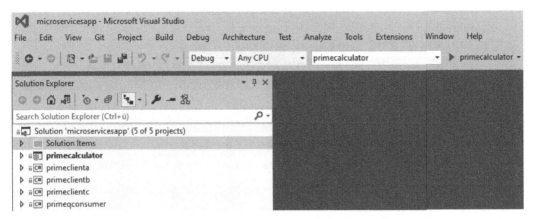

Figure 4.19 – How the complete solution looks in Visual Studio 2019

7. You are now ready to execute all the services via the `tye run` command and can see the output of each service in its logs via Tye's dashboard. The output of `tye run --tags mw --debug primeqconsumer` gives us the following:

```
[09:49:08 INF] Executing application from C:\Users\
YHAQ\source\repos\Adopting-.NET-5--Architecture-
Migration-Best-Practices-and-New-Features\code\Chapter04\
microservicesapp\tye.yaml

[09:49:08 INF] Dashboard running on http://127.0.0.1:8000

[09:49:09 INF] Docker image rabbitmq:3-management already
installed

[09:49:09 INF] Running image rabbitmq:3-management for
rabbitmq_fef100b4-5

[09:49:09 INF] Building projects

[09:49:11 INF] Running container rabbitmq_fef100b4-5 with
ID 3d6ffe5b7da4

[09:49:11 INF] Replica rabbitmq_fef100b4-5 is moving to a
ready state

[09:49:11 INF] Collecting docker logs for rabbitmq_
fef100b4-5.

[09:49:11 INF] Launching service primeqconsumer_
bd9f47c8-f: C:\Users\YHAQ\source\repos\Adopting-.NET-5--
Architecture-Migration-Best-Practices-and-New-Features\
code\Chapter04\microservicesapp\primeqconsumer\bin\Debug\
```

```
net5.0\primeqconsumer.exe
```

```
[09:49:11 INF] primeqconsumer_bd9f47c8-f running on
process id 8744
```

```
[09:49:11 INF] Replica primeqconsumer_bd9f47c8-f is
moving to a ready state
```

```
[09:49:12 INF] Selected process 8744.
```

```
[09:49:12 INF] Listening for event pipe events for
primeqconsumer_bd9f47c8-f on process id 8744
```

Note that in the Tye command here, I provided the mw tag, which I have set up in the YAML file and set to debug primeqconsumer. mw is the middleware tag and enables only RabbitMQ and primeqconsumer to run, and in this way, I can exclusively test only the selected services instead of running the whole stack.

8. Doing tye run will execute all of the services and we can verify their execution by seeing the logs of the service either via the Tye dashboard or via the logs from the Docker container when it runs from the K8s cluster:

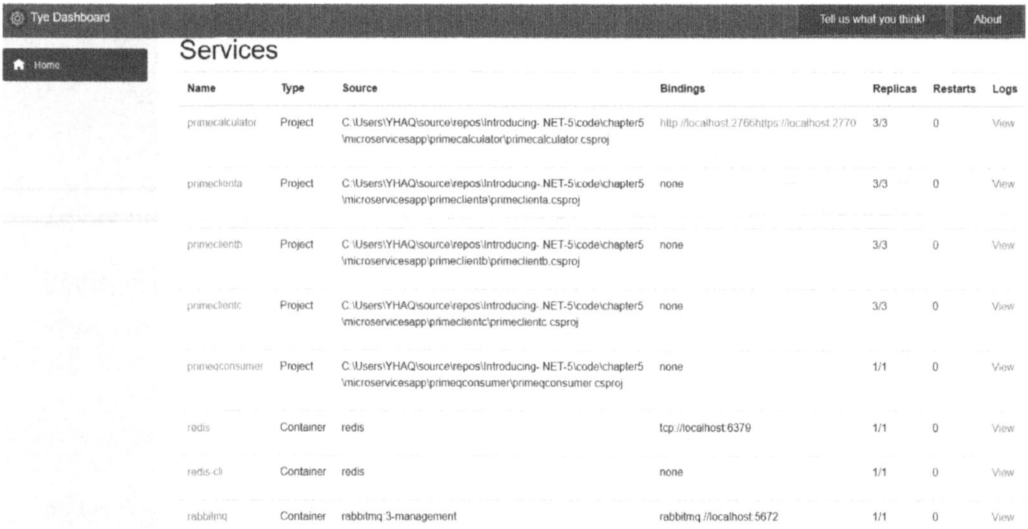

Figure 4.20 – The Tye dashboard after adding all of the services

We will now move on to our final step for deploying all of the microservices to the K8s cluster.

Deploying microservices to the Kubernetes cluster

In the previous section, *Infrastructure items you need to set up*, we already set up the container registry locally. The container registry is required now as we deploy to the Kubernetes cluster.

We will now deploy the microservices to the K8s cluster. Remember that we enabled the Docker integrated K8s cluster and its name is `docker-desktop`. It should be the current context for `kubectl`. This can be verified by running the following command:

```
PS C:\Users\YHAQ\source\repos\Adopting-.NET-5--Architecture-
Migration-Best-Practices-and-New-Features\code\Chapter04\
microservicesapp> kubectl config current-context
docker-desktop
```

Once verified, we are now ready to deploy workloads to the K8s cluster. We will be using Tye to deploy the services. While it supports launching external containers such as Redis when it is running as a kind of development time orchestrator, it does not deploy those external services automatically to Kubernetes.

In our example, we are using two external services in a container: RabbitMQ and Redis. This means we need to deploy these by ourselves. As mentioned before, to deploy to a K8s cluster, we need a deployment descriptor file. Therefore, we need two deployment files in YAML format. We have included these two files in the source code repository, which can be downloaded and applied to any K8s cluster. These are available with the names `rabbitmq.yaml` and `redis.yaml`.

The most important thing these YAML files are telling Kubernetes is to deploy these *pods* with the given name and use the given container image to execute the process inside the pod. In addition to that, it exposes the communication interface, such as the HTTP URL from one pod to other pods, using the `Service` value in the `kind` tag of the YAML file. Refer to the *Kubernetes basics* section if you need a refresher on these terms.

Now that we have the deployment YAML files for RabbitMQ and Redis, we are going to deploy them to our K8s cluster using the following command:

```
kubectl apply -f .\rabbitmq.yaml
```

We'll do the same for Redis, using this command:

```
kubectl apply -f .\redis.yaml
```

These commands will deploy our desired container images instantly and they will be up and running in a few seconds. Note that RabbitMQ could take from 30 seconds to a minute before it is completely ready. If you notice in the code, before the client services start to make calls, they all have a one-time delay of a few seconds, which is basically to give the whole system a bit of warm-up time before starting the activities.

You may also note that in `rabbitmq.yaml`, we have exposed an additional port, `30072`, with internal port `15672` as a type of NodePort. This is basically exposing RabbitMQ's MUI to the external world outside of the K8s cluster. With this, we will be able to access the MUI on our machine via `http://localhost:30072`, and then will be able to see the messages flow as we did with the `tye run` command earlier.

Now, to deploy our .NET 5 microservices to the cluster is very simple, thanks to Tye. Use the following command to deploy and execute the pods:

```
tye deploy --interactive
```

In the `tye.yaml` file, which Tye uses to deploy to the current K8s cluster, we have already specified to use the `localhost:5000` registry; otherwise, Tye will ask for it during the deployment. Tye will also ask us to give the URI of `redis` and `rabbitmq`, which we specified as external services in the `tye.yaml` file so that it can use them from the K8s cluster. You can specify them like this to match how we have defined them as a Service in the respective Kubernetes YAML files:

```
rabbitmq:5672
```

Similarly, you can use the following for Redis:

```
redis:6379
```

Following this, the deployment for microservices by Tye is complete. Once you see that Tye has finished its work, you can see the list of container images in Docker and they would appear something like this:

LOCAL   REMOTE REPOSITORIES

		TAG	IMAGE ID	CREATED	SIZE
localhost:5000/primeqconsumer	IN USE	1.0.0	50a73e99577e	less than a minute ago	187.7 MB
localhost:5000/primeclientc	IN USE	1.0.0	bad6891945d4	28 minutes ago	188.11 MB
localhost:5000/primeclientb	IN USE	1.0.0	56bd60157539	28 minutes ago	188.11 MB
localhost:5000/primeclienta	IN USE	1.0.0	ebce03180fc5	28 minutes ago	188.11 MB
localhost:5000/primecalculator	IN USE	1.0.0	29cefab4968f	about 19 hours ago	207.75 MB
mcr.microsoft.com/dotnet/runti...		5.0	05ba35a0558c	6 days ago	186.22 MB
rabbitmq	IN USE	3-management	263c941f71ea	10 days ago	185.9 MB
redis	IN USE	latest	74d107221092	18 days ago	104.27 MB

Figure 4.21 – The list of images in Docker

Note `localhost:5000` in front of the image names. This is because Tye automatically creates the Docker images, and so the Dockerfiles of our microservices, and uploads them to the local container registry that we have specified, while `redis` and `rabbitmq` are the names of images that were fetched from the public Docker Hub.

You can now log in to the MUI at `http://localhost:30072` and see the messages flow as they are executed within the Kubernetes cluster. Since our single-node K8s cluster is itself based on Docker, you can also see the list of running pods in the list of images currently running by Docker in your development machine. They would appear similar to that in *Figure 4.22* in your local development environment:

Figure 4.22 – RabbitMQ's MUI and the list of images of the running pods in Docker

From *Figure 4.22*, you may note that for each respective microservice, there is one container running for the pod and one container running for the image of the microservice itself. This is because in the Docker Desktop single-node cluster, Kubernetes itself is running in the Docker container and therefore, pods are also running in their own container. So, when you want to see the logs of a given microservice, you can view them from its container and not the container of the pod.

Finally, just for reference and visualization, I will show here how the logs appear for each microservice when it is deployed to the K8s cluster and then when viewing them from the container logs:

- The container logs for the `primecalculator` microservice would appear like this:

Figure 4.23 – The logs for the primecalculator service

- The container logs for the `primeclienta` microservice would appear like this:

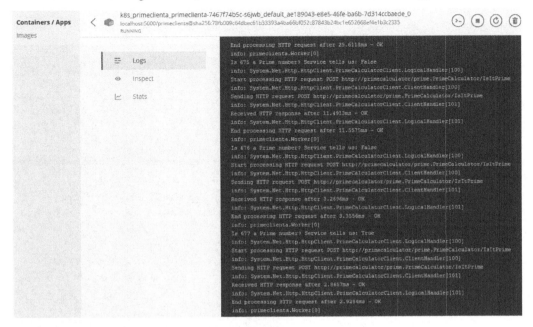

Figure 4.24 – The logs for the primeclienta service

- The container logs for the `primeqconsumer` microservice would appear like this:

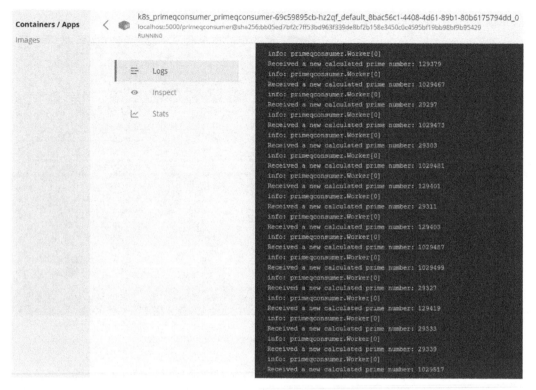

Figure 4.25 – The logs for the primeqconsmer service as it pulls messages from the queue

You can also see the list of everything that is running in the K8s cluster in the context of our demo microservices application. This can be seen, for example, in one console view by executing the list of some `kubectl` commands in order. You can execute the following commands and press *Enter*:

```
kubectl get deployment
kubectl get svc
kubectl get secrets
kubectl get pods
```

Executing these commands, for example, in PowerShell, can give you an output similar to in *Figure 4.26*:

```
PS C:\Users\YHAQ\source\repos\Introducing-.NET-5\code\chapter5\microservicesapp> kubectl get deployment
NAME            READY   UP-TO-DATE   AVAILABLE   AGE
primecalculator 3/3     3            3           56s
primeclienta    3/3     3            3           56s
primeclientb    3/3     3            3           56s
primeclientc    3/3     3            3           56s
primeqconsumer  1/1     1            1           56s
rabbitmq        1/1     1            1           54m
redis           1/1     1            1           53m
PS C:\Users\YHAQ\source\repos\Introducing-.NET-5\code\chapter5\microservicesapp> kubectl get svc
NAME            TYPE        CLUSTER-IP       EXTERNAL-IP   PORT(S)          AGE
kubernetes      ClusterIP   10.96.0.1        <none>        443/TCP          19h
primecalculator ClusterIP   10.105.92.228    <none>        80/TCP           57s
rabbitmq        ClusterIP   10.111.242.107   <none>        5672/TCP         54m
rabbitmq-mui    NodePort    10.99.63.100     <none>        15672:30072/TCP  54m
redis           ClusterIP   10.106.128.112   <none>        6379/TCP         53m
PS C:\Users\YHAQ\source\repos\Introducing-.NET-5\code\chapter5\microservicesapp> kubectl get secrets
NAME                               TYPE                                  DATA   AGE
binding-production-rabbitmq-secret Opaque                                3      52m
binding-production-redis-secret    Opaque                                1      53m
default-token-4nzv6                kubernetes.io/service-account-token   3      19h
PS C:\Users\YHAQ\source\repos\Introducing-.NET-5\code\chapter5\microservicesapp> kubectl get pods
NAME                             READY   STATUS    RESTARTS   AGE
primecalculator-95d5cf95b-h2pnn  1/1     Running   0          57s
primecalculator-95d5cf95b-n7pmb  1/1     Running   0          57s
primecalculator-95d5cf95b-xknqr  1/1     Running   0          57s
primeclienta-7467f74b5c-n7dqf    1/1     Running   0          57s
primeclienta-7467f74b5c-wjlsr    1/1     Running   0          57s
primeclienta-7467f74b5c-z8tcr    1/1     Running   0          57s
primeclientb-5d7647c784-dhdsd    1/1     Running   0          57s
primeclientb-5d7647c784-kvdrh    1/1     Running   0          57s
primeclientb-5d7647c784-xjbg6    1/1     Running   0          57s
primeclientc-c8dfbccbc-76rft     1/1     Running   0          57s
primeclientc-c8dfbccbc-7hjvr     1/1     Running   0          57s
primeclientc-c8dfbccbc-f5m7t     1/1     Running   0          57s
primeqconsumer-69c59895cb-ktfrb  1/1     Running   0          57s
rabbitmq-854d846986-2wmwl        1/1     Running   0          54m
redis-5957ddd4f4-hps99           1/1     Running   0          53m
PS C:\Users\YHAQ\source\repos\Introducing-.NET-5\code\chapter5\microservicesapp> |
```

Figure 4.26 – The state of the K8s cluster

Viewing the logs and the state of the cluster marks the end of our microservices exercise. I hope that you have followed through until the end and were successful in the creation and execution of the whole microservices and Kubernetes cluster setup.

With this, we have also completed the chapter, and we hope that you have enjoyed reading and following it as much as we did.

Summary

In this chapter, we learned about many modern technologies and also were able to use them in a hands-on practical exercise as we built a demo microservices application.

In particular, we covered the theory and practical implementation of services communication via the gRPC protocol. We also covered the hands-on application of modern WSL 2 for Windows with lots of tips.

We also learned the basics of container orchestration and were able to apply those concepts practically to a locally created Kubernetes cluster.

We successfully built, tested, and deployed a .NET 5 microservices application with the extensive usage of Tye. In our application, we were also able to easily use modern external services in containers such as Redis and RabbitMQ, and also deployed them to the K8s cluster. All of this was made very easy and quick with .NET 5's extreme flexibility and support in the code to use external components. By doing this exercise, not only did we learn about and build the architecture and its implementation from top to bottom, but we were also able to successfully deploy a whole cluster dedicated to a microservices application.

We hope that you were able to get a lot out of the knowledge compressed into this single chapter as well as the hands-on experience. All of this learning of concepts and the hands-on practice is going to benefit you not only in designing the microservices but also implementing them using .NET 5 with Docker as well as Kubernetes. We also hope that you have not only learned but also enjoyed it as much as we did!

After this chapter, the focus of the book moves toward application migration-related topics, which we hope are going to be very useful in your journey to upgrade to .NET 5.

Further reading

You can find more information on related topics here:

- More information on gRPC:

  MS docs: `https://aka.ms/grpcdocs`

  Core concepts: `https://grpc.io/docs/what-is-grpc/core-concepts/`

  Protocol Buffers: `https://developers.google.com/protocol-buffers/docs/overview`

- E-book from the Microsoft Architecture site: `https://docs.microsoft.com/en-us/dotnet/architecture/grpc-for-wcf-developers/`

- More information on WSL configuration: `https://docs.microsoft.com/en-us/windows/wsl/wsl-config`

- More information on containerd: `https://containerd.io/`

- More information on the `kubectl` CLI: `https://kubernetes.io/docs/reference/kubectl/cheatsheet/`

Section 3: Migration

This section provides guidance on upgrading existing .NET applications to the .NET 5 platform. Whether you have been developing on-premises applications and wish to migrate them to the cloud or simply want to use the latest tools and libraries for your on-premises applications, this developer-focused section discusses the scenarios in which migrating to .NET 5 makes sense, and then provides examples with hands-on exercises to upgrade a legacy application from .NET Framework 4.x to .NET 5.

It then talks about the advantages of hosting the applications on the cloud and leveraging cloud services such as **Azure SQL Database**, **Azure Web Apps**, **Azure Functions**, and **Azure Container Instances**. If you are new to the .NET Core, you will also learn about using platform-provided libraries for dependency injection and configuration management.

This section comprises the following chapters:

- *Chapter 5, Upgrading Existing .NET Apps to .NET 5*
- *Chapter 6, Upgrading On-Premises Applications to the Cloud with .NET 5*

5
Upgrading Existing .NET Apps to .NET 5

Upgrading an app to its latest platform version, just for the sake of upgrading, is usually not a fun exercise, especially if there is no new and exciting feature to be added. Fortunately, Microsoft has provided solid inter-compatibility between libraries developed for earlier versions of .NET and .NET 5 to make the migration process much smoother. The cherry on top is the underlying performance enhancement that will make the existing code run faster without any significant transformation by the app developer.

There are some technologies that Microsoft has decided not to port to the .NET 5 platform, such as **Windows Communication Foundation (WCF)** Server, **Windows Workflow**, and **ASP.NET web forms**. We will discuss the options to replace these technologies where it is feasible to do so.

In this chapter, we will learn about the following topics:

- Technical requirements for upgrading to .NET 5
- Choosing the migration approach
- Points to ponder regarding an as-is upgrade
- Learning by example in terms of migrating a .NET Framework app to .NET 5

Let's first review the technical requirements to complete the migration exercises in this chapter.

Technical requirements

You will need the following software installed on your computer to complete the migration walk-through shown in the *Upgrading a .NET Framework example app* section:

- Visual Studio 2019 16.8 or higher (any edition is fine). This is needed to work with .NET Framework and .NET 5 solution files.

- SQL Server Express LocalDB 2019. This is typically installed along with Visual Studio 2019, so separate installation is not required.

- .NET 5 SDK, which can be downloaded from `https://dotnet.microsoft.com/download/dotnet/5.0`.

- To run legacy code in the example app, you will need .NET Framework 4.7.2 and .NET Framework 4.8 installed.

- .NET Framework 4.7.2 can be downloaded from `https://dotnet.microsoft.com/download/dotnet-framework/net472`.

- .NET Framework 4.8 can be downloaded from `https://dotnet.microsoft.com/download/dotnet-framework/net48`.

- The GitHub repo for this chapter: `https://github.com/PacktPublishing/Adopting-.NET-5--Architecture-Migration-Best-Practices-and-New-Features/tree/master/Chapter05`.

The chapter assumes that you are already familiar with .NET Framework and Entity Framework as we are upgrading these to the latest platform. We will focus on the core aspects of these technologies that require transformation during migration to .NET 5.

Choosing the migration approach

In this section, you will learn about the big decisions that need to be made upfront before starting the migration process.

If you are upgrading from any previous version of .NET Core, the implications are less severe simply because .NET 5 is a continuation of the same platform and the upgrade process is much simpler.

Migrating from .NET Framework, however, requires a bit more thought. There are a number of factors that will impact the approach, including the following:

- The size and footprint of the solution
- The number of different technologies that comprise the solution (for example, desktop apps, web apps, and REST APIs)
- Whether an unsupported technology (such as WCF Server) or .NET runtime feature (such as .NET Remoting) is used

Let's now see how these factors can influence the migration approach.

Factors influencing the migration approach

Should we migrate the whole solution at once or try to do it in different stages? Let's review the pros and cons of both approaches.

Big bang approach

For small- and medium-sized solutions, it makes sense to upgrade the entire solution stack at once from .NET Framework to .NET 5. For large solutions, it might not be too practical due to time constraints. You would need to maintain two separate code bases, one each for .NET Framework and .NET 5, during the migration process, and if any new feature needs to be implemented, it could become hard keeping the two code bases in sync.

The benefit of this approach is its *simplicity*. Instead of worrying about compatibility issues between intermediate phases of the upgrade, we just have to ensure that the final version of all the solution pieces is compatible with .NET 5.

Gradual upgrade

An alternative approach is to identify the least dependent libraries first. These are the projects that do not depend on other projects in the code base. A common example of such projects is a library containing model definitions or shared helper functions. Once these libraries have been upgraded to .NET 5, we look for the next set of libraries that are only dependent on previously upgraded components. We then gradually move up the dependency ladder to migrate the components with all their dependencies previously migrated.

The .NET team has made it easier by making it possible to multi-target an assembly for multiple platforms. So, you can write code once and target it for both .NET Framework and .NET 5 platforms. This will obviously work for scenarios where features set across both platforms are the same, or similar. Once the shared libraries have been migrated, the executing app (desktop or web app) can be migrated to the latest platform to take advantage of .NET 5's specific features. The complexity arises with this approach when a particular API is not supported on .NET 5. We would have to write a conditional compilation code so that unsupported API is only used when code is compiled for the .NET Framework platform.

In this chapter, we will follow the first approach in the *Upgrading a .NET Framework example app* section, where we will migrate an example app from .NET Framework to .NET 5.

Once the choice between gradual versus big bang approach has been made, the next decision to consider involves the introduction of any changes in the solution architecture.

Lift and shift versus architectural transformation

In the lift and shift approach, we try to minimize any fundamental changes to code and its constituent components. Once the application is up and running on the latest platform, architectural changes are taken aboard as a separate project. This is a simpler approach and there is less risk of upgrade failure, but the new platform must support the components from the previous platform.

For example, if you have built a WCF Server instance or have implemented inter-process communication using .NET Remoting, it is simply not possible to upgrade these technologies on an as-is basis on .NET 5 as .NET 5 does not support these.

The architectural transformation makes sense when new features are expected to be implemented as part of an upgrade exercise or in the near future. It is best to leverage the latest platform features and technologies to reduce the technical debt on an older platform.

The final decision that we need to make is about whether and how we upgrade third-party libraries.

Replacing third-party libraries with platform-provided features

A similar concern to the architectural changes that are discussed in the previous section is about making code improvements. This is especially tempting for third-party libraries when a newer alternative is provided by the framework itself.

In .NET Core and .NET 5, Microsoft provides a system API for JSON parsing and serialization named `System.Text.Json`. Similarly, libraries for **dependency injection (DI)**, `Microsoft.Extensions.DependencyInjection`, and logging, `Microsoft.Extensions.Logging`, eliminate the need to use corresponding third-party libraries, especially for basic use cases. If you are using advanced features of existing libraries, then it is best to consult the documentation of the newer alternative to understand whether every feature is available as a drop-in replacement or whether significant development is required.

Also, sometimes it takes less effort to transform the feature than to keep trying to use the existing code or library in a backward-compatible fashion. For example, in .NET 5, it is easier to read application configuration from JSON files instead of `*.config` XML files, so it may be worthwhile upgrading the configuration reading code unless it is significantly customized in the existing code base.

In the *Upgrading a .NET Framework example app* section, we'll do a comparison of the `Microsoft.Extensions` and `System.Text.Json` namespace feature sets with popular alternative libraries such as `Newtonsoft.Json` and `AutoFac`.

We will now review the points that would generally be applicable to most .NET like-for-like migration projects.

Points to ponder regarding an as-is upgrade

A transformation project can easily get quite large and complex. In this chapter, we will primarily focus on as-is upgrades. However, we will also try and score some technical improvements in the solution, where comparatively less effort will bring reasonably good rewards in terms of code maintenance and performance.

Keeping this in mind, the following subsections will tell us about some general points that will be applicable to most upgrade projects.

Unsupported technologies

While most of the .NET Framework technologies can be migrated relatively easily to the .NET 5 platform, some features and technologies do not have a direct replacement and will require redesign or, at a minimum, replacing code from a different library. In addition, due to the fast-paced nature of .NET Core/.NET 5 development, many features in libraries such as **Entity Framework Core or ASP.NET Core** get marked as obsolete or deprecated in newer versions. So, it is best to review release notes when migrating to newer versions of these libraries.

In this section, we will review what major .NET Framework features are not available and the possible approaches to replace these features.

WCF Server

WCF was originally released in November 2006. Since then, it has been a very popular inter-service communication mechanism for .NET developers. It has vastly improved technology compared to ASMX web services. Its major strength is the support for various communication protocols, inter-server communication, and intra-server communication with minimal coding changes.

While still used in many legacy applications, Microsoft has decided to not support WCF Server on the .NET Core/.NET 5 platform in favor of modern technologies such as REST APIs over **HTTP** or **Google RPC** (commonly known as **gRPC**) for contract-based RPCs. Both alternatives are cross-platform and support the most popular programming languages and cloud platforms.

> **Tip**
> If you still want to continue development with WCF Server, one option is to consider the CoreWCF project, which is an open source port of WCF to the .NET Core platform: `https://github.com/CoreWCF/CoreWCF11`.
>
> At the time of writing this book, this project is still under development and not production-ready.

The recommended approach is to use the REST APIs or gRPC for new features. Alternatively, you can upgrade the WCF client to .NET 5 and continue to use the WCF Server on .NET Framework until you have the time resources available to do the migration.

ASP.NET Web Forms

ASP.NET Web Forms is another technology that is being axed in .NET 5. Microsoft recommends migrating to Blazor WebAssembly for modern web UX development. Blazor supports C# and is quite scalable. The transformation from Web Forms to Blazor is not a simple task and requires considerable planning. We will not cover Blazor technology in-depth in this book as it deserves a whole book in its own right.

The following Microsoft article has guidance on transforming ASP.NET Web Forms apps to Blazor WebAssembly: `https://docs.microsoft.com/en-us/dotnet/architecture/blazor-for-web-forms-developers/migration`.

ASP.NET Web Forms was introduced in 2002 and now (if not before) is a good time to port the code to newer technologies. If you could consider using a non-C# technology, modern JavaScript-based UI frameworks such as Angular and React provide a robust feature set to build a sleek UX.

Windows Workflow Foundation (WWF or WF)

WWF's primary feature set is to reduce coding for developing and automating repeatable business processes. It does so by providing an API, an in-process workflow engine that supports long-running processes, and a visual designer.

Compared to WCF Server and Web Forms, WWF's market footprint is somewhat reduced. There is no direct alternative to this technology on .NET 5, but most of its functionality can be redesigned using a combination of gRPC, REST APIs, Azure Logic Apps, and Power Automate.

Like CoreWCF, there is an open source fork of WWF available that is still in the experimental phase: `https://github.com/UiPath-Open/corewf`.

We will now review some Windows platform-specific features that cannot be used from code when targeting .NET 5.

Unsupported Windows OS-specific features

Aside from the technologies mentioned in the preceding section, some platform-specific features for Windows OS are not available in .NET 5 platform libraries. These features should generally be of concern to Windows desktop developers when migrating to .NET 5.

AppDomains

AppDomains were primarily used to *isolate* application processes from each other. For modern applications, a better alternative for process isolation is to use containers, which are more versatile and flexible. There is also the `AssemblyLoadContext` class, which supports dynamically loading assemblies at runtime.

For ease of migration, .NET 5 provides some of AppDomains' APIs; however, not all methods are guaranteed to behave in the same way. Some will throw `PlatformNotSupportedException`, while some will do nothing and others will continue to function as per previous behavior.

Remoting

A related feature to AppDomains is remoting, where processes living in different app domains can communicate with each other. This is no longer supported.

For communications across the network, REST and gRPC are recommended. For inter-process communication on the same machine, `MemoryMappedFile` or `System.IO.Pipes` can be used.

In the next chapter, we will also review some of the modern messaging technologies available on the Azure Cloud platform.

Code Access Security (CAS)

Sandboxing applications on the Windows platform allowed applications to execute in a constrained environment with restricted access to resources. This feature has been retired from .NET Framework itself, and so has not been ported to .NET Core or .NET 5.

The cross-platform alternative is to restrict process privileges by using containers and/or constrained user accounts.

Security transparency

Security transparency was used in sandboxed applications to declaratively specify access privileges required by code. This is generally used in Silverlight applications. As CAS is not supported, the related feature of security transparency is also not supported. The alternative is also the same as CAS, which is to use virtualization, containers, and user accounts to control the process privileges.

Transforming application configuration

In .NET Framework, application configuration is typically specified in `app.config` or `web.config` files in XML format.

An example `appSettings` section appears as follows:

```
<appSettings>
    <add key="MaximumRowsPerPage" value="10" />
</appSettings>
```

.NET Framework implemented a hierarchy of configuration files, where a parent file's settings can be inherited or overridden by a more specific file. For example, machine-specific settings can be specified in `machine.config` and then a web application can inherit or override these settings for its process in a `web.config` file.

These settings are accessed by developers using the `System.Configuration` namespace. This namespace is still available in the .NET Core world, but a more flexible approach with usually minor code changes to use the `Microsoft.Extensions.Configuration` namespace, which offers considerable improvements.

Some of the benefits of using the `Microsoft.Extensions.Configuration` namespace are as follows:

- Support for hierarchical **plain old CLR object** (**POCO**)-based settings
- Built-in binding and validation for non-string values, such as `int`, `bool`, and `decimal`
- Uniform handling and choice of configuration store, such as JSON files, XML files, in-memory objects, command-line arguments, and environment variables
- Support for encrypted and cloud-specific stores, such as Azure Key Vault or Azure App Configuration

In the *Migrating BookApp.Models* section, we'll see a practical example of transforming our code to switch from using `System.Configuration` to the `Microsoft.Extensions.Configuration` namespace.

Choosing the Entity Framework version

The majority of applications need to access databases for one use case or another. Entity Framework is a very popular choice for .NET developers as an **object-relation mapping** (**ORM**) tool to access the data layer in .NET Code.

The most recent major version of Entity Framework is Entity Framework 6. It is fully supported by Microsoft on the .NET Core platform, but all new development should be done on Entity Framework Core. EF Core supports .NET Framework (up to EF Core v3.1) and .NET 5 (all EF Core versions).

EF Core and Entity Framework do not have 100% feature parity; there are many new features in EF Core and some that will never be ported from Entity Framework to EF Core (due to low usage or radical design change), while some features are slated to be ported in future EF Core versions.

Refer to the official documentation for a detailed overview of the features that are not available on either platform: `https://docs.microsoft.com/en-us/ef/efcore-and-ef6/`.

In the *Upgrading a .NET Framework example app* section, we will go through the migration process from Entity Framework to EF Core.

Using .NET Framework compatibility

A common migration approach is to port your libraries to .NET Standard first. .NET Standard libraries can be referenced from both .NET Framework and .NET 5 assemblies, which work great as an interim solution until both frameworks are in use in the organization.

With .NET Framework compatibility mode, .NET Standard projects can make references to .NET Framework libraries as if they were compiled for the .NET Standard platform. This helps remove a major migration blocker where migrating dependent libraries to newer platforms is not feasible in a short time frame.

Of course, having a compatibility layer does not automatically guarantee that all .NET Framework APIs will work on the .NET 5 platform. The APIs that are not supported will either throw `PlatformNotSupportedException` or might do nothing in some cases.

The vast majority of APIs are now ported on the .NET 5 platform, so using .NET Standard is a useful way to reference third-party NuGet packages that have not been updated by their developers despite having full API availability on the new platform.

During our example migration exercise, we will learn about using the .NET Portability Analyzer tool, which can detect and inform about potential API incompatibility on the new platform.

Upgrading third-party NuGet packages

When using third-party NuGet packages, you can use one of the following approaches:

- If the current NuGet package version is .NET 5- or .NET Standard 2.1-compatible, then use that version.

- If the current version does not support .NET 5/.NET Standard 2.1, but the later NuGet package version does, it's likely a good candidate to be used. We need to review any breaking changes in the new version to assess the code refactoring effort required to use the new version.

- The vast majority of active and popular NuGet packages fall under the first two cases. However, if there is no compatible version, then it is possible to use the .NET Framework library from .NET Standard code using the compatibility mode as described in the preceding section.

- Another option is to use an alternative library, but this could potentially take significant time and costs to implement.

We have now covered enough theoretical ground to understand the considerations and pitfalls of migration. Let's now dive into a practical example of upgrading a fictional real-world app.

Upgrading a .NET Framework example app

We will now see the previously discussed concepts in action. It's time to do the hands-on exercise, folks! In this section, we will go through a step-by-step approach of migrating an example app named **BookApp** from .NET Framework 4.7.2 to .NET 5.

The sample code for this exercise is provided in two folders:

- The code to begin this exercise is the `netframework472` folder: `https://github.com/PacktPublishing/Adopting-.NET-5--Architecture-Migration-Best-Practices-and-New-Features/tree/master/Chapter05/netframework472`.

- The code in its final form after being upgraded to .NET 5 is in the `net5` folder: `https://github.com/PacktPublishing/Adopting-.NET-5--Architecture-Migration-Best-Practices-and-New-Features/tree/master/Chapter05/net5`.

During this upgrade journey to the latest .NET platform, we will come across, review, and make decisions to resolve various issues that any typical .NET application would face during migration.

We will walk through the following exercises:

- Migrating from Entity Framework to EF Core
- Replacing third-party libraries with new platform features
- Upgrading a WPF desktop application to .NET 5
- Upgrading an ASP.NET MVC 5 web application to .NET 5

Without further ado, let's jump into the process to upgrade BookApp.

Introducing BookApp

We will use a sample application named *BookApp*. This is a fictional book review application where users can post reviews and ratings about the books.

The current logical component diagram of *BookApp* is as follows:

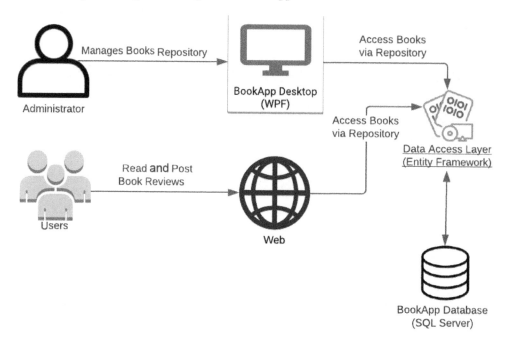

Figure 5.1 – BookApp component diagram

In the next subsections, we will learn about the aforementioned *BookApp* components.

BookApp database

For this app, we have used SQL Server Express LocalDB. The schema is quite simple as it uses only two tables to store the book's metadata and reviews:

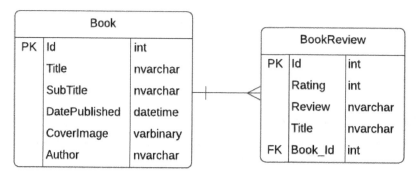

Figure 5.2 – BookApp database schema

Each book can have multiple reviews. For simplicity, we are storing the author's name in the `Author` field as an `nvarchar` value. In a real-world design, the author details would likely be stored in a dedicated table.

Domain definitions (BookApp.Models)

This is a .NET class library to hold definitions for `Book` and `BookReview`. In a well-designed application, the database models should be separately defined from application models. For the sake of simplicity and focusing on the actual migration process, we have used a single version of definitions for both purposes.

DataAccess layer (BookApp.DAL)

The purpose of this .NET class library is to provide a service layer in the form of `IBookRepository`. The layer uses Entity Framework 6. The database context definition, with database initialization and seeding information, is also included.

Admin Desktop – WPF App (BookApp.AdminDesktop)

The admin desktop app is developed in WPF. It allows the administrator to upload and manage book metadata, such as the book's authors and cover image.

The administrator can also export any book metadata, including its reviews, to a JSON file:

Id	Title	SubTitle	Author(s)	Date Published	Cover Image	Upload	Export
1	Introducing .NET 5	Building & migrating apps using mo	Hammad Arif, Habib Qureshi	1/1/2021		Browse	Export
2	Python Machine Learning	Machine learning and deep learning	Sebastian Raschka, Vahid Mirjalili	12/1/2019	Python Machine Learning	Browse	Export
3	Learn Microsoft PowerApps	Build customised business applicatio	Matthew Weston	11/1/2019	Learn Microsoft PowerApps	Browse	Export
						Browse	Export

Figure 5.3 – BookApp admin desktop

The steps to migrate a WinForms desktop application are similar to the case for a WPF application, so you can still follow this exercise if you want to upgrade WinForms applications.

Web Application (BookApp.Web)

This is an ASP.NET MVC 5 web application that allows users to read and post book reviews and assign ratings to the books:

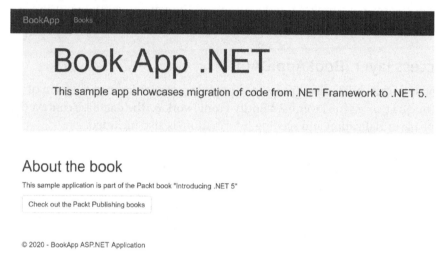

Figure 5.4 – BookApp web home screen

The home page is similar to the admin desktop, but it doesn't let users edit book details. There is a reviews screen where users can read and post book reviews:

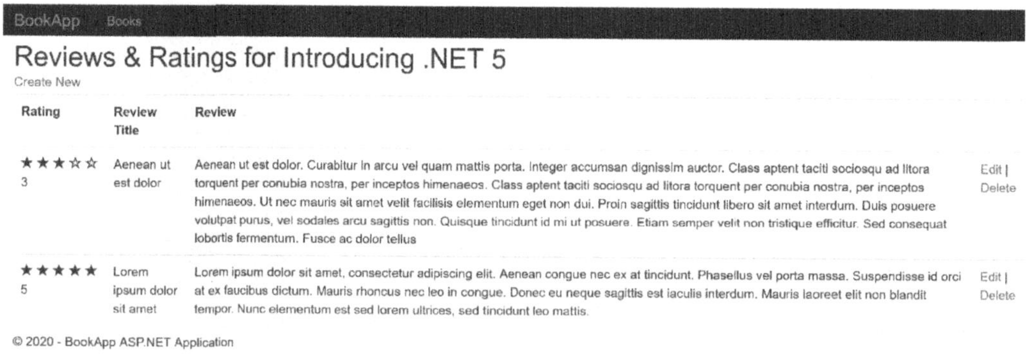

Figure 5.5 – BookApp web reviews and ratings screen

Note that this app does not follow all the best practices to develop a production-grade app. The focus of this chapter is to learn about common migration techniques, so the code has intentionally been kept simple, but with enough use cases so that a variety of upgrade scenarios can be discussed.

There are many ways to upgrade this app. In the next section, we will provide the details of the chosen approach and then implement the migration process for *BookApp*.

Preparing for migration

We will migrate the *BookApp* solution by migrating one project at a time. We'll start the preparations for migration by creating the backup and then upgrading the project's version to .NET Framework 4.8.

Creating the backup (optional)

Your real-world code would likely be stored in some source control repository. This example app is also available on GitHub, so making a backup is not critical. If you like, you can create a backup of the original application code in a different folder so you can execute and compare the two applications side by side.

Upgrading the projects to .NET Framework 4.8

BookApp is developed using .NET Framework 4.7.2. It is a good idea to upgrade all projects in the *BookApp* solution to the latest .NET Framework version 4.8. This way, if things do not work as expected at this stage, we can troubleshoot knowing that the problem is not caused by the .NET 5 upgrade.

As specified in the *Technical requirements* section, you would need .NET Framework 4.8 installed on your computer.

In Visual Studio 2019, the process to change the .NET Framework version is the following and needs to be repeated for each project in the *BookApp* solution:

1. Right-click on the project name and select **Properties**.

2. Make sure that the **Application** tab is selected.

3. Choose **Target Framework** to be .NET Framework 4.8.

4. Click **Yes** if you get a warning about the project reloading:

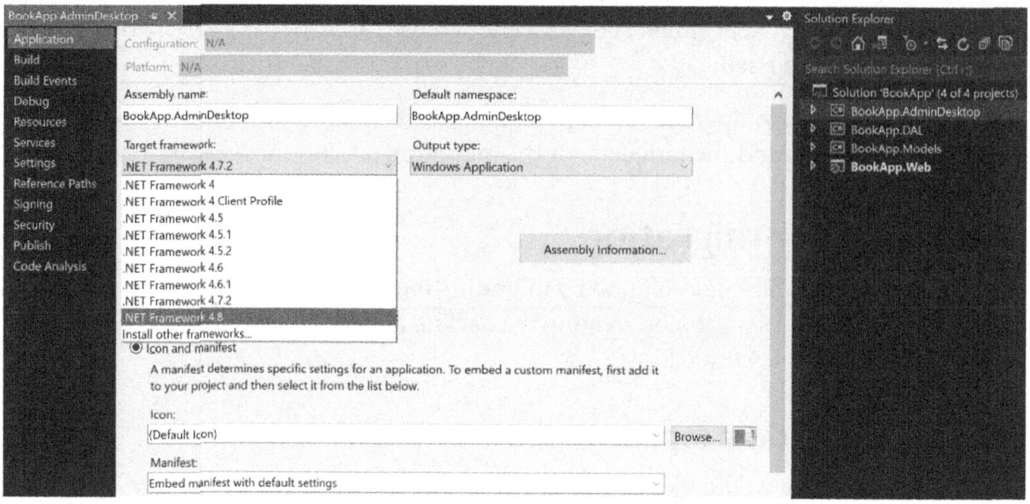

Figure 5.6 – Changing the .NET Framework version

5. After updating all the projects, run and see whether both desktop and web applications are still working as expected.

> **Tip – Automated testing**
>
> For a production-grade app, it is extremely important and helpful to have automated unit tests and integration tests that provided complete feature coverage. For a large application, it is not feasible to manually test all the features after each step of migration.
>
> For *BookApp*, we will stick to the poor man's testing approach, that is, manually browsing and testing each screen.

Migrating BookApp.Models

We will start with a class library that is at the bottom of the dependency tree. That is, it does not require any other class library in the solution. The advantage of this approach is that we can independently test (assuming we have unit tests written) the library without worrying about the other projects in the solution.

Migrating the packages.config file

In classic .NET projects, the project references to external packages are stored in the `packages.config` file. For the `BookApp.Models` project, this file content looks like the following.

```xml
<?xml version="1.0" encoding="utf-8"?>
<packages>
  <package id="EntityFramework" version="6.4.4"
targetFramework="net48" />
  <package id="Newtonsoft.Json" version="12.0.2"
targetFramework="net48" />
</packages>
```

.NET Core and .NET 5 have a cleaner approach in terms of using the `ProjectReference` attribute inside the `csproj` file, which covers external packages as well as internal project references. There is no need to keep the `packages.config` file in this case. Fortunately, this new format is also supported in .NET Framework.

We need to migrate package references by performing the following steps:

1. In Visual Studio Solution Explorer, expand the project and then right-click on the `packages.config` file.

2. Choose **Migrate packages.config to PackageReference…**:

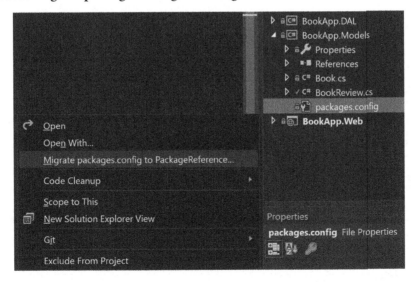

Figure 5.7 – Migrating the packages.config file

3. Once the migration is complete, you will notice that the `packages.config` file is deleted and that the `csproj` file has a section like the following added:

```
<ItemGroup>
  <PackageReference Include="Newtonsoft.Json">
    <Version>12.0.2</Version>
  </PackageReference>
</ItemGroup>
```

After migrating the `packages.config` file, we need to check the compatibility of our existing code with the target platform library. Fortunately, Microsoft has provided a tool that makes this job somewhat easier. Let's now see how we can use the .NET Portability Analyzer tool.

Checking dependency compatibility using .NET Portability Analyzer

.NET Portability Analyzer is a tool provided by Microsoft. It analyzes the code base and prepares a detailed report on .NET APIs that are missing for the applications or libraries that we wish to migrate from one .NET platform to another.

As we will see during the migration, this is not a bullet-proof tool. We still need to fix subtle behavioral changes in the app due to new platform features that we will use. However, if this tool reports a compatibility issue with the new platform, we will need to work on fixing that issue first.

Here is how to use this tool:

1. If you have not already done this, then install .NET Portability Analyzer as a Visual Studio extension from `https://marketplace.visualstudio.com/items?itemName=ConnieYau.NETPortabilityAnalyzer`.

2. Right-click on the project name and then click **Portability Analyzer Settings**.

3. Choose only **5.0** (under **.NET + Platform Extensions**) as your target platform:

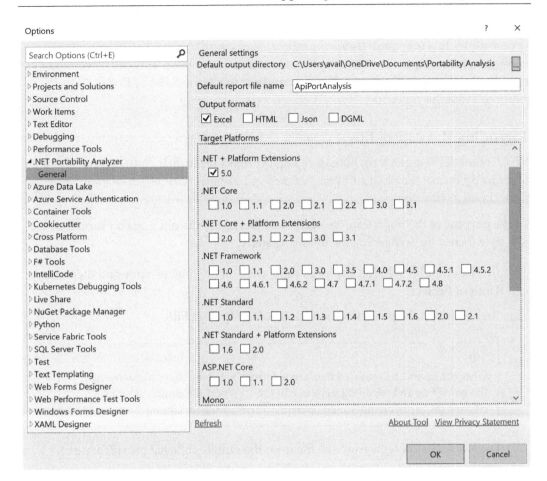

Figure 5.8 – .NET Portability Analyzer settings

4. Click **OK**.

5. Right-click on the project name again, and this time choose **Analyze Project Portability**.

6. This should generate the compatibility report. Click **Open Report** to view the report in Excel:

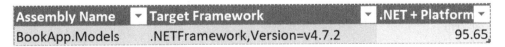

Figure 5.9 – Analysis report by .NET Portability Analyzer

For the `BookApp.Models` project, you would notice that only about 95% of the code is compatible. This is because `Newtonsoft.Json.JsonIgnoreAttribute` is not natively supported in the new `System.Text.Json` namespace. This can be verified from the **Details** tab in the report. We can continue to use the `Newtonsoft.Json` library to avoid this issue.

Upgrading the csproj file

.NET Core/.NET 5 uses a lean, human-readable project file format. You can read about the full `csproj` format details at `https://docs.microsoft.com/en-us/dotnet/core/tools/csproj`.

For the purpose of the migration, we need to convert from the old `csproj` format to the SDK style format by performing the following steps:

1. In Visual Studio Solution Explorer, right-click on the project name and then click **Unload Project**.

2. Right-click on the project name and click **Edit Project File**.

> **Tip**
> Once the project is converted into a new format, we do not have to go through the unloading and reloading steps to edit the `csproj` file. Simply double-clicking the project name would open the `csproj` file for editing.

3. Overwrite the contents from the file from the sample code file provided: `net5\ BookApp\Models\BookApp.Models.csproj`.

   The key element that we've changed in the new project file is the `TargetFramework` attribute, which has been changed to `net5.0`:

```
<PropertyGroup>
    <TargetFramework>net5.0</TargetFramework>
</PropertyGroup>
```

This target framework moniker specifies that the project is targeting the .NET 5 platform.

> **Tip**
> I did not create the new file by hand. I created a new .NET 5 class library project in a temporary folder and copied most of the `csproj` contents from there.

Deleting the AssemblyInfo.cs file

.NET 5 projects automatically generate an `AssemblyInfo.cs` file. If we leave the old file in the project, it will create conflicts for the compiler. To avoid this, delete this file from the `Properties` folder under the project.

Congratulations! We have completed the migration of the first project in the solution. Let's now move to a more complex migration of the data access layer.

Upgrading the BookApp.DAL project

In this exercise, we will not only upgrade the `BookApp.DAL` project itself, but also upgrade our data access framework to EF Core. In addition, we will replace the DI framework from `AutoFac` with the one provided by the .NET 5 platform, which is available in the `Microsoft.Extensions.DependencyInjection` namespace.

These changes and their impact are described as we go along.

Upgrading the project format to .NET 5

Perform the following steps to upgrade the `BookApp.DAL` project:

1. Migrate the `packages.config` file and delete the `AssemblyInfo.cs` file using similar steps to those described in relation to the `BookApp.Models` project.

2. Overwrite the contents of the `csproj` file using the following file from the example code provided: `net5\BookApp\BookApp.DAL\BookApp.DAL.csproj`.

3. In the new `csproj` file, the package references for `EntityFramework` and `AutoFac` have been replaced with `EntityFramework.Core` and `Microsoft.Extensions.DependencyInjection`. In subsequent sections, we will talk about code changes that need to be made to use these libraries.

4. Replace the contents of the `BooksDBContext.cs`, `BookRepository.cs`, and `BookAppDBModule.cs` files from the example code provided.

5. Delete the `BooksDBInitialiser.cs` file.

We have changed a lot in the `BookApp.DAL` project using the preceding steps. Let's now understand the reasons and implications of the changes we have just made.

Upgrading Entity Framework to EF Core

There are several fundamental changes in Entity Framework Core due to which simply changing the package reference will not work. In this exercise, we will walk through all the changes that need to be made to make the *BookApp* migration successful.

For your real-world projects, it is worthwhile reviewing the full list of changes between the two frameworks to see which functionality of your application is impacted. The official porting guide can be read from the following link: `https://docs.microsoft.com/en-us/ef/efcore-and-ef6/porting/`.

Refactoring database initializers

BookApp uses a database initializer strategy named `CreateDatabaseIfNotExists`. This ensures that the database is created the first time the WPF application is used.

This mechanism has significantly changed in EF Core. We can instead use `DbContext.Database.EnsureCreated()` to ensure that a database is created if it doesn't already exist.

We will apply this code change in the admin desktop application during its migration process.

Seeding the database

BookApp seeds some sample data when the database is created. This seeding mechanism has also changed in EF Core. We have to use the `HasData()` method to ensure that sample data is always present in the database. This can be specified as part of the model configuration itself.

As shown in the following code snippet, the code change has been made to the new `BooksDBContext.cs` file:

```
var books = new[]
{
    new Book
    {
        Id=1,
        Author="Hammad Arif, Habib Qureshi",
        DatePublished=new DateTime(2021,1,1),
        Title="Introducing .NET 5",
        SubTitle="Building & migrating apps
        using modern architecture on latest
        .NET platform"
    },
    ..........
```

```
        }
    };
```

In the preceding code snippet, the HasData() method cannot automatically create foreign key IDs for navigation properties. Therefore, we have explicitly specified these IDs.

It is also not simple to specify parent and child entities (Book and BookReview in our case) to be seeded in a single statement. So, we need to create another HasData() statement for child entities:

```
modelBuilder.Entity<Book>().HasData(books);
modelBuilder.Entity<BookReview>().HasData(new
{
    Book_Id = 1,
    Id = 1,
    Rating = 3,
    Title = "Aenean ut est dolor",
    Review = "Aenean ut est dolor. Curabitur in
    arcu vel quam mattis porta. "

});
```

As shown in the preceding code snippet, we had to add child entities in separate HasData() statements and specify the same Book_Id value that was used to create the Book object.

Replacing the System.Data.Entity namespace

This is a relatively simple change. The using references to System.Data.Entity has been replaced with the new Microsoft.EntityFrameworkCore namespace in all the cs files.

Specifying model conventions

The conventions assumed by the EF Core framework to understand the data model properties are mostly the same as they were in Entity Framework. There are a couple of changes we need to make for the unsupported conventions.

The following line from the old code is not supported in EF Core:

```
modelBuilder.Conventions.
Remove<PluralizingTableNameConvention>();
```

As a result, EF Core would assume that database table names are in their plural form (that is, `Books` instead of `Book`).

To resolve this, we can explicitly specify the table names in the `OnModelCreating` method:

```
modelBuilder.Entity<Book>()
    .ToTable("Book");


modelBuilder.Entity<BookReview>()
    .ToTable("BookReview");
```

Another issue is that for the `BookReview` entity, EF Core assumed that its parent key field for the table book must be named `BookId`. However, Entity Framework generated this field as `Book_Id` by convention. So, we need to explicitly specify this in the `OnModelCreating` method:

```
modelBuilder.Entity<BookReview>()
    .HasOne(b => b.Book)
    .WithMany(b => b.Reviews)
    .HasForeignKey("Book_Id");
```

More changes have been made to the `BooksDBContext.cs` and `BookRepository.cs` files that are related to DI. Let's discuss these changes in the next section.

Replacing the DI framework

The .NET Framework version of *BookApp* used `AutoFac` as the DI framework. `AutoFac` is a popular DI framework. It has some advanced features that are not found in .NET 5's built-in DI framework provided via the `Microsoft.Extensions.DependencyInjection` namespace. One example of such features is the automatic registration of the classes by scanning the assemblies.

So, here is a question for you:

Should we replace AutoFac with Microsoft.Extensions.DependencyInjection even though AutoFac has a more comprehensive feature list?

Using a built-in feature reduces the maintainability requirements and would be a good choice if the existing code base is not heavily dependent on the third-party framework.

As our use case for DI is quite standard, we will replace the third-party framework with the built-in library.

To accommodate this change, the following changes have been made to the `BookApp.DAL` project:

1. The NuGet package reference for `Microsoft.Extensions.DependencyInjection` has been added to the `csproj` file:

    ```
    <PackageReference Include="Microsoft.Extensions.
    DependencyInjection" Version="5.0.0-rc.1.20451.14" />
    ```

2. A new method named `AddBookAppDB()` has replaced the `Load()` method in `BookAppDBModule.cs`.

Other DI changes are specifically implemented to accommodate some best practices for configuring EF Core dependency injection.

Configuring dependency injection for EF Core

The `DbContext` instance in EF Core requires access to the `DbContextOptions` object. It uses it to identify connection configuration, such as a connection string, query tracking behavior, and error handling and caching.

The constructor of `BooksDBContext.cs` has been updated to receive an instance of the `DbContextOptions` class:

```
public BooksDBContext(DbContextOptions<BooksDBContext> options)
        : base(options)
    {
    }
```

In the .NET Framework version of the constructor, we also had the `SetInitializer()` method call to initialize the database. We are now initializing the database using the `SeedData()` method in the `OnModelCreating()` event, as explained in the *Seeding the database* section.

Updating BookRepository for short-lived contexts

EF Core does not support the operations in the same context from multiple threads and the official documentation recommends using a separate `DbContext` instance for operations that execute in parallel. To implement this recommendation, most operations in the `BookRepository` class have been updated to create and dispose of `DbContext` during the life of the operation.

Here is the code snippet for one of the methods that has changed:

```
public IEnumerable<Book> GetBooks()
{
    using (var context = new
    BooksDBContext(dbOptions))
    {
        return context.Books
        .Include(b => b.Reviews)
        .ToList();
    }
}
```

The complete `DbContext` configuration guidance can be read in the following article: `https://docs.microsoft.com/en-us/ef/core/miscellaneous/configuring-dbcontext`.

We are now done with the data access layer upgrade process. Phew! Now, let's move on to upgrading the admin desktop app.

Migrating the admin desktop app

So far, we have not been able to see the results of the upgrade effort in action. The good news is that after upgrading the admin desktop app, we will be able to see the .NET 5 WPF application in full motion. Let's go through the migration exercise.

Perform the following steps to perform the upgrade:

1. Migrate the `packages.config` file and delete the `AssemblyInfo.cs` file using similar steps to those carried out in relation to the previous two projects.

2. Replace the contents of the `csproj` file from the example code provided. You will need to unload and reload the project.

3. You'll notice that we are now referencing two packages from the `Microsoft.Extensions.Configuration` namespace. These are discussed in detail in the next section.

4. Replace the contents of the `MainWindow.xaml.cs` and `App.xaml.cs` files from the example code files provided. The changes to these files are done to accommodate DI and configuration changes, which we will discuss in the next section.

5. Delete the `app.config` file and copy `appsettings.json` from the example code provided. Ensure that its **Copy to Output Directory** property is set to **Copy if Newer**.

Using the Microsoft.Extensions.Configuration namespace

As described in the *Replacing third-party libraries with platform-provided features* section, the mechanism for managing application configuration in the .NET Core and .NET 5 world is quite superior to .NET Framework's XML-based `*.config` files. The effort to make this replacement is usually low, so it is a low-hanging fruit waiting to be picked.

The changes made to the code related to this replacement are as follows:

1. The `appsettings` file has a JSON schema. Currently, it only specifies the connection string for `BooksDB`, but it is capable of holding application settings in tightly bound POCO objects:

```
{
    "ConnectionStrings": {
      "BooksDB": "Data
      Source=(LocalDb)\\MSSQLLocalDB;Initial
      Catalog=BookApp;Integrated Security=True;"
    }
}
```

2. The `Application_Startup` code in `app.xaml.cs` reads the settings from the `appsettings.json` file:

```
var builder = new ConfigurationBuilder()
.SetBasePath(Directory.
GetCurrentDirectory())
    .AddJsonFile("appsettings.json",
    optional: false, reloadOnChange: true);

Configuration = builder.Build();
```

The .NET 5 configuration management functionality is quite versatile and can read the application configuration from environment variables, command-line arguments, or even cloud services such as Azure Key Vault.

Can you think of an advantage of using external sources such as command-line arguments or Azure Key Vault when storing the application configuration?

It is a good practice to externalize the application configuration from its code. This helps in centrally managing the configuration across different environments (such as dev, test, and prod) or services (such as frontend and backend). Sensitive configurations, such as database credentials, can be encrypted and secured, and configuration changes can easily be managed without redeploying the application code.

If you want to read more about .NET 5 configuration management, please refer to the following Microsoft article: `https://docs.microsoft.com/en-us/aspnet/core/fundamentals/configuration/?view=aspnetcore-5.0`.

Updating dependency injection code

Just like we did in `BookApp.DAL`, the DI code has been updated to replace `AutoFac` with the `Microsoft.Extensions.DependencyInjection` library:

```
var serviceCollection = new
ServiceCollection();
ConfigureServices(serviceCollection);

ServiceProvider =
serviceCollection.BuildServiceProvider();
```

The following lines have been added to ensure that the database gets created if it does not already exist:

```
var dbOptions = ServiceProvider.GetService
<DbContextOptions<BooksDBContext>>();
using (var context = new
BooksDBContext(dbOptions))
{
    context.Database.EnsureCreated();
}
```

We have now completed all the steps needed to upgrade the admin desktop WPF app. Before we run the app, let's understand the reason behind not upgrading the `Newtonsoft.Json` library in the case of this particular project.

Using System.Text.Json instead of Newtonsoft.Json

In the *Replacing third-party libraries with platform-provided features* section, we have talked about `System.Text.Json` as an alternative for `Newtonsoft.Json`.

In the admin desktop app, we are using an export book feature that requires a specific serialization setting, namely, `PreserveReferencesHandling`. This is needed to avoid a circular reference from `Book` to `BookReview`, and then from `BookReview` to the same `Book` as its parent.

This feature is not supported by `System.Text.Json`, so we have decided to use `Newtonsoft.Json`, which is fully supported on the .NET 5 platform.

For full guidance on migrating from `Newtonsoft.Json` to `System.Text.Json`, refer to the following article: `https://docs.microsoft.com/en-us/dotnet/standard/serialization/system-text-json-migrate-from-newtonsoft-how-to`.

Executing the .NET 5 admin desktop WPF app

It is now time to see our desktop app in action! Run the admin desktop app in Visual Studio. It should work in the same way as it did prior to migration.

The bulk of the migration job is completed. However, the process to migrate the ASP.NET MVC app has some unique steps that we will go through in the next section.

Migrating BookApp.Web

This is the final piece of the migration exercise for *BookApp*. The approach is a bit different this time, since instead of changing the project files directly, we will create a new ASP.NET Core project targeting .NET 5 and then move our existing code to the new project. This is done because there is no built-in support in Visual Studio 2019 to migrate `packages.config` files to ASP.NET MVC projects and it's usually easier to plumb controllers and views from the existing code base to the new pipeline infrastructure of ASP.NET Core.

If you choose to make in-place changes to the existing ASP.NET MVC project instead, please refer to the following article: `https://docs.microsoft.com/en-us/aspnet/core/migration/proper-to-2x/?view=aspnetcore-3.1`.

Let's begin the upgrade journey for `BookApp.Web`.

Creating the new project

We will create a new ASP.NET Core project by performing the following steps:

1. Add a new project to the BookApp solution by right-clicking the solution name and then choosing **Add a New Project**.

2. Choose **ASP.NET Core Web Application** from the project templates selection window. Click **Next**.

3. Set the name as **BookApp.Web.V2** and then click **Create**.

4. Ensure that **ASP.NET Core 5.0** and **Web Application (Model-View-Controller)** are selected on the **Create a new ASP.NET Core web application** screen:

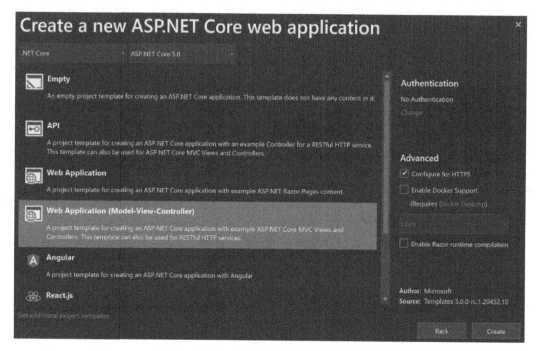

Figure 5.10 – Creating a new ASP.NET Core web application

5. Click **Create**.

This will create a new project in the *BookApp* solution. We will now begin transforming the code from an existing web project to make it .NET 5-compatible.

Updating the Startup.cs file

The `Startup.cs` file replaces the `global.asax` file from the ASP.NET MVC project. Replace its contents from the same file in the example code with the `net5` folder. The following key changes have been made:

1. A very basic global exception handling code has been added using the `app.UseExceptionHandler()` method. This is important to troubleshoot errors that you will invariably get while migrating your own app due to the framework differences. In a production-grade app, you can use the guidelines from this article: `https://docs.microsoft.com/en-us/aspnet/core/fundamentals/error-handling?view=aspnetcore-3.1`.

2. DI code has been added for the data access layer. This is very similar to the code added in the `BookApp.AdminDesktop` project:

```
services.AddBookAppDB(Configuration.
GetConnectionString("BooksDB"));
```

The next step is to upgrade controllers and the views files.

Copying controllers and views

Controllers and views are copied from the existing `BookApp.Web` project, but some changes have been made to them. For convenience, you can directly copy the final contents from the example code provided. The changes are described here:

1. From all controllers, `using Microsoft.AspNetCore.Mvc;` has been added and the unnecessary `using` statements have been removed.

2. `Privacy.cshtml` from the home view is deleted as it not required for *BookApp*.

3. ASP.NET Core Razor does not support the `@Style.Render` tag. We have replaced it with the `link` tag in the `Shared/_Layout.cshtml` file that loads the `bootstrap.css` file:

```
<link rel="stylesheet"
      href="https://maxcdn.bootstrapcdn.com/
bootstrap/3.3.7/css/bootstrap.min.css"
      integrity="sha384-BVYiiSIFeK1dGmJRAkycuHAHRg32O
mUcww7on3RYdg4Va+PmSTsz/K68vbdEjh4u"
      crossorigin="anonymous">
```

4. Similar to the preceding point, ASP.NET Core Razor does not support the @ `Script.Render` tag. We have replaced it with a series of `script` tags in the `Shared/_Layout.cshtml` file that loads the `jquery` files for client-side validation:

```
<script src="~/lib/jquery/dist/jquery.min.js"></script>

<script src="~/lib/jquery-validation/dist/jquery.validate.min.js"></script>

<script src="~/lib/jquery-validation-unobtrusive/jquery.validate.unobtrusive.min.js"></script>

<script src="https://maxcdn.bootstrapcdn.com/bootstrap/3.3.7/js/bootstrap.min.js"
integrity="sha384-Tc5IQib027qvyjSMfH
jOMaLkfuWVxZxUPnCJA712mCWNIpG9mGCD8wGNIcPD7Txa"
crossorigin="anonymous"></script>
```

Interestingly, the `jquery-validation-unobtrusive` folder is not placed under the `dist` folder, unlike the other two `jquery` files. This is likely a bug that should be fixed in future releases. For now, you can copy the same code as provided in the snippet, which should work fine.

5. In all the controller methods, the code to return the `BadRequest` HTTP status code has been updated as follows:

```
// Old code
return new BadRequestResult();
//New code
return new HttpStatusCodeResult(HttpStatusCode.BadRequest);
```

6. Similar to the preceding point, the code to return the `NotFound` HTTP status code has been updated as follows:

```
//Old code
return HttpNotFound();
//New code
return NotFound();
```

7. The syntax for `BindAttribtue` has been changed slightly in ASP.NET Core and has been updated in all the controller methods:

```
//Old code
public ActionResult Create([Bind(Include =
"Id,Title,SubTitle,DatePublished,CoverImage,Author")]
Book book)
```
```
//New code
public ActionResult Create([Bind("Id,Title,SubTitle,
DatePublished,CoverImage,Author")] Book book)
```

8. In the old code base, the `Create`, `Edit`, and `Delete` views for `BookReviewController` use a hidden field to pass on the parent book ID to the controller's `POST` method:

```
@Html.HiddenFor(m => m.Book.Id, new { Name="bookId"})
```

This code incorrectly generated the hidden field ID as book_id instead of `bookId` in the ASP.NET Core app. This has been corrected using the following code.

```
       @Html.Hidden("bookId",Model.Book.Id, new { @Id =
"bookId" })
```

Note that the corrected code should have been used in the old code base in the first place as this is the correct approach to generate the field ID. However, I left it intentionally to demonstrate that there could be subtle behavior changes between the frameworks when the code behavior is not strictly defined.

9. The connection string has been copied to the `appsettings.json` file. This is the same connection string as used in `BookApp.AdminDesktop`:

```
  "ConnectionStrings": {
    "BooksDB": "Data Source=(LocalDb)\\
MSSQLLocalDB;Initial Catalog=BookApp;Integrated
Security=True;"
  },
```

With all these changes in place, we are now ready to test the upgraded application.

Testing the upgraded app

This is the time to reap the rewards of all the effort spent during migration. Build and execute the `BookApp.Web.V2` app. It should behave in the same manner as the original .NET Framework app. Hooray!

Cleaning up the solution

You can now delete the `BookApp.Web` project from the solution and rename the `BookApp.Web.V2` project to `BookApp.Web`. The beauty of the new SDK style projects is that Visual Studio will rename the physical filename as well.

As you can see, we had to make a considerable number of code changes to upgrade this simple app. For large real-world apps, it is always best to review the official migration guides to understand the impact of required changes.

We will now conclude with a summary of what we have learned from this chapter.

Summary

In this chapter, we learned about different migration approaches and the pros and cons of each of these approaches. There is no one-size-fits-all solution. The preferred approach depends on the compatibility of the technologies involved, the size of the existing code base, and the extent of dependence on the third-party NuGet libraries.

It is not always possible to use the legacy technology, as we saw in the case of WCF Server, WWF, and Web Forms. We learned that potential technologies, such as gRPC, Blazor, and REST, can be used to replace the existing solutions in such cases.

We then migrated a sample book review app from .NET Framework to .NET 5. Most of the code was usable as it was, but we still had to make considerable changes due to behavioral differences in new versions of libraries, particularly around Entity Framework Core and ASP.NET Core usage. These changes could be applied in most real-life .NET applications that need to be migrated to .NET 5. Additionally, the coding examples would also help in developing .NET 5 applications from scratch.

In the next chapter, we'll focus on leveraging the strength of cloud platforms, such as Microsoft Azure and Amazon Web Services, to run .NET 5 applications in a scalable, reliable, and cost-effective fashion.

Further reading

We have covered the most common migration scenarios of migrating WPF-, ASP.NET-, and Entity Framework-based applications from .NET Framework to .NET 5 while largely keeping the feature set as-is. You may also find the following resources helpful when migrating from other versions of .NET Core or upgrading a WinForms application to Blazor:

- There is a video titled *Porting Projects to .NET 5* from the .NET 5 launch event on YouTube. It discusses the migration approaches from .NET Framework and .NET Core to .NET 5 with live demos: `https://www.youtube.com/watch?v=bvmd2F11jpA`.

- If you are looking to replace Window Forms applications with Blazor, this YouTube video titled *Migrating a Windows Forms App to Blazor* from the .NET 5 launch event could be a good starting point: `https://www.youtube.com/watch?v=bvmd2F11jpA`.

- Every version of ASP.NET Core has breaking changes compared with the previous major version. You can review the official documentation for breaking changes and the migration guide for each version at the following Microsoft article: `https://docs.microsoft.com/en-us/aspnet/core/migration/31-to-50?view=aspnetcore-5.0&tabs=visual-studio`.

6

Upgrading On-Premises Applications to the Cloud with .NET 5

Cloud, microservices, containers, serverless, Platform as a Service, and so on – these are all the buzzwords that you frequently hear these days. If you have developed a new application in the last 3-5 years, chances are that it has already been deployed to the cloud using one or more of the aforementioned technologies. But what about the applications that are still hosted on-premises? This could be either because they were developed in the pre-cloud era, or there are legitimate reasons to run it off-cloud (such as dependency on on-premises resources).

In this chapter, we will talk about the available platforms and services on the Microsoft Azure cloud that can help us migrate on-premises applications to the cloud, without us having to significantly rebuild and rearchitect the whole solution.

We will cover the following topics:

- Planning for cloud-optimized application transformation
- Migrating SQL Server databases to the cloud
- Deploying .NET 5 applications on Azure App Service
- Deploying to the serverless – Azure Functions
- Deploying .NET 5 applications to containers

By the end of this chapter, you'll have learned about the advantages of building cloud-optimized and cloud-native applications. You'll be equipped with practical knowledge of deploying .NET 5 applications on the Azure cloud platform, and you'll also be able to choose the appropriate Azure service for different types of .NET 5 applications and SQL Server databases.

First, let's review the technical requirements that we'll need in order to complete the exercises in this chapter.

Technical requirements

This is a practical chapter, so there are a number of technical requirements you'll need to complete the exercises presented:

- Visual Studio 2019 16.8 or higher (any edition is fine). This is needed to work with the sample .NET 5 application (BookApp) that is included with this chapter's code.
- SQL Server Express LocalDB 2019 is typically installed along with Visual Studio 2019, so a separate installation is not needed.
- The .NET 5 SDK, which can be downloaded from here: `https://dotnet.microsoft.com/download/dotnet/5.0`.
- A Microsoft Azure Subscription. A free account is sufficient to complete this chapter's exercises. You can create one by going to `https://azure.microsoft.com/en-au/free/`.
- The last section of this chapter, *Deploying .NET 5 applications to containers*, shows you how to create a Linux-based container. You will need Windows 10 for this, preferably version 1903+ with WSL 2 enabled to run Linux containers on Windows. Please refer to `https://docs.microsoft.com/en-us/windows/wsl/install-win10` for the installation process for WSL 2.

- Optionally, you can install Docker Desktop from `https://www.docker.com/products/docker-desktop`. If it is not installed already, Visual Studio will install it for you when you try to use containerization features.

- Another piece of optional software is **SQL Server Management Studio (SSMS)** v18.7 or higher, which can be downloaded from here: `https://docs.microsoft.com/en-us/sql/ssms/download-sql-server-management-studio-ssms?view=sql-server-ver15`.

  We will only use SSMS to query the databases for migration verification. This can also be done from the Azure portal UI, so having SSMS installed is not a mandatory requirement.

We will use a sample book review application named **BookApp** throughout this chapter for all the migration exercises. If you have already read *Chapter 5*, *Upgrading Existing .NET Apps to .NET 5*, then you have sufficient background knowledge of this application. If you don't, you will need to run the application at least once so that the application database is created. The steps for running the BookApp application are provided in the *Setting up the sample BookApp application* section.

Using the source code provided for this chapter

Just like the previous chapter, the sample code is provided with two different copies in two different folders.

You will use the code from the `https://github.com/PacktPublishing/Adopting-.NET-5--Architecture-Migration-Best-Practices-and-New-Features/tree/master/Chapter06/onprem/BookApp` folder as your starting point to walk through the exercises provided.

In some steps, I will ask you to copy files from the final solution folder. That folder contains the final form that your working solution will transform into once all the exercises have been completed. The path to the final solution folder is `https://github.com/PacktPublishing/Adopting-.NET-5--Architecture-Migration-Best-Practices-and-New-Features/tree/master/Chapter06/azure/BookApp`.

Many of the exercises in this chapter require Azure CLI commands to be executed. You can copy and paste the commands directly from this chapter's content. If you are using the hard copy version of this book, you can copy the scripts from the CLI scripts folder at `https://github.com/PacktPublishing/Adopting-.NET-5--Architecture-Migration-Best-Practices-and-New-Features/tree/master/Chapter06/cli%20scripts`.

Now that we've covered the technical requirements, it is time to understand the strategies involved in cloud migration.

Planning for cloud-optimized application transformation

The key benefit of having cloud-native applications is the scalability, agility, and cost-effectiveness that we can get from using cloud services. However, cloud-native applications typically require major architectural changes and code to be rewritten if the legacy application is too old and has been built with a monolithic architecture.

There is no one-size-fits-all approach to suit all scenarios. Depending on an organization's appetite to modernize and rebuild, there are a few options that can be used directly or in phases to transform a legacy monolith application into a cloud-native application using microservices and serverless architecture. Let's look at these options one by one.

Infrastructure as a Service (IaaS)

With IaaS, the applications are simply re-deployed on virtual machines hosted in the cloud. Compared to the other options, this approach disrupts the application code the least but brings minimal benefits since most software infrastructure maintenance is still the customer's responsibility.

Cloud-optimized applications

For legacy monolith applications, this option typically brings the best *effort-to-value ratio*. As we will see during the hands-on exercises in this chapter, without the significant code or architectural changes, we can host our applications using a managed Azure App Service or as containers. This takes away lots of software infrastructure concerns, such as OS installation, patching, scaling, and monitoring, and so on. This transformation can be done gradually as it is possible for an on-premises service, such as a web application, to talk to a resource such as a SQL database deployed in the cloud.

Cloud-native applications

This is the ultimate goal for cloud applications. For cloud-native applications, the architecture is designed and the code is written while keeping the cloud features in mind. Major cloud platforms offer hundreds of platform features, such as asynchronous messaging, event-driven programming, big data storage and query, and so on. This can all be leveraged best if the code is explicitly written to take advantage of these services.

This option best suits new applications. For most organizations, it is also suitable to transform into the cloud-optimized application first and then rearchitect it as a cloud-native application in the next phase.

Now that we've provided this brief overview, we will go through the practical options and perform some exercises so that we can transform application components such as databases and web applications into a cloud-optimized form. To get a taste of cloud-native applications, we will also develop a new Azure Functions app and integrate the existing BookApp application with it.

Migrating SQL Server databases to the cloud

In the previous chapter, when we were migrating a .NET Framework app to the .NET 5 platform, we chose to migrate the least dependent component first. Then, in the next cycle, we migrated the components that relied on the components that were migrated in the previous cycle.

A similar approach works when migrating applications to the cloud as well. In the case of BookApp, the database can function on its own, but the application cannot function without the database. So, we will migrate the database to the cloud first. Then, in the next section, we will migrate the BookApp web application to the Azure cloud to complete the migration process.

Let's learn how to migrate the SQL Server database to the Azure cloud.

Comparing Azure SQL options

There are a number of SQL Server offerings on the Azure platform. Collectively, these are known as the **Azure SQL family**. Here is a brief introduction to the salient points of each offering.

Option 1 – SQL Server hosted on Azure VM

This option provides nearly the same experience as SQL Server hosted on-premises. The hardware is managed by Azure. The customer chooses the virtual machine specifications and then performs the installation and ongoing maintenance by themselves. This is recommended for organizations that are not ready for a cloud-native styled architecture and need full control over SQL Server features and its upgrade cycle.

Let's take a look at this option's strengths and weaknesses:

- **Key strengths**:

    Complete control over the software installation and patching cycle.

    All SQL Server features are supported.

    It is the only option where **SQL Server Reporting Services** (**SSRS**) can be used.

    Third-party extensions such as custom full-text search word breakers can be installed.

- **Key limitations**:

    Requires full database administration skills to manage the server.

    High availability and replication of databases is complicated to implement.

Now, let's look at the second option.

Option 2 – Azure SQL Managed Instance

With this option, Azure manages the SQL Server software but provides most of the control to the customer so that they can fine-tune it according to their needs. Unlike hosting on VMs, as with the previous option, the client does not have to worry about OS and software maintenance. However, general database administration is still the client's responsibility. This option is recommended for organizations that need to use features that are not supported via Azure SQL Database, such as cross-database queries or linked servers.

The key points for this option are as follows:

- **Key strengths**:

    Near 100% feature parity with SQL Server on-premises.

    Cross-database queries and linked servers are partially supported.

    High availability and replication of databases is easier to implement and manage.

- **Key limitations**:

    SSRS is not supported.

    Windows authentication is not supported.

    Compared to the Azure SQL Database offering, some database server maintenance skills are still needed.

Now, let's look at the third option.

Option 3 – Azure SQL Database

This is the most modern option that's suitable for cloud-native applications. Azure manages everything to do with software installation and maintenance. All the resources required to provision the databases are also managed by Azure. The client can provision and deprovision databases without having to worry about any underlying infrastructure concerns.

This is the recommended approach for most new applications, as well as existing applications that can be transformed into cloud-native architectures. We will use this option when we walk through the migration process.

The key points for this option are as follows:

- **Key strengths**:

  The easiest option to set up and provision databases.

  A serverless option is available, where the client only pays when the database is in use.

  High availability and auto-scaling are built-in and require no maintenance by the client.

  Only database application-level skills (such as query tuning) are needed.

- **Key limitations**:

  SSRS is not supported.

  Windows authentication is not supported.

  Cross-database queries and some system-level stored procedures are not supported.

  Migrating from an on-premises SQL Server is slightly more complex compared to the other options.

For a detailed comparison of these Azure SQL options, please refer to the following Microsoft article: `https://docs.microsoft.com/en-us/Azure/Azure-sql/Azure-sql-iaas-vs-paas-what-is-overview`.

Migrating the BookApp database to Azure SQL Database

As we saw in the previous section, Azure SQL Database is the most hassle-free and modern option for migrating the BookApp database to the cloud. Let's walk through the hands-on exercise to perform the actual migration.

Setting up the sample BookApp application

If you have not followed the exercises in *Chapter 5, Upgrading Existing .NET Apps to .NET 5*, then you will need to run this application at least once so that our source database is created. You can skip to the next section, *Creating a free Microsoft Azure account*, if the BookApp database already exists on your development machine.

Follow these steps to run the BookApp application:

1. Download the sample code from the provided GitHub repository:
    `https://github.com/PacktPublishing/Adopting-.NET-5--Architecture-Migration-Best-Practices-and-New-Features/tree/master/Chapter06`.

2. In Visual Studio, open the `BookApp.sln` file in the `Chapter06\onprem\BookApp` folder.

3. Run the `BookApp.Web` application.

4. On the home screen, click the **Books** link to get to the books page.

This process will initialize the BookApp database using the LocalDB edition of SQL Server on your local machine. We will use this database for the migration exercise.

Creating a free Microsoft Azure account

If you have not done this already, then create a free Microsoft Azure account by visiting `https://Azure.microsoft.com/en-us/free/`.

For brevity, detailed steps have not been provided. The signup process is quite straightforward. Note that you'll need a credit card to sign up, but Azure offers most services for free under a trial account. Azure also currently provides enough free credits that you will not be charged for using any resources that are shown in this chapter's example exercises.

Reminder – Cleaning up cloud resources

In the last section of this chapter, resource cleanup instructions will be provided so that you can delete any of the resources that you'll have provisioned in this exercise. Please ensure that you follow those instructions to avoid any unintended resource usage and getting billed for that by the cloud provider.

As we'll see in the rest of this chapter, having an Azure account is a great way to explore the latest and greatest technology in the cloud without having to go through the tedious process of setting up hardware, or even installing software, on a personal computer. The next requirement is to configure Azure Cloud Shell.

Configuring Azure Cloud Shell

To configure resources in Microsoft Azure, we can use the Azure portal UI, PowerShell scripts, or the **Azure Command-Line Interface (Azure CLI)**.

All these options have good use cases. For this chapter, we will use the Azure CLI using a cloud shell as the portal experience can change over time. Azure CLI commands can be repeated relatively quickly and reliably when needed.

If you haven't used Azure Cloud Shell before, go to `https://shell.azure.com/` to set it up. Ensure that you log in using the same account that you created in the previous section. When you're asked about a preferred shell type, choose **Bash** instead of **PowerShell**.

Downloading and installing Microsoft Data Migration Assistant

Microsoft **Data Migration Assistant (DMA)** helps in detecting compatibility issues between source and target versions of SQL Server for migrations. In our case, the source version for the BookApp database is SQL Server LocalDB, and the target version is Azure SQL Database. The tool can also migrate the schema and the data from the source to the target database.

This is an ideal tool for simple migrations. For migrating large databases at scale, an Azure service named Azure Database Migration Services can be used.

DMA can be downloaded and installed from this URL: `https://www.microsoft.com/en-us/download/details.aspx?id=53595`.

The next step is to create an Azure SQL database. We will use this as a target to perform data migration using the same DMA tool.

Creating an Azure SQL database

In this exercise, we will create an Azure SQL Server and then an Azure SQL database on it.

All the Azure CLI commands that are required for this section can also be copied from the code folder for this chapter; that is, `code\Chapter06\cli scripts\sql migration scripts.txt`.

Follow these steps to create a new Azure SQL database:

1. Go to `https://shell.Azure.com/` in your preferred browser. Ensure that **Bash** is selected as the environment in the top-left corner.

2. We will now set up various configuration settings, such as a SQL administrator password and data center region. Edit the highlighted values as per the explanation provided here and then press *Enter* to execute the script:

    ```
    resourceGroupName=bookAppResourceGroup
    location=australiaeast
    ```

    `resourceGroupName` is the name of the group under which we will create all the resources for this chapter, such as the Database, Application, Azure Function, and so on. This will help us manage these resources as a single unit for billing and cleaning up.

    `location` is the name of the Azure data center region where these resources will be created. I've chosen `austrliaeast`, which is the closest to my physical location (Sydney). You can choose the data center that is the closest to your location.

3. To get the full list of all available data center locations, you can run the following command from the Azure CLI shell:

    ```
    az account list-locations -o table
    ```

4. Create the resource group using the following command:

    ```
    az group create --name $resourceGroupName --location
    $location
    ```

    If the command executes successfully, you will see the following output, with the `provisioningState` value showing **Succeeded**:

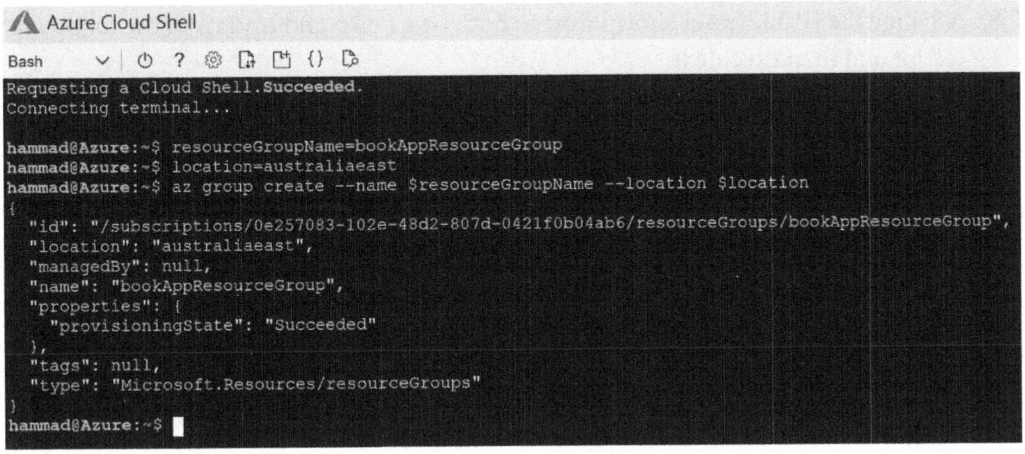

Figure 6.1 – Resource Group creation result in Azure Cloud Shell

5. Specify the SQL Server admin username, password, and server name using the following commands:

```
adminlogin=sqlserveradmin
password=ASampleP@ssw0rd!
serverName=BookAppSQLServer2020
```

The server name must be unique across your chosen Azure region. If, in later steps, Azure complains about the name being not unique, try any other random four digits or your name instead of **2020**. Also, change your `adminlogin` and `password` if you plan to continue to use this server after completing this chapter.

6. Create the SQL server using the following command:

```
az sql server create \
    --name $serverName \
    --resource-group $resourceGroupName \
    --location $location  \
    --admin-user $adminlogin \
    --admin-password $password
```

7. Once the server has been created successfully, the next step is to the configure firewall rules. By default, SQL Server can only be accessed from the resources that have been created within the Azure portal. To access the server from our local machine, we need to add the local machine IP to the firewall. You can find your IP by visiting https://whatismyipaddress.com/.

8. Change the IP addresses shown next to both `startip` and `endip` in the following
    script and then execute it:

```
startip=118.211.162.81
endip=118.211.162.81
az sql server firewall-rule create \
    --resource-group $resourceGroupName \
    --server $serverName \
    -n DeveloperLocalIP \
    --start-ip-address $startip \
    --end-ip-address $endip
az sql server firewall-rule create \
    --resource-group $resourceGroupName \
    --server $serverName \
    -n AzureServices \
    --start-ip-address 0.0.0.0 \
    --end-ip-address 0.0.0.0
```

Note that we are running the `firewall-rule create` command twice. The
first command adds the local machine IP address to the firewall whitelist, while the
second command adds all Azure portal services to the firewall whitelist. This will be
useful when we deploy Azure App Services and containers and want those to access
the same database server.

9. The final command we'll use will create the database on the server. Use the following
    command for this purpose:

```
az sql db create \
    --resource-group $resourceGroupName \
    --server $serverName \
    --name BookApp \
    --service-objective Basic
```

This should create a database named BookApp on the Azure SQL Server.

10. To verify that the database is accessible from the Azure portal, log into
    `https://portal.Azure.com` and then type BookApp into the search bar.
    This should display the BookApp database in the list of available resources. You
    can click it to go to the overview page for the database:

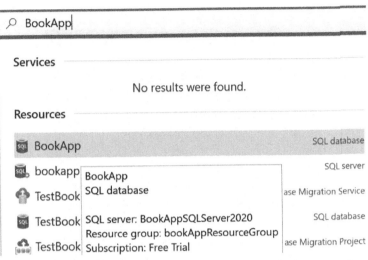

Figure 6.2 – Navigating to the BookApp database in the Azure portal

Creating the database is only half the job. We still need to migrate the data from the
existing database to complete this exercise.

Migrating data using Data Migration Assistant

We will now migrate the existing data from the SQL Server LocalDB-based database
to Azure SQL Database. For small-scale migrations where some downtime (usually
in minutes) is acceptable, DMA can be the perfect tool. For zero downtime, advanced
services such as Azure Data Migration Service can be used, which can keep the data
synchronized between the source and target database server and allow you to cut over to a
new database in real time.

Follow these steps to begin the migration process using Database Migration Assistant:

1. Launch Database Migration Assistant and click the + sign.

2. Enter or select the following values:

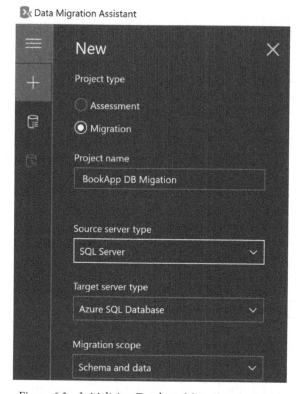

Figure 6.3 – Initializing Database Migration Assistant

3. Click **Create**.

4. In the **Select Source** tab, enter `(LocalDb)\MSSQLLocalDB` for **Server Name**. Leave **Authentication type** as `Windows Authentication`.

5. Ensure that the **Encrypt connection** and **Trust server certificate** options are unchecked.

6. Click **Connect**.

7. Choose **BookApp** from the list of available databases. Ensure that the **Assess database before migration** option is checked. This option will make an assessment if any database feature is not compatible with the migration. An example of such a feature could be having a stored procedure that makes cross-database queries.

8. Click **Next**.

9. In the **Connect to target server** dialog, type in the server name as `BookAppSQLServer2020.database.windows.net`. This is the name we chose for the Azure SQL Server in the previous exercise.

10. Enter the username and password that we configured when we created the Azure SQL Server. If you used the provided values, these will be as follows:

    Password: `ASampleP@ssw0rd!`

    Username: `sqlserveradmin`

11. Ensure that the **Encrypt connection** options are checked this time. Then, press **Connect**.

12. From the list of available databases, choose **BookApp**. We created this database in the previous section of this exercise.

13. On the **Select objects** screen, ensure that both tables (**dbo.Book** and **dbo.BookReview**) are selected. The right-hand side of the screen should state that no issues were found for this object during migration.

14. Click **Generate SQL script**. This will generate the scripts that will create a database schema.

15. Click **Deploy schema**. This will execute the scripts that were generated in the previous step.

16. Click **Migrate data** and then **Start data migration**.

17. Migration should complete in the next few seconds. You should see a success message under the **Migration details** column.

This completes the database migration task. We will now verify that the data has indeed been migrated.

Verifying the migration's success

We will now query some sample data from the migrated database using SSMS. Let's get started:

1. Launch SSMS (v18.7 or later) on your computer.

2. In the **Connect to Server** dialog, enter the target server details:

    Server Name: `BookAppSQLServer2020.database.windows.net`

    Authentication: `SQL Server Authentication`

Login: `sqlserveradmin`

Password: `ASampleP@ssw0rd!`

3. Click **Connect**. This should make the server available in the **Object Explorer** window.

4. Under **Databases**, click **BookApp** and then click **New Query** in the standard toolbar. Alternatively, press *Ctrl + N*.

5. Execute the following query:

```
SELECT TOP 10 * FROM [Book]
   Inner Join BookReview
   ON Book.Id = BookReview.Book_Id
```

This should return three or more rows of data from the book table.

> **Using the Azure portal to query the database**
>
> An alternative to SSMS is to use the Azure portal UI to query the database. You can access the database from the Azure portal and then go to the Query Editor (preview) screen for a query editing experience.

The database migration is now completed. The final part of this exercise is to connect the `BookApp.Web` application to the newly migrated database.

Connecting BookApp.Web to Azure SQL Database

Now that the database has been migrated to Azure, we need to change the connection string in the web application so that it can start communicating with the migrated BookApp database.

> **Whitelisting the application server IP for the SQL Server firewall**
>
> When we followed the database creation exercise in the *Creating an Azure SQL database* section, we whitelisted our local machine's IP address in *step 6*. If you intend to run the web application on a different machine or your local machine's IP has changed since then, you will need to add that new IP to the whitelist again. Repeat *step 6* in the *Creating an Azure SQL database* section to ensure that your application is allowed to access SQL Server.

Follow these steps to change the connection string in the BookApp web project:

1. In Visual Studio 2019, open the `BookApp.sln` file from `code\Chapter06\onprem\BookApp`.

2. Under the `BookApp.Web` project, change the connection string in the `appsettings.json` file to the following. Change `user ID` and `password` if you have been using a different user ID or password for this exercise:

```
"ConnectionStrings": {
    "BooksDB": "Server=tcp:BookAppSQLServer2020.
    database.windows.net,1433;Database=BookApp;
    User ID=sqlserveradmin;Password=ASampleP@ssw0rd!;
    Encrypt=true;Connection Timeout=30
    },
```

3. Save the file and run the application. It should display the home page correctly.

4. Try creating a sample review by clicking **Books** in the navigation bar, and then clicking the **Reviews** link for any book. Then, press **Create New**.

5. Enter some review details and click **Create**:

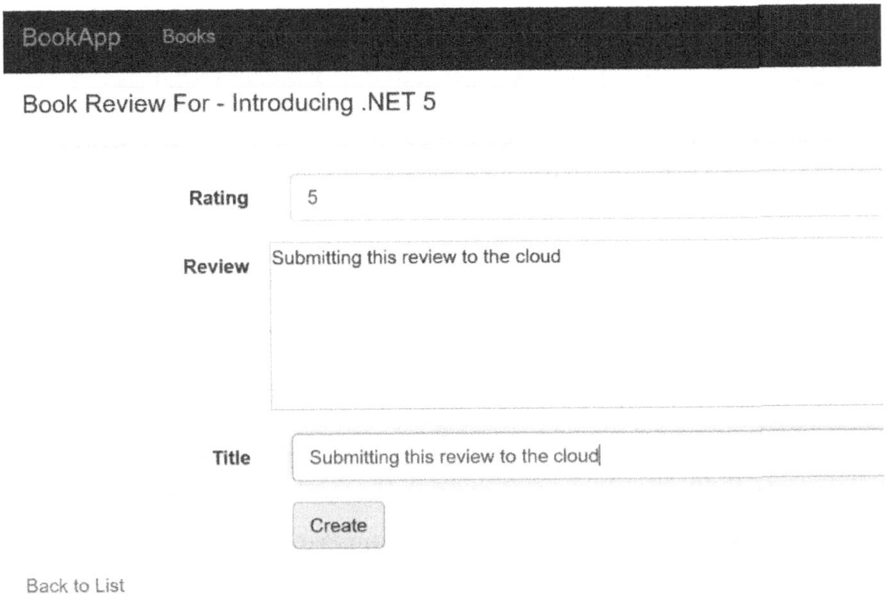

BookApp   Books

Book Review For - Introducing .NET 5

Rating   5

Review   Submitting this review to the cloud

Title   Submitting this review to the cloud

Create

Back to List

Figure 6.4 – Creating a book review in BookApp

6. Verify that the new review has been saved to the cloud by following the steps provided in *Verifying the migration's success* section.

Congratulations! You have now learned how to migrate an on-premises database to the cloud as an Azure SQL Database. However, this is only one of the 600+ services that Azure Services offers. In the next section, we will learn how to migrate a web application to the Azure App Service platform, which can greatly simplify the operational management that's required for the application.

Deploying .NET 5 applications on Azure App Service

To run a web application successfully in a production environment, just writing the application code is not enough. There are a number of operational concerns such as hosting, monitoring, scaling, tracing, and so on that need to be addressed. Azure App Service offers to take care of all these operational concerns so that developers can focus on writing the application-specific code.

App Service is not the only option you can use to host application code in Azure. Let's understand the circumstances in which deploying an application to App Service is ideal (or not ideal).

When should I use Azure App Service?

Azure App Service is a great deployment option in the following scenarios:

- When you do not want to be concerned with OS and web server patching, monitoring, and load balancing. App Service provides built-in support for all of these features.

- If your on-premises app is already being hosted on IIS or Kestrel on Windows and it doesn't have lots of dependencies on OS-specific features, chances are that it could run on App Service with minimal or no changes. Linux-based applications on .NET Core, Node.js, Java, and so on would work fine too.

- If your application scaling requirements change dynamically, for example, based on season or time of the day, Azure App Service can automatically scale the allocated resources up or down, which can significantly save operational costs.

In summary, .NET applications typically require minimal changes and gains lots of operational benefits when deployed on Azure App Service. Now, we'll look at the features of alternative application hosting services on the Azure platform.

Alternatives to Azure App Service

There are also some use cases when using a different Azure service for application hosting could be more suitable. Here are some examples of such cases:

- For an application that doesn't need to run 24/7 and is primarily schedule- or event-driven, **Azure Functions** is an excellent choice, and it is a significantly cheaper option to run on a consumption plan.

- **Azure Container Instance (ACI)** allows us to bundle an application, along with its dependencies, into a single container. This could be beneficial for deploying Python or Node.js applications, along with all its dependent packages, or .NET applications with Windows OS-specific features that are not supported on Azure App Service.

- **Azure Kubernetes Service (AKS)** is ideal for running N-tier- or microservices-based applications as it provides greater control over the life cycle of each microservice. It also allows superior control over the deployment and placement of related services on the same nodes for better latency.

For our monolithic BookApp application, Azure App Service is a perfect choice. Now, we will deploy the `BookApp.Web` application to Azure App Service.

Deploying BookApp.Web to Azure App Service

The BookApp database has already been deployed as a Azure SQL database. We will now go through the steps of deploying the `BookApp.Web` ASP.NET Core application.

All the Azure CLI commands that will be used in this exercise can be copied from the sample code folder; that is, `code\Chapter06\cli scripts\ Azure App service scripts.txt`.

Creating the App Service plan and web application

An App Service plan is a container that can host one or more web applications. All the web applications under the same App Service plan share the physical resources that have been allocated to that plan.

Follow these steps to create the App Service plan:

1. Launch Azure Cloud Shell by going to `https://shell.Azure.com/`.

2. The App Service plan is an abstraction that's used to manage all the resources that are required to run the web application.

3. Execute the following code from the cloud shell:

```
resourceGroupName=bookAppResourceGroup
location=australiaeast
appServicePlanName=bookAppServicePlan
az appservice plan create --name $appServicePlanName
--resource-group $resourceGroupName --sku F1
```

In the first two lines, we are using same the resource group and location that we did while creating the Azure SQL database in the previous section. In the third line, we defined the App Service plan's name, while in last line, we created the App Service plan using a Free tier plan.

Now that we've successfully created the App Service plan, the cloud shell will show the newly created App Service plan's properties, as shown in the following screenshot:

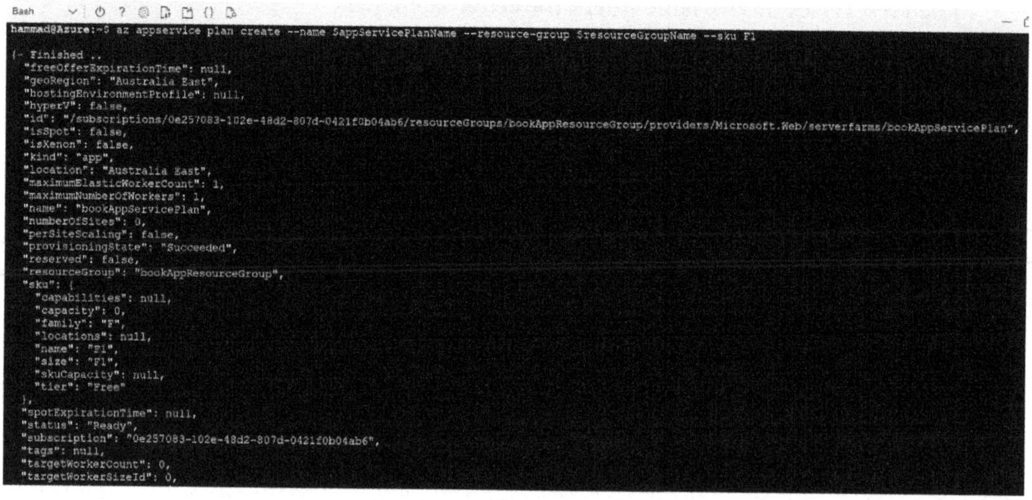

Figure 6.5 – App Service plan properties in cloud shell

4. Create the web application using the following commands:

```
webappName=bookApp2020
az webapp create --resource-group $resourceGroupName
--plan $appServicePlanName --name $webappName
```

Note that the web application's name must be unique across the entire Azure portal. If you receive a message stating that the application already exists, then try adding some unique bits to the webappName variable (for example, bookApp2020_v2).

Installing the .NET 5 runtime

At the time of writing this book, Azure App Services does not have the .NET 5 runtime installed by default. It might take a few weeks or months for the Azure platform to support this after the official release of .NET 5, so we'll install it manually:

1. Run the following command from cloud shell to see a list of available runtimes:

    ```
    az webapp list-runtimes
    ```

    If the returned list contains **DOTNETCORE|5.0** or **DOTNET|5.0**, then skip *step 2* and go directly to next section, *Publishing the BookApp application*. Otherwise, follow the next step to manually install the .NET 5 runtime.

2. Execute the following command to install the ASP.NET Core 5 runtime, which is needed to run our .NET 5 web application:

    ```
    az resource create --resource-group $resourceGroupName
    --resource-type 'Microsoft.Web/sites/siteextensions'
    --name $webappName'/siteextensions/AspNand so
    onoreRuntime.5.0.x86'  --properties '{}'
    ```

    The preceding command will install the ASP.NET Core 5 runtime on the BookApp2020 web application we created previously.

Alternatively, we can skip this step and bundle the ASP.NET Core 5 runtime along with our application when we publish the app. This option will be explained when we publish the application. However, it is better to install the runtime now as bundling will increase the time it takes to publish the application.

Publishing the BookApp application

Now, we will publish the application code to the newly created web application:

1. Log into the Azure portal by going to `https://portal.Azure.com/`.

2. Go to **App Services** and click **BookApp2020**.

3. Click **Get Publish Profile**. This will download the published profile, which will be called `bookApp2020.PublishSettings` on your local computer. We will use this file to deploy the application from Visual Studio.

If you would prefer to download the publish profile via cloud shell instead, you can run the following CLI command:

```
az webapp deployment list-publishing-profiles --name
$webappName --resource-group $resourceGroupName --xml
--output tsv
```

The preceding command will generate the publish profile's contents, which you can then save as a file named bookApp2020.PublishSettings on your local computer.

4. Launch Visual Studio 2019 and open BookApp.sln by going to \code\ Chapter06\onprem\BookApp.

5. In the **Solution Explorer** window, right-click BookApp.Web and click **Publish**.

6. On the **Publish** screen, click **Start** to start the Wizard, then choose **Import Profile** to import the profile.

7. Click **Next**, then browse to the publish profile we downloaded in *Step 8*.

8. Optional: If you did not install the ASP.NET Core 5 runtime in *Step 5*, you can choose to bundle the framework along with the application by changing the deployment mode from **Framework-Dependent** to **Self-Contained**. This will deploy the .NET 5 framework to the web application.

9. Click **Publish**. The application should be published in a few minutes. Once you've done this, the output window should contain the following message:

```
Web App was published successfully
```

10. Browse the newly published web application in your browser by going to http://bookapp2020.Azurewebsites.net. It should work as expected.

Yay! With that, we have a fully functional web application running in the cloud without the overhead of us having to manage a web server or database server ourselves. In the next section, we will briefly discuss some of the best practices for deploying applications to Azure App Service.

Best practices for deploying applications to Azure App Service

For a production-grade application, there are some best practices that should be followed if we wish to deploy and run Azure App Service. We did not follow these practices in the preceding exercise to keep this chapter and book's size manageable. However, these are worth mentioning as these concepts can be applied to most cloud-native application platform services, such as Azure Functions and ACIs.

Let's briefly review these practices from a cloud-native application architecture perspective.

Managing secrets and configuration

Secrets such as passwords, connection strings, and authentication keys should never be stored in the source control. Ideally, the non-secret application configuration should also be stored in a different configuration management tool.

Use the following resources to learn more about Azure services that can help you manage secrets and configuration:

- Azure App Service settings features: `https://docs.microsoft.com/en-us/Azure/app-service/configure-common`.

- Azure Key Vault: `https://docs.microsoft.com/en-us/Azure/key-vault/`.

- Azure App Configuration Service: `https://docs.microsoft.com/en-us/Azure/Azure-app-configuration/overview`.

There are a number of advantages when it comes to separating the configuration from the application code in a cloud-native architecture. The configuration can be updated with zero downtime and can be injected from sources such as a **Continuous Integration/ Continuous Deployment (CI/CD)** process. Having a CI/CD process is the next best practice that we are going to discuss.

Continuous Integration and Deployment

We have used Azure Cloud Shell as our primary tool for deployment in this chapter. This method is superior to UI-based deployment because CLI commands are the same on most environments and can easily be stored in source control for future reference.

An even better approach is to have a formal pipeline that can build the code, perform automated tests on it, get approvals from stakeholders if needed, and deploy the code on dev, test, and production environments.

It will take longer to set the pipelines up for the first time, but the ongoing deployments will become a matter or pressing just a few buttons.

To read more about the continuous deployment options available in Azure, please refer to this article: `https://Azure.microsoft.com/en-au/solutions/architecture/Azure-devops-continuous-integration-and-continuous-deployment-for-Azure-web-apps/`.

A good CI/CD process significantly reduces deployment complexity. In the next section, we'll review what we can do to reduce this service provisioning complexity by defining Infrastructure as Code.

Infrastructure as Code

Just like the deployment process, the infrastructure provisioning process, such as creating an App Service plan and a web app, should also be specified as code to make it repeatable, trackable, and scalable. A consistent environment provisioning process will eliminate many issues that arise due to environment differences.

Using the Azure CLI is a good starting point to ensure you have repeatable provisioning instructions. At an advanced level, **Azure Resource Manager** (**ARM**) templates a full-featured infrastructure provisioning services you can use.

You can read more about implementing the Infrastructure as Code practice on Azure at `https://docs.microsoft.com/en-us/dotnet/architecture/cloud-native/infrastructure-as-code`.

As exciting as it was to have our web application running on the cloud, it is now time to explore another modern option we can use to run our code in the cloud in serverless mode.

Serverless deployment – Azure Functions

Azure Functions is a serverless offering from Azure. This does not mean that there is no server running the code. What this means is that the concept of the underlying server is completely abstracted away from the application developer. The code might run on Server A on the first request, Server B the second time, and on both of them when there is enough request load.

There are tremendous benefits to this approach, some of which are listed in the next section.

Benefits of using Azure Functions

Azure Functions could be a good choice in the following scenarios:

- By default, Azure Functions run on a consumption plan. Hence, you only pay for the time when the request is actually executed. If your application mostly remains idle, you'd be paying a small fraction of the cost compared to Azure App Service.

- Azure Functions has built-in support that can be triggered in response to events such as when a new message arrives at the Service Bus. This makes it an ideal choice for event-driven architectures. It can also be triggered on schedule or on an ad-hoc basis via HTTP requests.

- For simpler microservices-based architectures, Azure Functions is a suitable alternative to Kubernetes-based solutions. Each function app can act as a microservice that's responsible for a specific domain-based task.

- Azure Functions has superior scalability features. A function can be called from a few dozen times to a few million times in a day without any adjustment from the operational team. Azure Functions' infrastructure will automatically take care of scaling in most cases.

> **Serverless architecture**
>
> Azure Functions is an implementation of the serverless architecture. To read more about serverless architecture, refer to the *Serverless architecture* section of *Chapter 3, Design and Architectural Patterns*.

That's enough theory about Azure Functions. Now, let's learn more about it by covering a practical example of developing an Azure Function for sentiment analysis.

Developing a function app project

In this example, we will develop an Azure Function that will take a book review as its input text and analyze the sentiment of the review as positive, neutral, or negative. Follow these steps to develop this function:

1. Copy `BookApp.SentimentAnalysisFunction` from the final project folder to the working folder.

2. Launch Visual Studio 2019 and open the BookApp solution from the working folder.

3. In **Solution Explorer**, right-click the BookApp solution and then, from the context menu, choose **Add | Existing Project**.

4. Add the `BookApp.SentimentAnalysisFunction.csproj` file from the folder we copied in *step 1*. This should add the project to the solution.

There are a number of code items that are worth explaining in this project, all of which we will cover in the next section.

Specifying an Azure Functions runtime

If you look at the `BookApp.SentimentAnalysisFunction.csproj` file, you'll notice that the target framework is .NET Core 3.1 with Azure Function runtime version 3:

```
<TargetFramework>
netcoreapp3.1</TargetFramework>
<AzureFunctionsVersion>v3</AzureFunctionsVersion>
```

Azure Function runtimes typically get upgraded a few months after a new .NET version is released. At the time of writing, the latest runtime version is version 3, which supports .NET Core 3.1.

Dependency injection in Azure Functions

When you create an Azure Function project from one of the default templates provided by Visual Studio, the generated code doesn't create any placeholder code for setting up **dependency injection** (**DI**). However, it is completely possible to use all .NET DI practices that you typically use in ASP.NET Core applications. In fact, the code that's use to set up DI is almost identical to ASP.NET Core web applications. Here is what I have done to set up DI:

1. First, I added the reference to the `Microsoft.Azure.Functions.Extensions` NuGet file in the project file:

```
<PackageReference Include="Microsoft.Azure.Functions.
Extensions" Version="1.1.0" />
```

2. Then, I added the `Startup.cs` file, which does a couple of things differently compared to the ASP.NET Core web application; that is, the `Startup` class inherits from `FunctionsStartup` and a `FunctionsStartup` attribute has been added to the namespace. This ensures that when this assembly executes, the `Startup` class is called to register services.

3. The actual DI code is in the `Configure()` method:

```
public override void Configure(IFunctionsHostBuilder
builder)
{
    builder.Services.AddSingleton
    <ISentimentAnaysisService,
    SentimentAnaysisService>();
}
```

We are only using one service class to perform sentiment analysis, so the registration code is quite simple. If your function app has a large number of dependencies, then the dependency setup code can grow here accordingly.

Core function logic – Sentiment Analysis Services

The core sentiment analysis logic is in the `SentimentAnaysisService` class. The algorithm does the following:

- Breaks down the text into individual words.
- Counts the number of positive words in the text from a pre-defined list of positive words (for example, good, happy, ideal, and so on).
- Counts the number of negative words in the text from a pre-defined list of negative words (for example, disappointing, wrong, fails, and so on).
- If there are more positive words than negative words, then it returns a positive sentiment, while if there are more negative words, then it returns a negative sentiment. If both are equal, then a neutral sentiment is returned.

> **Using machine learning for sentiment analysis**
>
> As you can guess, the preceding approach to determine sentiment from a piece of text is quite simplistic and not very accurate. In the next chapter, we will learn how to use the **ML.NET** library, which can use more sophisticated machine learning models to predict and learn the sentiment from text.

Function entry point

A function entry point is specified using the `FunctionName` attribute. This is specified on the `Run()` method in the `SentimentFunction` class. You can see that this class is receiving `ISentimentAnaysisService` as one of its dependencies.

Defining a function trigger

This GetSentiment function is intended to be executed as an **HttpTrigger**; that is, the consuming code will make an HTTP request to execute the function. This is specified using the HttpTrigger attribute on the HttpRequest parameter in the function signature.

The req parameter, which is of the HttpRequest type, will contain all the request context data (for example, Headers, Cookies, Query String parameters, and so on).

An Azure Function can also trigger on a pre-defined schedule or from other events; for example, when a new item is added to a Service Bus. To read about all the triggers that are supported, please refer to the following Microsoft article: https://docs.microsoft.com/en-us/Azure/Azure-functions/functions-triggers-bindings?tabs=csharp.

Using a request body versus a query string as input

To receive text as input, our function must check the query string parameter and then request body as a fallback:

```
string text = req.Query["text"];
string requestBody = await new StreamReader(req.Body).
ReadToEndAsync();
dynamic data = JsonConvert.DeserializeObject(requestBody);
text = text ?? data?.text;
```

The request body is more flexible and can receive complex and large input types. I have left the query string option in the code as well as this makes it a bit easier to test the function from a browser. To pass the request body, we can use a tool such as Postman, which helps us test HTTP trigger-based Azure Functions.

Now that we have understood the function code, let's run the function locally and see how it performs.

Testing the Azure Function locally

An HTTP trigger-based Azure Function can be tested locally by running the function from Visual Studio and then triggering the function from the browser. Follow these steps to test the function:

1. Run the `BookApp.SentimentAnalysisFunction` project from Visual Studio. If this is the first time you are executing any Azure Function on your machine, then Visual Studio might take some time to download and configure the Azure Functions runtime.

2. To test the function, open your browser and enter the following URL: `http://localhost:7071/api/GetSentiment?text=i feel good and happy about it`.

   This should display **1**, indicating positive sentiment in the browser window.

3. To test whether negative sentiments are detected, change the value of the text parameter with a negative sentence and try it in your browser. The following is an example URL: `http://localhost:7071/api/GetSentiment?text=i feel bad and unhappy about it`.

   This should return **-1** as a result, indicating a negative sentiment in the text.

The function is now good to be deployed on Azure. In the next section, we will push this function to the cloud.

Deploying the sentiment analysis function

A function that's been deployed to Azure is hosted under a function app. In this section, we will create a storage account and the function app for the function to be deployed. The commands we'll be using in this exercise can be copied from `code\Chapter06\cli scripts\Azure Functions scripts.txt`.

Creating a storage account

A storage account is needed for a function for storing its function keys, files, and binding information. We can create a storage account using the following CLI script from Azure Cloud Shell:

```
resourcegroupname=bookAppResourceGroup
locationname=australiaeast
storageaccountname=bookappstorageaccount
az storage account create -n $storageaccountname -g
$resourcegroupname -l $locationname --sku Standard_LRS
```

Remember to use same resource group name and location name that you used while creating the Azure SQL Database in the *Creating an Azure SQL database* section.

Creating a function app

We will create the function app on a consumption plan that grants us about 1 million free function executions per month.

Execute the following CLI commands to create the function app:

```
functionappname=sentimentanalysis2020
az functionapp create --consumption-plan-location $locationname
--name $functionappname --os-type Windows --resource-
group $resourcegroupname --runtime dotnet --storage-account
$storageaccountname --functions-version 3
```

Just like Azure App Service, the function app's name must also be unique within the Azure portal. So, you might have to change the `functionappname` variable value so that a unique name is appended to it.

Publishing the function app project

The publishing process is very similar to what we did when we published `BookApp.Web` to Azure App Service. Follow these steps:

1. Browse the Azure portal by going to `https://portal.Azure.com/`.

2. Go to **App Services** and click on the **sentimentanalysis2020** function app.

3. On the overview page, click **Get Publish Profile**. This will download the **sentimentanalysis2020.PublishSettings** publish profile onto your local computer. We will use this file to deploy the application from Visual Studio.

4. In Visual Studio's **Solution Explorer** window, right-click `BookApp.`
    `SentimentAnalysisFunction` and click **Publish**.

5. On the **Publish** screen, import the profile and then click **Publish**. The application
    should be published in a few minutes.

6. Browse the newly published function app in the browser by going to
    `https://sentimentanalysis2020.Azurewebsites.net`. This should
    show the default home screen:

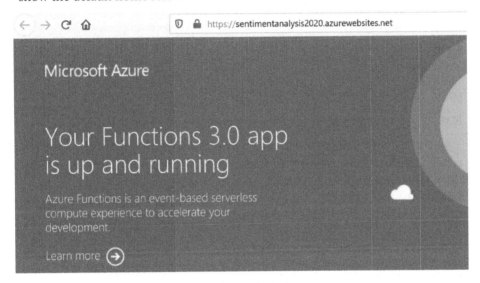

Figure 6.6 – Azure Function App default home page

This is the default home screen for the function app. We will test its functionality in the
next section.

Testing the Azure Function we deployed in the cloud

By default, Azure functions are protected by an authentication key. So, we can't test the
function in the browser without knowing the authentication key. Azure generates the
default key when the function is deployed. It is possible to reset the key or create a new
one. For our testing purposes, it is fine to use the default one created by Azure. Follow
these steps:

1. To retrieve the authentication key, execute the following CLI commands:

```
functionname=GetSentiment
az functionapp function keys list -g $resourcegroupname
-n $functionappname --function-name $functionname
```

The `functionapp function keys list` command lists all the keys associated with the function. You should see an output similar to the following:

```
hammad@Azure:~$ az functionapp function keys list -g $resourcegroupname -n $functionappname --function-name $functionname
{
  "default": "1jCLHNSdZCTT2sXxB5XyJhScfObpnY1BdApeAsOnNrdRXMzZFPvzuQ==",
  "id": null,
  "kind": null,
  "name": null,
  "properties": null,
  "type": null
}
```

Figure 6.7 – Retrieving Azure Function keys using the CLI

2. Copy the value of the default key, as shown in the preceding screenshot.

3. Craft the URL to test the function in a browser. The URL will take two query string parameters:

   code: This is the authentication key value we copied previously.

   text: This is the text parameter we want to use to gauge the sentiment.

   Make sure you replace the values of code that were copied previously. If you created the function app with a different name, you'll need to change the application name (`sentimentanalysis2020`) in the URL as well:

   `https://sentimentanalysis2020.Azurewebsites.net/api/GetS entiment?code=1jCLHNSdZCTT2sXxB5XyJhScfObpnY1BdApeAs-OnNrdRXMzZFPvzuQ==&text=i%20am%20happy.`

   You should get a value of **1** as a response to this URL in the browser.

The function app is working as expected. We will now learn how to integrate this function from our main web application; that is, BookApp.

Integrating the Azure function with BookApp

We want to provide the sentiment analysis functionality on the review creation and editing pages. We want to display the detected feedback on the review as soon as user types it in.

For this purpose, we'll use jQuery to send the review text to the backend controller action as soon as the review text changes. Then, the text will be sent to the sentiment analysis function app and the results from it will be passed back to the view.

In the view, we'll use jQuery to format the result in red, amber, or green, depending on the sentiment of the text, which could be negative, neutral, or positive, respectively. Follow these steps:

> **Consuming Azure functions from the client side**
>
> You might be wondering why we can't call the Azure Function directly using jQuery without using an ASP.NET controller action as an intermediary. This is technically possible, but it is a poor idea to consume an Azure Function directly from the client-side JavaScript. This is because this will expose the authentication key to the end user, who could then consume and misuse the function without your knowledge. Any code that requires secrets to be used, such as an authentication key, should always be consumed from the backend.

1. Add the following section at the end of the `appsettings.json` file. You can also copy this from the file with same name from the final solution folder:

```
"SentimentAnalysisService": {
    "URL": "https://sentimentanalysis2020.Azurewebsites.
net/api/GetSentiment",
    "Code": "1jCLHNSdZCTT2sXxB5XyJhScfObpnY1BdApeAs0nNr
    dRXMzZFPvzuQ=="
}
```

These settings will be utilized by the controller action method, which we'll create shortly. Change the value of `Code` as per your function app key and adjust `URL` if needed.

2. Add the following lines at the end of the `ConfigureServices` function in the `Startup.cs` file:

```
var sentimentAnalysisServiceSettings = new
SentimentAnalysisServiceSettings();
        Configuration.
GetSection("SentimentAnalysisService").
Bind(sentimentAnalysisServiceSettings);
        services.
AddSingleton(sentimentAnalysisServiceSettings);
```

This code snippet ensures that the `sentimentAnalysisServiceSettings` object from the `appsettings` file can be injected into any service that needs it.

3. Overwrite the `BookReviewsController.cs` class using the file with the same name from final the solution folder.

The key change here is that we have added the `GetSentiment` action to the controller class, as shown in the following code:

```
[HttpGet]
[Route("GetSentiment")]
public async Task<int> GetSentiment(string text)
{
    HttpClient _client = new HttpClient();
    HttpRequestMessage sentimentRequest = new
    HttpRequestMessage(HttpMethod.Get,
    $"{sentimentAnalysisServiceSettings.URL}
    ?Code={sentimentAnalysisServiceSettings.Code}
    &text={text}");
    HttpResponseMessage response = await
    _client.SendAsync(sentimentRequest);

    var resultString = await
    response.Content.ReadAsStringAsync();
    return Convert.ToInt32(resultString);
}
```

This method receives text as input. It then calls the sentiment analysis Azure Function using the service settings we configured in the `appsettings` file. The result is then sent back to the calling view, which we will configure in the next step.

4. Copy a partial view file named `_GetSentiment.cshtml` from the final solution folder to the `BookApp.Web.V2\Views\BookReviews` folder in the current solution.

This partial view file is responsible for calling the backend controller action named `GetSentiment` that we created in the previous step.

The view file also contains the jQuery code to color-code the result of the function as red, amber, or green.

We are using the `debounce` function from a well-known JavaScript library named `underscore.js`. This function allows us to throttle the consecutive calls of the function since we want to update the result on every keystroke when the user is writing a book review. It could end up calling the Azure Function several times in quick succession, which is not efficient.

The following code ensures that if there are multiple calls to the `getReviewSentiment()` function within a time span of 300 milliseconds, it gets called only once:

```
_.debounce(getReviewSentiment, 300);
```

So, if a user is typing the book review too fast, we'll keep rechecking the sentiment of the text every 300 milliseconds or so.

5. In the `Views/BookReviews` folder, replace the `create.cshtml` and `edit.cshtml` files with the files in the final solution folder.

In the new files, the following line has been added to reference the partial view we created in the previous step:

```
<partial name="_GetSentiment" />
```

In addition, the review edit control is now bound to the `getReviewSentimentDebounced` method on every keystroke that's pressed by the end user:

```
@Html.TextAreaFor(model => model.Review, 5, 100,
htmlAttributes: new { @class = "form-control", @onkeyup =
"getReviewSentimentDebounced();" })
```

Lastly, a row has been added to the display sentiment analysis result right after the review editor control:

```
<div class="form-group">
    <span class="col-md-9"></span>
    <span>Review Sentiment: </span>
    <span id="reviewSentiment"></span>
</div>
```

The text inside the `reviewSentiment` span segment will be populated by the jQuery code in the partial view that we created in the previous step.

This is all we needed to do to integrate the sentiment analysis function app from BookApp. Let's test it to see the sentiment analysis functionality in action.

Testing the integrated application

Now, it's time to test if the integrated code is working correctly. Follow these steps:

1. Run the BookApp application locally.

2. Click the **Books** link in the top navigation menu.

3. Click the **Reviews** link for any book.

4. Click **Create New** to create the review.

5. When the review field is empty, you should see that the value of **Review Sentiment** is **Neutral**:

Book Review For - Introducing .NET 5

Rating	
Review	
	Review Sentiment: Neutral
Title	
	Create

Figure 6.8 – Neutral sentiment for an empty review

6. Try entering positive and negative words in the review. You should see that the review sentiment is updated accordingly:

Book Review For - Introducing .NET 5

Rating	
Review	Wow. I like the book as ample code examples have been provided
	Review Sentiment: Positive

Figure 6.9 – Positive sentiment for a positive review

7. There is no need to save the review as we always do sentiment analysis on the fly. You can test this by editing any of the existing reviews.

Hooray! We are now able to use an Azure Function directly from our ASP.NET Core web application. We will now redeploy the BookApp web application so that recent changes can be published to the Azure cloud.

Publishing the integrated application

In the last step of this section, we will update the BookApp web application with the latest changes. You published this app when you completed the exercise in the *Deploying BookApp.Web to Azure App Service* section. The republishing steps are quite simple.

Visual Studio has already stored the publish profile for Azure App Service. Just right-click the `BookApp.Web` project and click **Publish** from the context menu.

On the publish dialog, click **Publish** again and you are done.

Before we conclude chapter, there is one more option we can use to host our applications in the cloud; that is, containers. We'll quickly explore this option and then summarize what we've learned.

Deploying .NET 5 applications to containers

Azure App Service and Azure Functions are both great options when we purely want to focus on application logic and don't want to worry about the OS, web server, patching, and so on. Sometimes, we do need some control over these parts of the infrastructure. Some example requirements are as follows:

- We might want a .NET Framework assembly deployed to the **Global Assembly Cache (GAC)**. This is not allowed in Azure App Service.
- We might want to run the application on a specific flavor of Linux.
- We might want to deploy related microservices on the same physical node to reduce latency.
- We might to control the life cycle of multiple microservices as a single unit for ease of management.

For all of these scenarios, running applications on containers could address these requirements. Let's briefly talk about two widely used container orchestration options for Azure.

Azure Container Instances

Azure has a number of offerings we can use to run applications on containers. The simplest of these services is called **Azure Container Instances (ACI)**. Without worrying about the underlying server, we can define application dependencies in one or more containers and then host them using ACI. We only pay for the time when the containers are running, so this could be quite a cheap option compared to other container orchestration options.

Azure Kubernetes Services

Azure Kubernetes Service (AKS) is a hosted Kubernetes service that is suitable for microservices architecture-based cloud-native applications where a number of services need to be configured and run together for an end-to-end solution.

AKS provides significant control over how services are created and deployed, as well as options for fine-tuning service connectivity, scaling, upgrading, and rollout. As a consequence, there is a learning curve involved in running production-grade applications on AKS.

In the rest of this section, we'll focus on understanding the deployment process for ACI.

Deploying a BookApp web application to ACI

In this exercise, we will configure the BookApp web application so that it runs on a container. Then, we will host the container on the ACI service to see it in action. The dependent services – that is, the BookApp database and the sentiment analysis function – will continue to run as an Azure SQL database and an Azure Function, respectively.

Adding container support to BookApp.Web

In this part of this exercise, we'll configure the BookApp.Web project so that it runs on a Docker container. As we mentioned in the *Technical requirements* section, you must have Docker Desktop installed and, preferably, the WSL 2 feature enabled on your Windows 10 computer. Follow these steps:

1. Right-click the BookApp.Web project and choose **Add -> Container Orchestrator Support** from the context menu.

2. In the **Add Contrainer Orchestrator Support** dialog, choose `Docker Compose` as your orchestrator.

3. Choose `Linux` as your **Target OS** and then click **OK**.

   This operation will create a Dockerfile in your project, as well as a `docker-compose.yml` file under the `docker-compose` folder.

   This Dockerfile contains instructions for building the container with `mcr.microsoft.com/dotnet/aspnet:5.0-buster-slim` as a base image so that we know that .NET 5 SDK is being used to build and run the app.

   The `docker-compose.yml` file is useful for scenarios where we have multiple containers that need to interact with each other. In our case, there is only a single container running the web application, so just a single service definition has been included.

Running the containerized application locally

If the preceding steps were completed successfully, we should be able to run the application locally on a docker container. Let's test this to see if that is the case:

1. On the standard toolbar, choose **Docker Compose** as your preferred Debug Target:

Figure 6.10 – Choosing Docker Compose as a Debug Target

2. Press *F5* to run the application. It might take some time to build the container for the first time. Once the container has been built, the application should work as expected.

   The **Logs** tab in the **Containers** window will show that the application has been started successfully.

Running the Docker container locally is half the success. Now, we just need to publish it to Azure.

Publishing a container to Azure Container Registry

Containers require a repository where the container image can be stored. We could host our container image on a public or private Docker repository. Alternatively, if we want to keep the image within the Azure cloud, Azure offers **Azure Container Registry** (**ACR**) for hosting container images. It has built-in support for authentication and replication. So, in this section, we'll publish the BookApp container to ACR.

The commands that will be used in this exercise can be copied from code\Chapter06\ cli scripts\azure container instance scripts.txt. Follow these steps to publish the container:

1. Create a container registry instance by executing the following command in Azure Cloud Shell:

```
resourcegroupname=bookAppResourceGroup
containerRegisteryName=bookapp2020
az acr create --resource-group $resourcegroupname --name
$containerRegisteryName --sku Basic
```

Like other resources in Azure, you might have to come up with a unique `containerRegisteryName`. Keep it all lowercase as some subsequent commands will fail if we use a capital letter in the container registry name.

2. In Visual Studio, right-click the `BookApp.Web` project and click **Publish**.

3. Choose **New** on the publish dialog to create a new publish profile.

4. Choose **Docker Container Registry** as the publish target.

5. Choose **Azure Container Registry** as the specific target.

6. On the **Select existing or create a new Azure Container Registry** screen, choose the container registry we created in *step 1* (that is, `bookapp2020`) under the `bookAppResourceGroup` resource group.

7. Click **Finish** and then **Publish** to publish the container.

    Visual Studio will publish the container to the registry using the Docker CLI tool.

The container image is now stored in the ACR. The next step is to create a container instance that will run the BookApp web application.

Creating and testing our Azure Container Instance application

This is the last part of this exercise. In this section, we'll create an instance of the container that Azure will automatically execute and host on a public IP so that we can use the web application. Let's do this:

1. To perform operations against the newly created container registry, we need to authenticate with an access token. You can retrieve an access token by executing the following CLI command:

    ```
    az acr login --name $containerRegisteryName --expose-
    token
    ```

    Copy the value of `accessToken` from the response of the preceding command.

2. From cloud shell, execute the following commands:

    ```
    containerName=bookapp2020
    az container create --name $containerName --resource-
    group $resourcegroupname --os-type linux --image
    bookapp2020.Azurecr.io/bookappweb --ip-address public
    ```

3. When you're asked for a username, enter an empty GUID; that is, `00000000-0000-0000-0000-000000000000`.

4. When you're asked for a password, enter the access token we copied in *Step 2*.

5. After a few minutes, you should receive a success message. Copy the `ipAddress` value as we'll need this to test the app in the next section:

```
"ipAddress": {
  "dnsNameLabel": null,
  "fqdn": null,
  "ip": "20.53.140.152",
  "ports": [
    {
      "port": 80,
      "protocol": "TCP"
    }
  ],
  "type": "Public"
},
"location": "australiaeast",
"name": "bookapp2020",
"networkProfile": null,
"osType": "Linux",
"provisioningState": "Succeeded",
"resourceGroup": "bookAppResourceGroup",
"restartPolicy": "Always",
"tags": {},
"type": "Microsoft.ContainerInstance/containerGroups",
"volumes": null
}
```

Figure 6.11 – Copying the IP value from the container creation message

6. In a new browser window, type in the container instance's application URL. The URL will start with `http://`, followed by the IP address we copied in previously; for example, `http://20.53.140.152`.

7. You should see the BookApp application's home page.

This was a basic walkthrough of deploying a web application as a container instance to Azure. For more complex applications with multiple microservices, please explore AKS. You can read more about it at `https://docs.microsoft.com/en-us/azure/aks/intro-kubernetes`.

Cleaning up resources

We have created a number of publicly available resources in Azure while completing hands-on exercises in this chapter. Now, we need to delete these resources. Fortunately, it is very simple to delete a related group of resources since we have created all the resources under the same resource group. Follow these steps to delete all the resources we created in this chapter:

1. Log into Azure Cloud Shell by logging into https://shell.azure.com/ using the Microsoft account you created for this chapter.

2. Execute the following code from cloud shell:

```
resourcegroupname=bookAppResourceGroup
az group delete --name $resourcegroupname
```

Just like the other scripts in this chapter, your might have to change the value of the resourcegroupname variable if you chose a different resource group name for the other exercises.

Summary

In this chapter, we discussed the strategies we can use to transform legacy applications into cloud-optimized or cloud-native architectures. We then explored some of the most commonly used Azure services, such as Azure SQL Database, Azure App Service, Azure Functions, and Azure Container Instances.

All modern applications strive to follow cloud-native application principles, which include defining infrastructure dependencies as a code, keeping the configuration separate from the code, building an application for scale, designing the application components as microservices, and using CI/CD.

Azure services help us achieve these principles. We learned that web applications and database servers can be provisioned in a few minutes in the cloud. This is in stark contrast to traditional IT environments in large organizations where similar resources could take several weeks to be made available.

In the next chapter, we'll learn about an exciting new .NET library named ML.NET, which opens the door for .NET developers to incorporate machine learning services in their client-facing and backend .NET 5 applications.

Section 4: Bonus

Among the cadre of .NET 5 technologies, **ML.NET** is an exciting library by Microsoft that enables the development of machine learning services in .NET code. The last section introduces ML.NET to .NET developers. It shows how to integrate machine learning workflows and services into .NET 5 applications. It discusses typical uses of machine learning scenarios for application developers and then provides hand-on exercises to develop example machine learning services using ML.NET in .NET 5 applications.

The final exercise shows how to deploy a machine learning service as a serverless function in the cloud that enables machine learning features to be consumed from web, desktop, and mobile applications.

This section comprises the following chapters:

- *Chapter 7, Integrating Machine Learning in .NET 5 Code*

7
Integrating Machine Learning in .NET 5

Developing **machine learning (ML)** solutions is a highly sought-after skill. But it is not limited to data scientists only. Traditional .NET application developers are increasingly being asked to integrate ML algorithms into their client-facing apps. ML.NET makes it very easy for .NET developers to leverage the power of ML in .NET applications, without going through the learning curve of another language such as Python or R.

This chapter is all about the ML.NET API to give you a taste of how to use ML in .NET. In this chapter, we will familiarize ourselves with the ML concepts and how ML.NET can help us build ML models and services, and then consume these from traditional .NET web and desktop projects. Finally, this chapter will point you to additional resources, should you be interested in building more advanced machine learning-based solutions on the .NET platform.

We will cover the following topics in this chapter:

- Machine learning explained for .NET developers

- Building an ML.NET-based service to predict the shopping score

- Building Azure Functions using ML.NET models

First, let's review the technical requirements that we'll need to complete the exercises in this chapter.

Technical requirements

You will need the following software installed to work with the exercises presented in this chapter:

- Visual Studio 2019 16.8 or higher (any edition is fine). This is needed to work with the sample .NET 5 applications that are included with this chapter's code.

- The .NET 5 SDK, which can be downloaded from here: `https://dotnet.microsoft.com/download/dotnet/5.0`.

- ML.NET Model Builder is a Visual Studio extension. The instructions for installing and enabling this extension are provided in the *Enabling ML.NET Model Builder* section.

- A Microsoft Azure Subscription is an optional requirement, and only needed if you are planning to deploy the Azure function-based service we will develop in this chapter to the Azure cloud. A free account is sufficient for this purpose and you can create one at `https://azure.microsoft.com/en-au/free/`.

> **Note**
>
> It is helpful but not mandatory to complete the exercises provided in *Chapter 6, Upgrading On-Premises Applications to the Cloud with .NET 5*. We will improve upon an Azure function that we developed in that chapter and integrate it with ML.NET. The ML.NET work is fairly independent of the context of the previous chapter, so you should still be able to grasp the concepts and complete the exercises in this chapter if you haven't been through the aforementioned chapter yet.

The sample code for this chapter can be downloaded from `https://github.com/PacktPublishing/Adopting-.NET-5--Architecture-Migration-Best-Practices-and-New-Features/tree/master/Chapter07`.

There is one folder for each of the two exercises, and a third folder for the datasets. The instructions for using the code files and datasets are provided in the relevant places during the exercises.

Now, we will go through some fundamental concepts we need to understand in order to work with the machine learning-based solutions available in .NET.

Machine learning explained for .NET developers

If you are new to the ML world, you are the intended audience of this section. As developers, we are usually keen to learn by completing a practical exercise. The machine learning knowledge domain is significantly broad, and it would help to get a basic understanding of some of its commonly cited concepts before we start writing code. I promise to keep it brief and relevant to the exercises that we are going to follow later in this chapter.

Let's start by understanding the most common ML terminology.

Understanding the jargon

In the ML world, some of the terms are the same as those used in the software development world, but they have a completely different meaning. For example, did you know that models in the ML world are not the same as the C# classes that are used to define object properties? Then, there are other ML terms that would be fairly unknown to software developers. Let's take a look at some ML jargon as this will help us understand the ML.NET API documentation, and also improve our conversation quality with fellow data scientists:

- **Dataset**: A dataset is the source data provided to an ML algorithm so that it can learn the patterns in the data to make predictions about it. The data is mostly structured (such as customer shopping orders) but could also be unstructured (such as the text from novels). For production-grade applications, the datasets typically consist of millions or even billions of data points.

- **Features**: Features are one or more attributes in data that serve as input to an ML algorithm. For example, if we want to learn about customer shopping behaviors, then customer income, age, gender, products and so on could all be features of the dataset.

- **Label**: A label is the output of classification- and regression-based machine learning algorithms. We will learn about the different types of ML algorithms later in this chapter. Think of it as an attribute that we want an ML algorithm to predict about. So, if an ML algorithm says that a person is likely to spend $200 on shopping, then this value of $200 is a label for that prediction.

- **Algorithm**: A machine learning algorithm is a set of instructions and operations that run on a dataset. The algorithm tries to understand the patterns in the data and then produces a model as output.

- **Model**: A model produced by the algorithm defines the relationship between features and labels. We can use the model to build programs that can leverage the knowledge that's learned by the algorithm and stored in the model.

- **Prediction**: Once a model is ready, it contains the algorithm to produce the label from the provided input features. This process of producing an output using the model is called prediction.

You will also frequently hear about testing, training, evaluating, and retraining the models. We will cover these terminologies in a later section, where we'll describe a typical machine learning workflow.

But first, let's quickly review the types of problems ML usually addresses.

Common types of ML problems

Every coffee table discussion about the future of the human race these days inevitably leads to the role that ML will play in it. There is no shortage of predictions that says that machines will become so smart that most manual jobs will become redundant. Some even argue that machines will be able to write a book like the one you are reading right now. Are these predictions really true? We cannot prophesize the future with certainty, but a good starting point is to understand what kind of problems ML can already solve for us.

In this section, we will summarize the common problem areas where machine learning is used. When machine learning gets sufficiently advanced, we hope that it will automatically update this section with more use cases all by itself:

- **Binary classification**: In this class of problems, a machine learning model takes some input and classifies it into one of two possible values. For example, a piece of text could be identified with a positive or negative sentiment, or a candidate hiring decision could come back as a *Yes* or *No*, and so on.

- **Multiclass and image classification**: This is more versatile than binary classification. In these types of problems, an ML model can categorize input data into two or more categories. For example, it could determine the risk of giving a loan to an applicant as high, medium, or low. It could even be used to classify images. As an example, an image could be labeled under either the food, animal, or object category.

- **Regression and forecasting**: In regression, a label is a numeric value that the model predicts from the set of features. An example usage could be evaluating the fair price for a stock or forecasting the probability of an air flight becoming sold out in the next 3 days.

- **Clustering**: This is an example of unsupervised learning. In these classes of problems, we do not get too specific about what we want to know. It is the job of the machine learning model to find interesting patterns in the data. For example, it could investigate the Facebook Ad click data and group the customers who belong to a certain demographic and always buy similar products.

- **Anomaly detection**: This is also an example of unsupervised learning. The ML model tries to find unusual patterns in the data. This could be used to find credit card fraud, suspicious computer network activity, or a broken IoT device sending incorrect data.

- **Recommendations and ranking**: A widely used feature on e-commerce websites is to display recommended and related products. This is typically implemented as an ML recommendation model that groups the input data and then provides a similarity ranking between each pair of data. Another example of this algorithm is to detect plagiarism by ranking a pair of texts based on how similar their content is.

Regardless of the class of problem being worked on, the machine learning workflow is fairly standard. We will review this process in the next section.

ML workflow

Machine learning has two or sometimes three distinct phases. These phases can be visualized as follows:

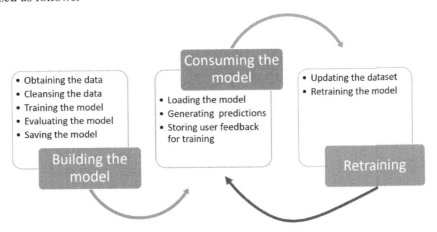

Figure 7.1 – Typical machine learning workflow

If the data that's used for the model remains static over the long term, then there is no need to include the third phase of retraining in the ML workflow. Retraining helps keep the model up to date if the training data changes frequently.

Let's go through the details of the activities included in each of the ML workflow phases.

Building the model

Acquiring and cleansing the data is typically the most effort-consuming part of the whole process. The datasets are usually huge and fixing data quality issues is not always simple. Imagine finding all the variations of the same name spelled differently, or an address to the same location written in two different ways.

Training the model is the process of applying the operations in the algorithm to produce the model as output. Typically, a model is trained several times with competing algorithms and then the best model is chosen using the evaluation process.

For the purpose of post-training evaluation, a subset of the data (typically 20%) is deliberately kept out of the training process. Once the model has been built, it is tested to see if its predictions on the rest of the dataset are accurate or not. Various mathematical measures exist to determine this accuracy.

Once the best model has been chosen, it is saved and published to be consumed by application developers.

Consuming the model

The model consists of algorithmic instructions that can produce output (that is, predictions) from the provided input.

The model that was produced in the previous phase is then used by the application. Some applications have a mechanism to store user feedback. For example, if a retail website uses machine learning to recommend a product, it can then store a fact stating whether the customer bought the recommended product or not. This feedback data is extremely valuable for retraining and improving the model.

Retraining the model

Using the data that's been obtained from a user's feedback or other sources, the model can be continuously improved and retrained. This process is very similar to the initial training phase. Retraining can be done on a continuous basis (that is, as soon as user feedback is received) or on a periodic basis (for example, once a month with a new batch of data).

The last conceptual topic I want to cover is the importance of data in the machine learning world. Let's see why there is a need to dedicate a whole section to this topic.

The importance of oil – I mean, data!

As software developers, we are familiar with the term *garbage in, garbage out*. A machine learning model is as good as the quality of its data. Arguably, it is more important to find the right dataset than choosing the right algorithm to solve the ML problem. Some experts have gone as far as to suggest that having data in the 21st century is like owning oil in the 18th century.

So, where we do source the data from? Let's take a look at some useful resources we can use to gather sample data that are useful for beginners and experts alike.

Getting datasets for machine learning

There are thousands, if not millions, of great quality datasets available on the internet under various licensing terms. I personally find these two websites to be very useful for finding practice datasets:

- Kaggle (a data science company by Google): `https://www.kaggle.com/`
- University of California Irvine, Machine Learning Repository: `https://archive.ics.uci.edu/ml/index.php`

Before using the data from any website, including the sites I just mentioned, we must check its usage permissions.

Attributing the data source

Data has tremendous commercial value in the machine learning world. Before you use a dataset in your code, please read its licensing terms to ensure that you can use this data for personal or commercial use. Also, check whether you are required to attribute the data to its original source in case you do use it.

The sample datasets that will be used in this chapter are clearly attributed to their creators. Both datasets (mall customers and sentiment labeled reviews) allow the free use of the data included for personal and commercial use.

Alright! We are now set to start working with the ML.NET library to build some machine learning applications. Let's take a look at a quick introduction to ML.NET. Then, we'll build a couple of services to see machine learning in action.

Building an ML.NET-based service to predict the shopping score

In this section, we will provide a quick introduction to the ML.NET API. After that, we'll perform an exercise in which we'll build a machine learning service that will predict the spending score of a shopping mall customer based on the customer's gender, age, and annual income. The score has been standardized from 1 to 100. The higher the score indicates the higher the spending potential of the customer. Let's see how ML.NET can help us build this service.

Introduction to ML.NET

ML.NET is a free cross-platform .NET Standard library provided by Microsoft so that developers can easily build machine learning-based solutions. It provides APIs for all the usual ML features, such as data acquisition, cleansing, model training, evaluation, and deployment. All major problem types are covered with plenty of well-known machine learning algorithms provided as a built-in feature.

The library is extensible and even supports the consumption of models by some of the most popular ML frameworks available, such as Infer.NET, TensorFlow, ONNX, and so on. This is a great feature as it enables .NET developers to work in collaboration with data scientists who typically prefer to build models in the aforementioned technologies.

In this chapter, we'll also use a feature of ML.NET named **ML.NET Model Builder**. Let's take a quick look at this component.

AutoML and ML.NET Model Builder

AutoML is part of the ML.NET API that automates the task of training, evaluating, and then choosing the best algorithm for a given dataset. It comes with a **command-line interface (CLI)** that can be used on any supported platform.

ML.NET Model Builder is currently a Visual Studio-only extension that provides a GUI for a developer to easily consume AutoML.

Throughout the rest of this chapter, we'll learn more about the ML.NET API by building some example services. Let's start our journey to build our first sample application.

Obtaining the dataset

The dataset file we'll be using for this chapter is named `mall_customers.csv` and is available in `datasets` folder, under the provided code files for this chapter.

I originally got this dataset from the Kaggle website: `https://www.kaggle.com/shwetabh123/mall-customers`.

This dataset is in the public domain, so we are free to download and modify it for any use we intend.

The `csv` data is straightforward and contains 200 rows and five columns. For our exercise, we are not interested in the `CustomerID` column. We'll use the `Gender`, `Age`, and `AnnualIncome` columns as features and then train the machine learning model to predict `SpendingScore` after learning from the sample data. The annual income is expressed in a thousand dollars as a unit, so a value of 15 means that the customer in question has an annual income of $15,000.

Once we have the data, we need to choose an algorithm so that we can build the model. To choose an algorithm, we need to identify the class of the problem we are trying to solve.

Classifying the problem

This is an example of a regression problem as we are predicting a numerical value (spending score) based on other features of the dataset (age, gender, and annual income).

Can you think of other problems where this dataset could be useful?

One easy answer is to include `SpendingScore` in the feature set and then use a different column as a label. For example, if a loan officer knows the age and gender of a loan applicant and can also determine their spending score from their credit card statements, the officer can make use of an ML service to provide the estimated annual income of the applicant.

We can even use this dataset for a different class of problems; that is, **clustering**. We can use unsupervised learning algorithms to find interesting customer groups, patterns, and anomalies based on all the available features.

In this exercise, we will focus on the originally stated problem of predicting the spending score of a customer.

While performing this exercise, you will notice that the steps for building and consuming this service are loosely based on the machine learning workflow we described in the **ML workflow** section, in *Figure 7.1*.

We will not use the retraining phase as our sample data is static. One of the prerequisites for this exercise is to have the ML.NET Model Builder feature enabled. Let's enable it so that we can start building our first ML.NET-based application.

Enabling ML.NET Model Builder

At the time of writing, the ML.NET Model Builder feature is currently in preview. If you have not enabled it in Visual Studio 2019 already, follow these steps to enable it now:

1. Launch the Visual Studio Installer and then click the **Modify** button to update the installed feature set.

2. In the **WorkLoads** tab, expand the **.NET Core cross-platform development** section under **Installation details** and then ensure that **ML.NET Model Builder (Preview) feature** is checked:

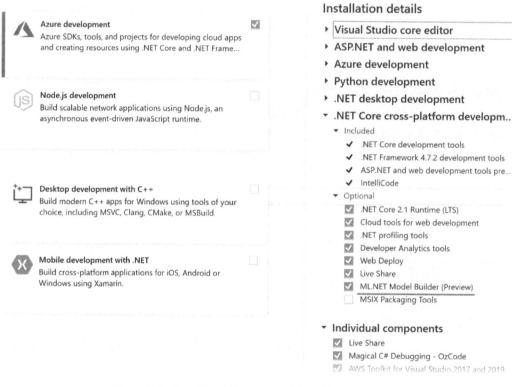

Figure 7.2 – Installing ML.NET Model Builder (Preview)

3. Continue with the installation until the installation process is completed.

4. Launch Visual Studio 2019. From the menu, click **Tools | Options**.

5. In the **Search Options** text box, type `preview` and then click **Preview Features** from the list of available options.

6. Check the **Enable ML.NET Model Builder** option and then click **OK**:

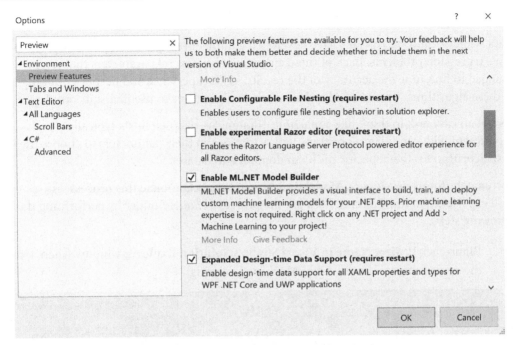

Figure 7.3 – Enabling the ML.NET Model Builder feature

This feature will allow you to auto-generate the code for building and consuming machine learning models from .NET applications.

We are now ready to build the spending score prediction app.

Creating the solution file

Now, let's get into the action. Perform the following steps to create the barebones application:

1. Launch Visual Studio 2019 and then click **Create a new project**.

2. Choose **Console App (.NET Core)** as our C# template. The template we choose is not important as we will let ML.NET Model Builder generate the sample project for us. For now, we just need a placeholder so that we can add a machine learning feature to it.

3. Type in SpendScorePredictor for **Project name**. Use the same value for **Solution name**.

This should create a sample console application for us to work with. In the next section, we'll be using ML.NET Model Builder to train the model using the mall customers dataset.

Training the model

Data scientists and statisticians have developed a number of algorithms over the years to solve regression problems. Each of these algorithms has several parameters that can be changed to fine-tune the accuracy of the results. With experience and deeper knowledge of these algorithms, we can decide which of these algorithms to use that suits our data.

It's not an easy task to think like a machine, though. So, data scientists typically experiment with candidate algorithms with variations in their parameters to choose the best algorithm for their specific problem domain and dataset.

Fortunately, for us developers, Model Builder can largely automate this process, as we'll experience in this exercise. Let's use the power of Model Builder by performing the following steps:

1. Right-click **Project Name** in Visual Studio's **Solution Explorer** window. Then, from the context menu, choose **Add | Machine Learning**:

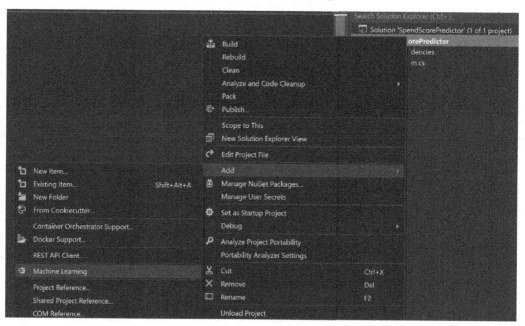

Figure 7.4 – Starting the ML.NET wizard by adding Machine Learning to a project

2. The preceding step will launch the ML.NET Model Builder wizard. From the **Select a scenario** screen, choose `Value prediction` since we are going to predict the value of a mall customer's spending score:

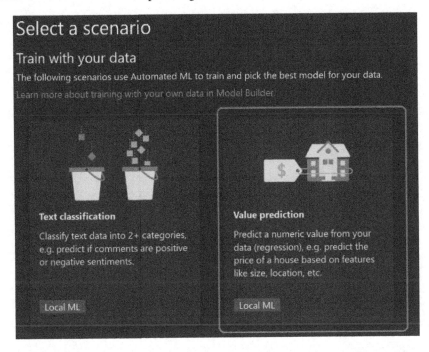

Figure 7.5 – Choosing Value prediction as the problem type that we want to solve

3. The next step is to choose the training environment. For the value prediction scenario, Model Builder only supports training on a local machine. For compute-intensive scenarios such as image classification, ML.NET also supports using compute resources on the cloud. This is because the training process could potentially take a long time and require expensive resources. We'll leave the default selection as **Local**.

4. The next step is to provide data for training. Click **Data** and then click the **...** button next to the **Select a file** input to choose a data file. Use the `mall_customers.csv` file from the `datasets` folder.

5. In the **Column to predict (Label)** dropdown, choose `SpendingScore`.

6. In the **Input Columns (Features)** dropdown, deselect the `CustomerID` column as it is not relevant for this exercise. Leave the other columns selected:

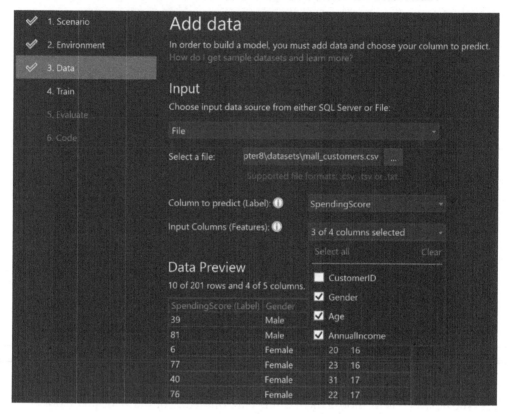

Figure 7.6 – The Label and Features dropdowns

7. The next step is to train the model. The wizard will automatically split the data, with 80% of it being used to train the model and the remaining 20% being used to verify the accuracy of the model. This 80-20 split is quite a common practice in the machine learning world. When using the ML.NET API directly from code, we can also choose to use a different split (for example, 70-30) or even two completely different datasets for training and testing the model. Click **Train** to proceed to the next screen.

8. For a small dataset like this, the default value of `10` seconds for the **Time to train (seconds):** input is fine. This will give Model Builder ample time to try and gauge the accuracy of various algorithms. For larger datasets, it's useful to allocate more time for training. Click **Start training** to begin the training process.

9. After 10 seconds, Model Builder will show the training output. In my case, it found that the `LightGbmRegression` algorithm was the most accurate because it has the highest `RSquared` value among the five models it explored. For regression-based algorithms, the value of `RSquared` depicts the accuracy of predictions. We want this value to be as close to 1 as possible. For our small dataset, the best we could obtain was **0.2566**:

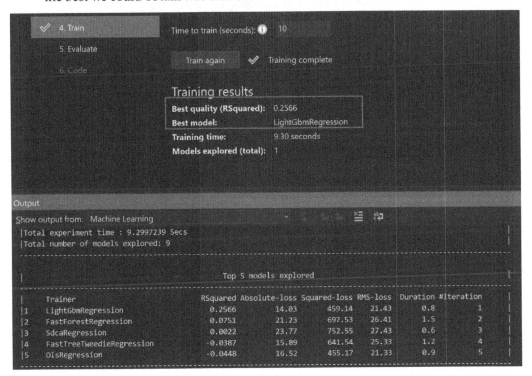

Figure 7.7 – Training results, as shown by Model Builder

> **Note**
> Due to the randomness of the selected training data and different hardware specifications, your results might vary a little.

The last step before generating the code so that we can consume the model is to evaluate the model generated by Model Builder.

Evaluating the prediction service

In this section, we will provide some test values and check the prediction that we received from the model to determine if the model is returning realistic values:

1. On the **Train** screen, click **Evaluate** to proceed to the next screen.

    Use any random values for the **Gender**, **Age**, and **AnnualIncome** inputs and then click **Predict** to see the result on the right-hand column. Here, I used `Male`, `19`, and `15` for these values and got a **SpendingScore** of **67.21**:

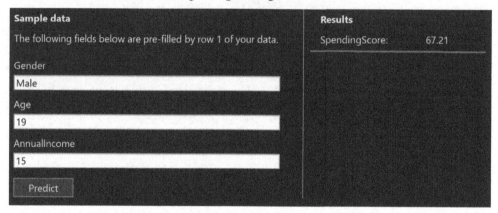

Figure 7.8 – Testing the model using random input values

2. You can try changing the input values and see how this impact the results. Which of the three variables made the biggest difference to the spending score?

In a real-world scenario, if the results look too weird, we can go back to the previous screens and choose a different algorithm. For us, it's time to generate the sample code that uses the selected model.

Generating the code that will consume the model

In this step, Model Builder will generate the sample code for us to build the same model programmatically, and then consume the generated model to make predictions on input data. On the **Evaluate** screen, click the **Code** button to generate the code.

This will generate some code and provide a summary using the sample code.

Let's explore this code that was generated by ML.NET Model Builder in detail.

Exploring the auto-generated code

Two projects are generated by ML.NET Model Builder:

- `SpendScorePredictorML.Model`: This project contains model classes for providing input to and getting output from the generated model. It also has the generated ML model in ZIP format and it called `MLModel.zip`. Lastly, it provides the `ConsumeModel` class for generating a prediction engine using the model file, which we can then use to create predictions on the input data.

- `SpendScorePredictorML.ConsoleApp`: This is a sample console app that's generated by Model Builder. It contains the `ModelBuilder` class, which contains the code for training and generating the model from the `mall_customers.csv` file. We don't need this class as ML.NET Model Builder has already generated the `MLModel.zip` file for us. This project has a reference to the `SpendScorePredictorML.Model` project. The console app can use this project to consume the generated model and make predictions.

> **Understanding the generated code**
>
> There is a lot more to explain about generated code. During the next hands-on exercise in this chapter, named *Building the sentiment analysis model*, we will create another machine learning service where we'll write the code by hand instead of using the Model Builder wizard. I will explain the ML.NET API in more detail during that exercise.

For now, let's test whether the console application is working as expected.

Testing the application

The application testing mechanism is very similar to what we did while we were on the **Evaluate** screen on the Model Builder wizard. This time, we'll change the input values in the code and check the output that's predicated by the model:

1. Under the `SpendScorePredictorML.ConsoleApp` project, in the `program.cs` file, change the values for the sample data. I am using the `Male`, `19`, and `15` values for the `Gender`, `Age`, and `AnnualIncome` fields, respectively:

```
ModelInput sampleData = new ModelInput()
{
    Gender = @"Male",
    Age = 29F,
```

```
                    AnnualIncome = 15F,
        };
```

The `ModelInput` class is generated by Model Builder and contains the same fields as the feature columns from our sample data file.

2. Set `SpendScorePredictorML.ConsoleApp` as the startup project and then run the application.

   The application will show the predicted score. For my example values, the predicted score is 75.27. Your result might vary a little:

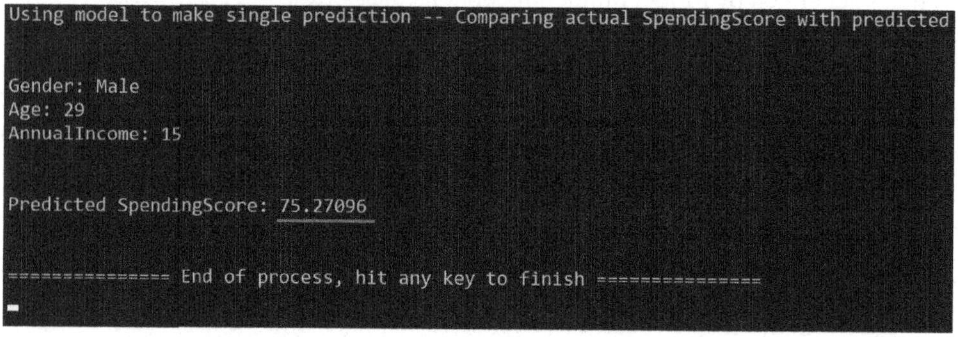

Figure 7.9 – Predicted spending score for the example customer

Great! We have learned how to consume the model programmatically once it has been generated. This is pretty cool in itself but in the real world, the machine learning service will likely be a part of a larger application. For example, Amazon uses the ML-based recommendation engine to display related products on their website.

In the next section, we'll learn how to deploy the ML service as an Azure function so that it can be consumed from an ASP.NET web application, such as the BookApp web application that we built in the previous chapter.

Building Azure Functions using ML.NET models

Once a machine learning model has been built, it can be consumed from any kind of .NET application, such as a WPF, Web Application, Web API, or even from microservices. In this section, we will use ML.NET to build a sentiment analysis service and then integrate it into an Azure function. This will replace the rudimentary sentiment analysis service that we built for the same purpose in the previous chapter.

We will then see the improved sentiment analysis service being used from the Azure function, which itself is being consumed by the BookApp web application we also built in the previous chapter.

> **Azure Functions and serverless architecture**
>
> If you are not familiar with Azure Functions, you can read an introduction to it in the *Deploying serverlessly – Azure Functions* section of *Chapter 6, Upgrading On-Premises Applications to the Cloud with .NET 5*. There is also information about serverless architecture in general in the *Serverless architecture* section of *Chapter 3, Design and Architectural Patterns*.

By performing this exercise, we will learn about the full cycle, from building an ML model to consuming it from the ASP.NET web application.

Building the sentiment analysis service

Like the shopping mall customer spending score service that we built in the previous section, we'll create another machine learning service. However, this time, instead of using the Model Builder wizard, we'll directly write code to build the sentiment analysis model.

Once the model has been built, instead of consuming it from the console application, we will use it from the Azure function.

Let's begin this journey by creating a machine learning-based sentiment analysis service.

Obtaining the data

There are a number of free datasets with sentiment tag annotations available on the internet. Many of them have restricted licensing permissions for commercial use. However, you should be able to use them freely for learning purposes.

For this exercise, I have sourced the data from the UCI website from the following link: `https://archive.ics.uci.edu/ml/datasets/ Sentiment+Labelled+Sentences`.

The credit for creating this dataset goes to the creators of the research paper, *'From Group to Individual Labels using Deep Features', Kotzias et al,. KDD 2015*.

The data files are available in the following source code folder: `Chapter07\datasets\ sentiment labelled sentences`.

The data is distributed into three different files. Each file contains 500 positive and 500 negative reviews. As the file's names suggest, the reviews have been taken from Amazon, IMDb, and Yelp.

The sentiment value of each sample review is either 0 (negative) or 1 (positive). Note that the sample data does not consciously include any reviews with neutral sentiments. Later in this exercise, we will look at a technique that helps determine neutral sentiment in a piece of text.

Walking through the solution files

Before we start the hands-on exercise, let me walk you through the solution components and the responsibilities of each of them.

The main solution file is `Chapter07\SentimentAnalysis\`
`SentimentAnalysis.sln`. It consists of the following projects:

- `SentimentAnalysis.Models` (.NET Standard class library)
- `ModelBuilderApp` (.NET 5 console app)
- `BookApp.SentimentAnalysisFunction` (.NET Core Azure function)

Now, let's look at each of these projects to understand the key code elements that contribute to the solution.

SentimentAnalysis.Models

This project only contains two classes that represent the input and output models for performing sentiment analysis. The input class, `SentimentInput`, will be used to read the data from `.csv` files. The output class, `SentimentOutput`, contains a `String` field named `Prediction` and a floating-point array value named `Score`. Both fields deserve some explanation.

The `Prediction` field will hold either **0** or **1** as a string value. There is a reason why this field is not of the `bool` type. The machine learning algorithm we will choose will perform binary classification (that is, the output label can only have two possible values), but the same algorithm can be used to perform multi-class classification (that is, it can associate multiple human emotions with a single piece of text). If we provide a dataset with multiple labels in future iterations, no model changes will be needed.

The `Score` array represents the confidence score associated with each classification label. So, for example, our model could say that it has 95% confidence that the text belongs to label number 1 (for example, negative) and 5% confidence that the text belongs to label number 2 (that is, positive). For binary classification, this array will always have two elements. If we use the algorithm with 10 possible emotion labels, this field will return 10 elements representing the confidence scores for each of the emotions.

ModelBuilderApp

This .NET 5 console app contains the code for generating the sentiment analysis model. Unless the source data changes, there is no need to rerun this application.

It contains a folder named `TrainingData` that contains source data files. There is another folder named `ModelOutput` where the generated model will be stored once the application is run.

The bulk of the code is in the `ModelBuilder.cs` class, which I will explain in the next section.

Here is a little secret, though: most of the code in this class is also auto generated by Model Builder for convenience. However, it is then manually fine-tuned according to the requirements and will not require Model Builder to be installed on the development or production environment to execute.

BookApp.SentimentAnalysisFunction

Once the model has been generated, it can be consumed from this Azure function app. The structure of this project is very similar to the project from the previous chapter. The main difference is that we've updated the `SentimentAnaysisService.cs` code so that it can consume the sentiment analysis model.

This was a high-level overview of the solution files. We will now perform the actual exercise. I'll explain the code in more detail along the way.

Building the sentiment analysis model

The end goal of this sub-exercise is to create a machine learning model that can predict a sentiment (positive or negative) from a piece of text. In the provided code files, there is already a model file named `Chapter07\SentimentAnalysis\ ModelBuilderApp\ModelOutput\sentiment_analysis_model.zip`.

You can directly use this model file in the next part of the *Consuming the model from an Azure function* section and skip this exercise. Alternatively, if you would like to learn how the model was generated and then practice generating a model by yourself, continue to follow these steps:

1. Open the `SentimentAnalysis.sln` file from the chapter code files in Visual Studio 2019.

2. Set the console app, `ModelBuilderApp`, as your startup project.

3.   Run the application. It should generate an output similar to the following:

```
Introducing-.NET-5\code\chapter8\SentimentAnalysis\ModelBuilderApp\bin\Debug\net5.0\ModelBuilderApp....
=============== Training  model =================
=============== End of training process ================
=============== Cross-validating to get model's accuracy metrics ===============
*****************************************************************************
*     Metrics for Multi-class Classification model
*---------------------------------------------------------------------------
*     Average MicroAccuracy:    0.797  - Standard deviation: (.008)  - Confidence Interval 95%: (.008)
*     Average MacroAccuracy:    0.797  - Standard deviation: (.008)  - Confidence Interval 95%: (.008)
*     Average LogLoss:          .573   - Standard deviation: (.037)  - Confidence Interval 95%: (.036)
*     Average LogLossReduction: .173   - Standard deviation: (.052)  - Confidence Interval 95%: (.051)
*****************************************************************************
=============== Saving the model ================
The model is saved to                              Introducing-.NET-5\code\chapter8\SentimentAnalysis\
\bin\Debug\net5.0\..\..\..\ModelOutput\sentiment_analysis_model.zip
=============== Model created successfully, hit any key to finish ===============
```

Figure 7.10 – ModelBuilderApp displaying successful model generation

After the successful run, the new model file will be stored as a file called
ModelBuilderApp\ModelOutput\sentiment_analysis_model.zip.
The other projects in the solution have already been configured to use this generated
model file.

Here is a brief explanation of how the ModelBuilder code in this project is working:

1.   The project is referencing the Microsoft.ML NuGet package in the csproj file:

```
<PackageReference Include="Microsoft.ML" Version="1.5.2"
/>
```

This package provides the ML.NET API so that we can build and consume machine
learning models.

2.   The names of the training data files are specified in a string array, as follows:

```
private static string[] TRAINING_DATA_FILES = new[]{
    @"TrainingData\amazon_cells_labelled.txt",
    @"TrainingData\imdb_labelled.txt",
    @"TrainingData\yelp_labelled.txt"
};
```

These three data files are included in the TrainingData folder of this project.

3. The files are then loaded into `IDataView` using the following code:

```
TextLoader textLoader = mlContext.Data.
CreateTextLoader<SentimentInput>(separatorChar: '\t',
hasHeader: false);

IDataView trainingDataView = textLoader.Load(TRAINING_
DATA_FILES);
```

In the `CreateTextLoader` function, we've specified that our CSV files do not have a header column and that the columns are separated by the tab character.

`IDataView` is an abstraction over the schema and the contents of the loaded data. You can think of it as a SQL table with rows and columns, but it also contains many more features that have been optimized to efficiently process large datasets and apply machine learning operations.

4. The `BuildTrainingPipeline` method then defines the pipeline (that is, the chained set of operations) that need to be performed on `IDataView` to train the model. Here are some lines of interest from that method:

```
.Append(mlContext.Transforms.Text.FeaturizeText("text_
tf", "text"))

                                    .Append(mlContext.
Transforms.CopyColumns("Features", "text_tf"))

var trainer = mlContext.MulticlassClassification.
Trainers.SdcaMaximumEntropy(labelColumnName: "sentiment",
featureColumnName: "Features")

                                    .Append(mlContext.
Transforms.Conversion.MapKeyToValue("PredictedLabel",
"PredictedLabel"));
```

In the preceding snippet, the first line is extracting key features from the text. This includes a number of operations, such as eliminating noise words (for example, *the*, *an*, and *of*), finding the parts of speech, and counting the frequency of words that appear in the text.

The second line specifies that the `Text` column will be used as a feature. The third line specifies `SdcaMaximumEntropy` as a chosen ML algorithm and lastly, the fourth line specifies that the `PredictedLabel` column in the `IDataView` schema will store the prediction output.

In the *Further reading* section of this chapter, a link to the official documentation for ML.NET has been provided, where you can read more about these features.

Note that the operations on `IDataView` are lazily evaluated. So, the preceding code snippet only defines how the operations should be performed to train the model. The actual execution begins when the `Fit` method is called, as described shortly.

5. The following line of code executes the training pipeline we defined previously:

```
ITransformer model = trainingPipeline.
Fit(trainingDataView);
```

The output of this line is a model encapsulated in the `ITransformer` schema that can then be saved to a file.

6. Before saving the model in a ZIP file, we must evaluate its performance using the following code:

```
        var crossValidationResults = mlContext.
MulticlassClassification.CrossValidate(trainingDataView,
trainingPipeline, numberOfFolds: 5, labelColumnName:
"sentiment");
```

Cross-validation is a technique in which data is sliced into several partitions, and the results are then evaluated on each of partition to eliminate any bias that could result from randomly selected test data. The `numberOfFolds` parameter in the method call specifies that the test data will be chosen five different times from the overall dataset. Each time, a different 20% subset of the data will be selected to evaluate the model's performance; the other 80% will be used to train the model. This usually improves the accuracy of smaller datasets as more data becomes available for training.

7. Finally, the model is saved to the local disk using the following line of code:

```
mlContext.Model.Save(mlModel, modelInputSchema,
GetAbsolutePath(modelRelativePath));
```

This will save the sentiment analysis model as a ZIP file in the `ModelOutput` folder of the solution.

Now that we have the model, we'll learn how this model can be used in an Azure function to make sentiment-based predictions.

Here is a question for you: *Can this model be tested with sample text before we use it in an Azure function?* You'd need to tweak the `ConsumeModel` class from the previous exercise a little bit and then copy and use it from the `ModelBuilderApp` console application to test the model. This isn't important, so I've left it as a practice exercise for you if you are interested.

Consuming the model from an Azure function

The function project has been copied from the BookApp solution from the previous chapter. There are three files in this project that have been changed so that they integrate with the ML.NET model that we built in the previous section.

The good news is that no changes have been made to the `SentimentFunction` class. What this means is that any application that is consuming the previous version of the Azure function will continue to work fine, without requiring any changes. This is because the function signature and its HTTP interface are still the same.

Let's review the changes that were made in the other files before testing the function.

Changes in BookApp.SentimentAnalysisFunction.csproj

In the `csproj` file, we have included the package references to the ML.NET library and linked the machine learning model ZIP file we generated from `ModelBuilderApp`. These changes are reflected in the following lines in the file:

- The NuGet package references can be included by using the following lines:

```
<PackageReference Include="Microsoft.Extensions.ML"
Version="1.5.2" />
<PackageReference Include="Microsoft.ML" Version="1.5.2"
/>
```

We've used the `Microsoft.ML` NuGet package in pretty much all the projects in this chapter. However, this is our first encounter with `Microsoft.Extensions.ML`. We need this package for a very handy service named `PredictionEnginePool`.

In the `SpendScorePredictor` solution, we used the `PredictionEngine` class from the ML.NET library to make predictions. This class is not thread-safe and is not an efficient operation for creating an instance of this class every time we want to make a prediction.

`PredictionEnginePool` solves this problem by using an `ObjectPool` for prediction engines. It's a somewhat similar concept to managing a connection pool for database connections. So, consumers can use pre-initialized prediction engines as and when needed. The `PredictionEnginePool` service assumes the life cycle responsibilities of creating and destroying the prediction engines as needed.

- The following lines ensure that the model ZIP file we generated in the `ModelOutput` folder of the `ModelBuilderApp` project is available as a link in the `MLModels` folder of the function project:

```
<None Include="..\ModelBuilderApp\ModelOutput\sentiment_
analysis_model.zip" Link="MLModels\sentiment_analysis_
model.zip">
        <CopyToOutputDirectory>PreserveNewest</
CopyToOutputDirectory>
</None>
```

The `CopyToOutputDirectory` tag ensures that the model file will be copied to the function output directory at build time whenever a newer model file is available.

Changes in Startup.cs

The `Startup.cs` file has gone through the following changes:

- The physical path on the disk for the model file will be different based on the Azure function hosting environment. We are determining this path using the following code:

```
environment = Environment.GetEnvironmentVariable("AZURE_
FUNCTIONS_ENVIRONMENT");


if (environment == "Development") {
  modelPath = Path.Combine("MLModels",
  "sentiment_analysis_model.zip");
}
else {
    string deploymentPath = @"D:\home\site\wwwroot\";
                 modelPath =
    Path.Combine(deploymentPath, "
  MLModels ", "
  sentiment_analysis_model.zip ");
}
```

If the `AZURE_FUNCTIONS_ENVIRONMENT` environment variable is set to `Development`, we can use the local disk file path. However, when the function is hosted in Azure, the executing environment's default directory is not the same as the function output directory. We can work around this by providing a hardcoded directory path, `D:\home\site\wwwroot\`, as the Azure function runtime if the app service is executed from this directory by default.

- The `PredictionEnginePool` service that we discussed in the previous section has been registered using the following line of code:

```
builder.Services.AddPredictionEnginePool<SentimentInput,
SentimentOutput>()
                        .FromFile(modelName:
"SentimentAnalysisModel", filePath: modelPath,
watchForChanges: true);
```

There are a couple of interesting ways to use the `AddPredictionEnginePool` method. Here, we are setting the `watchForChanges` parameter to `true`. If we retrain our model in the future, we can directly deploy the model file without redeploying or restarting the whole function app. This parameter value will ensure that the updated model file is used when the next `PredictionEngine` instance is created.

We can go one step further and use the `FromUri` method instead of `FromFile`, which can load models from any accessible URI, keep pooling the URI at a configurable interval, and then update `PredictionEngine` when changes in the model file are detected.

With that, the function has been set up to use ML.NET features. The `SentimentAnalysisService` class has been updated to replace the previous code-based logic with a machine learning service. Now, let's look at the code that's required to make this change possible.

Changes in SentimentAnaysisService.cs

The interface for `ISentimentAnaysisService` remains unchanged. So, the `SentimentFunction` function class will not require any changes. The two most notable changes that were made in `SentimentAnaysisService.cs` are as follows:

- We are injecting the `PredictionEnginePool` service into the class constructor using constructor injection:

```
private readonly PredictionEnginePool < SentimentInput,
SentimentOutput > predictionEnginePool;
public SentimentAnaysisService(PredictionEnginePool <
```

```
    SentimentInput, SentimentOutput > predictionEnginePool) {
        this.predictionEnginePool = predictionEnginePool;
    }
```

We must specify the input and output model classes (`SentimentInput` and `SentimentOutput`, respectively) for the `PredictionEnginePool` service. These model classes are defined in the `SentimentAnalysis.Models` project.

- The `GetSentiment` function has been updated like so:

```
public Sentiment GetSentiment(string text) {
    var input = new SentimentInput {
        Text = text
    };
    var prediction =
    predictionEnginePool.Predict(modelName:
    "SentimentAnalysisModel", example: input);
    var confidence = prediction.Prediction == "0" ?
    prediction.Score[0] : prediction.Score[1];
    if (confidence < 0.7) return Sentiment.Neutral;
    return (prediction.Prediction == "1") ?
    Sentiment.Positive: Sentiment.Negative;
}
```

First, this function converts the input text into a model that's suitable as a machine learning input model. Now, remember that our model only predicts positive and negative labels and that it has no knowledge of neutral sentiments. We can work around this by using confidence scores. The code in the `GetSentiment` function checks the confidence score of the predicted label. If the model predicts less than 70% confidence, the function returns the neutral sentiment. After all, no decision is better than an incorrect decision. When the confidence is more than 70%, the method returns the corresponding `Sentiment` enum value for the predicted label.

So, these were all the changes we needed to make to update the Azure function so that it can use the ML.NET-based model. Now, it's time to test the function and see if it's working as expected.

Testing the Azure function

The Azure function testing process is exactly the same as it was in the previous chapter. Here are the brief steps we need to follow to perform testing:

1. Set `BookApp.SentimentAnalysisFunction` as the startup project and run it locally.

2. Once the function has been started, browse to the following URL in your browser: `http://localhost:7071/api/GetSentiment?text=i%20feel%20 good%20and%20happy%20about%20it`.

3. You should see the value **1** being returned as output, which represents a positive sentiment.

4. Try providing a negative review, such as the following: `http:// localhost:7071/api/GetSentiment?text=i%20feel%20bad%20 and%20unhappy%20about%20it`.

5. You should see the value **-1** being returned as output, which represents a negative sentiment.

Congratulations! We have learned how to use ML.NET-based machine learning services from Azure Functions. The process would be very similar if you were to use ML models from an ASP.NET Core web application instead.

If you followed the exercises from the previous chapter, you may also want to deploy this function to the Azure cloud to test its functionality from within the BookApp application. You can simply repeat the process described in the *Publishing the function app project* section of *Chapter 6, Upgrading On-Premises Applications to the Cloud with .NET 5,* if you wish to do so.

In this section, we learned how to use and integrate ML.NET into our .NET applications. Now, it's time to wrap this chapter up. Do check out the *Further reading* section if you are interested in learning more about ML.NET.

Summary

In this chapter, we learned about the full machine learning-based .NET application workflow. We equipped ourselves with the requisite knowledge of machine learning terminologies that are commonly used in machine learning documentation all over the web.

We then learned how the ML.NET API and ML.NET Model Builder can help us quickly build applications by taking advantage of comprehensive algorithms, as well as using a model building library provided by ML.NET that supports the entire ML workflow.

After that, we built couple of sample .NET applications using the regression and binary classification algorithms. Then, we learned how in a real-world application, these machine learning services could be hosted as Azure Functions to be consumed by larger .NET applications. These skills will not only help you build smart applications that use ML services, but also integrate with data models that have been developed by other data scientists within and outside your organization.

Before finishing this chapter and this book, I will provide you with some resource links that can help you build advanced machine learning solutions using ML.NET.

Further reading

We have just covered the tip of the proverbial iceberg. Machine learning is a rapidly growing field with many types of specialized roles being created out of it. The following resources will help you continue your machine learning journey now that you've completed this chapter:

- The book by Packt Publishing titled *Hands-On Machine Learning with ML.NET* covers many advanced scenarios for using ML.NET with .NET applications: `https://www.packtpub.com/product/hands-on-machine-learning-with-ml-net/9781789801781`.

- This cookbook style guide by Microsoft provides comprehensive coverage of the day-to-day tasks that a developer would need to perform using ML.NET. It also provides a detailed explanation of all ML.NET classes and methods: `https://github.com/dotnet/machinelearning/blob/master/docs/code/MlNetCookBook.md`.

- Instead of building the machine learning services yourself, you might find it more useful to consume pre-created intelligent services from Microsoft that have been bundled together as a service named Azure Cognitive Services. These services can be used in the cloud or in on-premises containers. These services can perform advanced ML tasks such as speech recognition, language translation, face detection, and handwriting recognition. The following link will get you started: `https://docs.microsoft.com/en-au/azure/cognitive-services/`.

Other Books You May Enjoy

If you enjoyed this book, you may be interested in these other books by Packt:

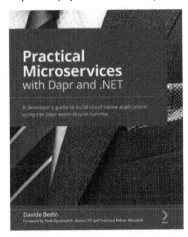

Practical Microservices with Dapr and .NET

Davide Bedin

ISBN: 9781800568372

- Use Dapr to create services, invoking them directly and via pub/sub

- Discover best practices for working with microservice architectures

- Leverage the actor model to orchestrate data and behavior

- Use Azure Kubernetes Service to deploy a sample application

- Monitor Dapr applications using Zipkin, Prometheus, and Grafana

- Scale and load test Dapr applications on Kubernetes

ASP.NET Core 5 for Beginners

Ed Price , Jeffrey Chilberto , Andreas Helland

ISBN: 978-1-80056-718-4

- Explore the new features and APIs introduced in ASP.NET Core 5 and Blazor
- Put basic ASP.NET Core 5 concepts into practice with the help of clear and simple samples
- Work with Entity Framework Core and its different workflows to implement your application's data access
- Discover the different web frameworks that ASP.NET Core 5 offers for building web apps
- Get to grips with the basics of building RESTful web APIs to work with real data
- Deploy your web apps in AWS, Azure, and Docker containers
- Work with SignalR to add real-time notifications to your app

Leave a review - let other readers know what you think

Please share your thoughts on this book with others by leaving a review on the site that you bought it from. If you purchased the book from Amazon, please leave us an honest review on this book's Amazon page. This is vital so that other potential readers can see and use your unbiased opinion to make purchasing decisions, we can understand what our customers think about our products, and our authors can see your feedback on the title that they have worked with Packt to create. It will only take a few minutes of your time, but is valuable to other potential customers, our authors, and Packt. Thank you!

Index

W

X

Made in the USA
Middletown, DE
30 June 2021